VIRTUAL SEARCHES

VIRTUAL SEARCHES

REGULATING THE COVERT WORLD
OF TECHNOLOGICAL POLICING

CHRISTOPHER SLOBOGIN

NEW YORK UNIVERSITY PRESS

New York

NEW YORK UNIVERSITY PRESS
New York
www.nyupress.org

© 2022 by New York University
All rights reserved

References to Internet websites (URLs) were accurate at the time of writing. Neither the author nor New York University Press is responsible for URLs that may have expired or changed since the manuscript was prepared.

Cataloging-in-Publication data is available from the publisher.
ISBN: 9781479812165 (hardback)
ISBN: 9781479812547 (library ebook)
ISBN: 9781479812172 (consumer ebook)

New York University Press books are printed on acid-free paper, and their binding materials are chosen for strength and durability. We strive to use environmentally responsible suppliers and materials to the greatest extent possible in publishing our books.

Manufactured in the United States of America

10 9 8 7 6 5 4 3 2 1

Also available as an ebook

Contents

Preface

This book is a sequel of sorts. In 2007, I published *Privacy at Risk: The New Government Surveillance and the Fourth Amendment*,[1] which summarized my thinking on how the Fourth Amendment's prohibition of unreasonable searches and seizures might apply to government surveillance. In this book, I continue to subscribe to the 2007 book's argument that all types of surveillance are Fourth Amendment "searches" and that they must be authorized by justification proportionate to their intrusiveness. But technological, legal, and political developments have since conspired to require a significant update of *Privacy at Risk*'s central message, as well as a new focus on sub-constitutional means of regulating government use of technology.

On the technological side, government's capacity to monitor its citizens has increased exponentially since 2007. *Privacy at Risk* talked about camera surveillance and drones, thermal imaging devices and beepers, data mining and digital dossiers. But this book will add into the mix facial recognition technology, automated license plate readers, cell phone tracking, and "geofencing" techniques, as well as familial DNA matching, predictive policing using algorithms, and government contracts with data brokers. All of these investigative practices have become routine since I wrote *Privacy at Risk*. A recent survey found that even many small police departments make use of cell phone tracking technology and that between a quarter and a third of the over 200 departments queried employ drones, CCTV (close-circuit television), and automated license plate readers for various purposes.[2]

Legal developments have been even more dramatic. While much of the technology just mentioned existed at least in nascent form in 2007, Fourth Amendment jurisprudence was still in a pre-technological Stone Age, wedded to a concept of police searches that focused on physical entry of houses, papers, and effects, and barely acknowledging the vast increases in data acquisition, storage, and analysis capacity that computers have brought. But in three decisions handed down in 2012, 2014, and 2018, the United States Supreme Court finally began to acknowledge that police access to tracking technology, data in phones, and data collected by private companies warrant constitutional regulation, even when the information thereby obtained was technically exposed to the public or voluntarily surrendered to another private party. These cases mark a sea change in Fourth Amendment law. Legal developments *outside* the courts have been at least as significant. Federal, state, and local legislatures have increasingly flexed their regulatory muscle in this area, with the result that there has been a significant upsurge in statutory treatment of surveillance technology as well.

Perhaps that is in part because the politics relevant to technological policing have also seen momentous change. Most importantly, in 2013, Edward Snowden famously leaked mountains of documents about America's national security surveillance programs. Almost overnight, it seemed, both the general public and the private companies that had facilitated those programs became noticeably more hostile to surveillance, no doubt in part because memories of the disaster on September 11, 2001, had faded. In the more recent past, the politics around policing has also undergone a transformation. The murder of George Floyd and the rise of the Black Lives Matter movement in particular have made the public more attuned to the power police wield and their willingness to abuse it.

For all of these reasons, the time is ripe for a new book about what I call "virtual searches"—police investigatory techniques carried out covertly, remotely, and technologically, rather than through physical intrusion. Despite the Supreme Court's signals that it is rethinking how the Fourth Amendment applies to virtual searches, the case law still tends to give law enforcement quite a bit of leeway in this area. In contrast, most scholarship has tended either to demand strict regulation of new virtual search techniques or to call for their outright abolition, both on general privacy grounds and because of the impact of surveillance on racial minorities. This book stakes out a middle ground in fashioning legal responses to technological policing. It tries to take into account the implications of new technological developments, the burgeoning judicial interest in expanding Fourth Amendment protections, and the rejuvenation of libertarian and anti-racism politics, without losing sight of the fact that crime, especially violent crime, is a serious problem in this country.

This book also takes a broader view of regulatory alternatives than did *Privacy at Risk*. That book focused on the judiciary as the main driver of surveillance regulation, and thus was mostly about the interpretation of the Fourth Amendment and other constitutional provisions. While this book also devotes considerable space to analyzing Fourth Amendment jurisprudence in the hopes of shaping its future contours, it is more attuned than the previous book to the potential of legislatures and other representative bodies to devise means of curbing government power. Whether or not the Fourth Amendment is read as broadly as I contend it should be, the precepts set forth here can inform the legislative and agency policies that we are beginning to see promulgated in much greater numbers than a mere decade ago.

Virtual Searches was essentially written from scratch, although parts of it borrow from articles I published in the *Georgetown Law Journal* and the *University of Pennsylvania Law Review* and chapters published in the National Constitution Center's *A 21st Century Framework for Electronic Privacy* and *The Cambridge Handbook of Surveillance Law*. In addition to the editors of those works, I am indebted to a number of people for their input on the issues addressed in this book, including the participants in workshops and panels that occurred over the past 15 years at the Privacy Law Scholars Conference (on more than one occasion), the Brookings Institute (including a convocation of federal and state judges), the Brennan Center for Justice, the Federal Judicial Center, the annual conferences of the Southeastern Association of Law Schools, several international symposia, and over 20 American law schools, including my home base, Vanderbilt, where the faculty had to put up with me prattling on about the topics in this book on many occasions. My work as a Reporter for the American Bar Association's Task Force on Technologically-Assisted Physical Surveillance, as a member of the ABA's Task Force on Government Access to Third Party Records, and as an Associate Reporter for the American Law Institute's Principles of Policing also greatly aided preparation of this work. Finally, I want to thank Brooke Bowerman, a student at Vanderbilt Law School, for her assistance on this project.

The Legislative Struggle over Virtual Searches

The third week in January 2021 saw three developments in the law governing technological policing that cemented the decision to write this book. None of the developments was earth-shattering. In fact, all three were fairly typical. But that is the point. The three events—occurring at the local, state, and federal levels—are representative of today's daily ferment over what I am calling "virtual searches."

One Week in January 2021

The first event occurred in Nashville, where I live and teach. In January 2021, Nashville, like the rest of the country, was in the midst of the COVID-19 pandemic, and the city was busy figuring out what to do about it. But on the night of January 13, the focus of the Nashville City Council's Committee on Public Safety, Beer, and Regulated Beverages was automated license plate readers (ALPRs), cameras that can record license plates and, in some versions, much more.[1] Several years earlier, the Council had passed an ordinance that prohibited operation of ALPRs "installed onto or within the public right-of-way," unless they were used to help identify vehicles suspected of involvement in a crime or violating emissions standards.[2] Then, in the fall of 2020, councilmember Freddie O'Connell proposed an amendment that, while leaving the criminal investigation and emissions exceptions in place, would otherwise have prohibited operation of ALPRs to capture occurrences on public spaces, no matter where they were installed, a provision that many thought would apply to use of Ring doorbell cameras and other privately owned devices that might pick up street activity. That proposed amendment prompted counterproposals, supported by the Metropolitan Nashville Police Department, that would have expanded permissible use of ALPRs to collection of license plate information even if, at the time, it was not pertinent to an existing criminal investigation, with the proviso that the license information had to be destroyed within 30 days unless it turned out to be evidence of a criminal offense or a civil traffic or parking offense within that period of time.

Given the ensuing controversy, there were also calls for public input on the issue. Thus, the Committee on Public Safety, Beer and Regulated Beverages, chaired by councilmember Jennifer Gamble, held a number of open sessions seeking input on use of ALPRs, including the one I attended on January 13. I was there (actually, in the Zoom room) only as an interested observer. I had testified at a previous meeting of the committee but had not taken a position on any legislation. Rather, I had described the likely impact of the Fourth Amendment's prohibition on unreasonable searches and seizures on surveillance of public thoroughfares (to sum up the gist of my testimony in a word, "none," for reasons explained in later chapters). I'd also noted that a number of jurisdictions had policies regarding ALPRs and that the typical statute or regulation identified the specific types of incidents that could be subject to surveillance and required policies governing the retention of, access to, and security of any information collected. One of the other principal speakers at that hearing had been the chief of police in Belle Meade (a suburb of Nashville), who testified that, in the two years after installation of 19 fixed ALPR cameras in his jurisdiction, burglaries had decreased by 50% and arrests for stolen vehicles and license plates (all from areas outside Belle Meade) had increased from one to 41, compared to the two years prior to installation of the cameras.

The January 13 meeting, held a month later, was principally meant to solicit comments about government use of ALPRs from public interest groups rather than experts, as well as look at the newest version of a bill authorizing greater use of ALPRs. The first several speakers, while members of the public, also sat on the Metro Human Relations Commission, a 17-person body appointed by the mayor with the goal of promoting "One City, for All People." All of them were against expansion of fixed ALPRs, and a couple indicated antipathy even toward the relatively common practice of mounting ALPRs on police cars, where they could signal police whether a license plate was on a "hot list" indicating that the car had been stolen or used to commit a crime.

The first of these Commission members focused on trust issues. She contrasted law enforcement's push for ALPRs with its foot-dragging on the city's policy regarding cameras on officers and squad cars that could record police–citizen interactions. In her view, "ALPR surveillance is antithetical to community policing and building relationships with the community" because of its constant monitoring of activities that would usually otherwise go unnoticed. Although she noted that a small online survey of Nashville citizens had found some support for ALPRs, she dismissed those results, arguing that the questionnaire was "an inelegant and inadequate means of ascertaining community sentiment," especially given the likelihood that many groups are not easily contacted through the internet. She also objected to ALPRs on the ground that the data they collect are often funneled through private companies that are difficult to monitor and that can use the information for their own profit-oriented ends. She ended with speculation that cameras would be placed, and data used, in ways that would harm disadvantaged communities.

The next member of the commission who spoke, a Vanderbilt University professor, picked up on this last thread, contending that ALPRs would do nothing to fix a society "full of inequities." Black and brown people will be disproportionately targeted by ALPR technology, he predicted, and that development will exacerbate differential treatment by the government. For instance, the professor suggested, ALPR data will likely be shared with Immigration and Customs Enforcement (the

federal agency known as ICE charged with enforcing immigration statutes) or used to surveil people who attend mosques. Further, if ALPR
data is maintained for the government by a private company, it will be
aggregated and shared nationwide in ways that local legislation passed
by the Nashville City Council could not affect. If, instead, it was maintained by the government, data could be exploited by political opponents or jealous lovers. Even limiting ALPR use to real-time hot list
alerts, with no additional recording capacity, would not prevent abuse,
he concluded, because hot lists can be wrong.

The speaker who followed headed the Nashville chapter of Neighbor 2 Neighbor, which in its many manifestations around the country
attempts to represent community interests and harness the power of
local residents to address local problems.[3] Based on his reading of the
polity, he, too, said that many people are not sure the government can
be trusted to protect their civil liberties. At the same time, this speaker
asserted, a "large group" of those he informally polled were concerned
about property theft (especially so-called porch pirates who steal
packages), drag racing, drug sales by gangs, and violent crime. He
noted that at least one neighborhood had installed cameras at its own
expense in the belief that surveillance could help with these problems.

However, the next several speakers, like those from the Human Relations Commission, were not convinced ALPRs were worth it. One
was concerned that the civilian oversight board recently established to
monitor Nashville police conduct had not been asked to examine any
of the proposals (the board has since come out against expansive use
of ALPRs).[4] Another noted that, unless the state legislature enacted
an exception to its public records statute, ALPR data in government
servers would be available to anyone who made a proper request. A
third pointed out that, even if camera data is encrypted or sequestered
in some other way, law enforcement could obtain it through a standard
subpoena (which is much easier to obtain than the "warrant" mentioned in the Fourth Amendment). And a fourth speaker, apparently
not privy to the Belle Meade police chief's presentation to the Council

the previous month, opined that there had been no concrete show-ing "connecting the dots" as to how ALPRs in Nashville would de-tect or deter crime, nor was there any information as to how much an ALPR system would cost or who would decide where ALPRs would be placed.

Then, toward the end of the meeting, two members of the City Council itself spoke up, and their comments clearly pushed the other way. The first, the only black person on the schedule other than Gam-ble (the committee chair), represented a district heavily populated by people of color. She asserted that a "majority" of her constituents favored use of LPR-type systems, given concerns about drag racing, stealing, and violent crime. "We don't have enough patrols, we need more assistance." ALPRs, she said, could make up for unequal police coverage. "I have Ring. There's a lot of sharing of Ring data and other security systems that folks have." An ordinance that banned this kind of surveillance, she claimed, would be rejected by an "overwhelm-ing" proportion of her district. The second Council member, a white woman who represented a "very diverse" jurisdiction, echoed these sentiments: "I get calls wanting more patrols, multiple times a week. And as I've met with different nationalities and races, I've seen that the immigrant population is victimized more times than not because the perpetrators know their victims are scared of deportation and won't call the police." Cameras, she contended, would "make com-munities safe for everyone" and "do not have racial bias. They rule out innocent people." She ended by saying, "I'm really passionate about this because I want to make my community safe for everyone, and I think there is way for us to do this, while providing a robust framework for auditing and reporting procedures."

The kind of debate Nashville is having about ALPRs is far from unique. Battles between those who think technology might help keep us safe and those who suspect it will not—between those who are rela-tively sanguine about technology's impact on privacy and those who believe it will exacerbate racial tensions, lead to police abuse, and increase the scope of the police state—are occurring all over the country, not only in local venues such as Nashville but also at the state and federal levels. In fact, just a few days after the Nashville meeting I attended, State Senator Becky Massey introduced a bill in the Tennessee legislature aimed at amending the state's drone surveillance statute. The previous Tennessee law on drones, enacted in 2013, carried the lofty title "Freedom from Unwanted Surveillance" and was passed during a national wave of similar statutes. It required police who wanted to use a drone to obtain a warrant from a court, except when there was "credible intelligence" of a "terrorist attack by a specific individual or organization" or when there was "reasonable suspicion" that the drone was needed "to prevent imminent danger to life" or search for escaped felons, missing persons, or evidence relating to accidents, crimes on public property, or fire.[5] Some privacy advocates resisted even this relatively restrictive approach, expressing concerns about "the further militarization of our civilian police forces" and the possibility that drone usage could "lead to fishing expeditions and invasive, all-encompassing surveillance that could seriously erode our privacy rights."[6]

Many law enforcement officials, in contrast, wanted more expansive authority to use drones, including in their campaign to discover illegal marijuana fields from the air.[7] Senator Massey agreed. Her amendment sought to change the law by allowing warrantless drone usage to investigate the scene of any crime, regardless of where it was committed, and by extending the time that images collected by a drone could be maintained from 24 hours to 30 days.[8] The amendment eventually passed both houses of the Tennessee legislature and was signed by Governor Bill Lee in May 2021.

The battle has also been joined at the federal level. The Breathe Act, a proposed federal law introduced in 2019 by several members of the United States Congress and supported by citizen groups such as the Movement for Black Lives, would prohibit all federal spending on aerial surveillance, facial recognition technology, predictive policing algorithms, or "any tool used to collect biometric data."[9] Yet the

Commercial Facial Recognition Privacy Act proposed in Congress the same year—while in most cases requiring explicit user consent before facial recognition data may be collected—specifically exempts from its provisions use of facial recognition technology if "intended to detect or prevent criminal activity, including shoplifting and fraud."[10] Similarly, the proposed federal Privacy Bill of Rights, introduced in 2019, would require all commercial enterprises to indicate the purposes for which personal information (broadly defined) is collected and to obtain affirmative consent from the customer for any alternative use,[11] but would still permit nonconsensual sharing of this information with law enforcement pursuant to a court order.[12]

That gets us back to the week of January 13, 2021. Two days after the Nashville hearing on ALPRs, and a day after Massey sent her bill to the Tennessee legislature, U.S. senator Amy Klobuchar of Minnesota introduced in Congress "A Bill to Protect the Health Data of All Americans." Proffering a similar bill two years earlier, Klobuchar had stated: "New technologies have made it easier for people to monitor their own health, but health tracking apps and home DNA testing kits have also given companies access to personal, private data with limited oversight."[13] The intent behind the legislation, she explained, is to "protect consumers' personal health data by requiring that regulations be issued by the federal agencies that have the expertise to keep up with advances in technology."[14] But the current version of the bill, like the Consumer Facial Recognition Privacy Act and the Privacy Bill of Rights, also states that any regulations that are promulgated under it should take into account "differences in sensitivity between genetic data, biometric data, and general personal health data," the needs of researchers who use such data, and—most relevant to this book—the needs of law enforcement.[15]

Virtual Searches, Legislatures, and the Courts

The three bills introduced during a single week in January 2021—involving ALPRs, drones, and health data legislation—are emblematic of the struggles cities, states, and the federal government face in deciding whether and how to deal with the relatively new phenomenon of technologically enhanced searches by law enforcement. Traditionally, police investigating crime engaged in physical searches of property or visual observation of someone's travels and transactions. Today, police are just as likely to resort to surveillance and data acquisition procedures that do not require physical intrusion, but rather can be carried out virtually, from headquarters or even a squad car. Without ever leaving their computers, police can access feeds from ALPRs, CCTV, and drone and satellite cameras that can both capture images of our public activities in real-time and maintain a record of those activities, data that can then be used to track people's movements or compared to hot lists and facial recognition data banks. An even greater information bonanza exists in the Cloud and other cyberspaces, because every aspect of our daily experience—communications, financial transactions, and even our health needs—are datafied and stored under the auspices of our credit card company, cell phone carrier, internet service provider, or some other third party.

Even activities inside the home are vulnerable to virtual searches. Unless users save their activities only on their hard drives, everything they do on a computer sits on a third-party server that can be accessed by the government, usually with a subpoena and often simply upon request. With the right equipment, law enforcement can, unbeknownst to the user, activate the computer's camera and monitor the keys being typed.[16] Phones can be hacked, cloned, or turned into a microphones. And those helpful friendly devices known as Alexa and Echo can record every word spoken within range unless they are unplugged.[17]

Law enforcement has been quick to take advantage of all these technological means to find out what people are up to. Some of these techniques—especially interception of phone and email communications—are strictly regulated by warrant requirements and other special legal rules.[18] But in most states, outside of restrictions that police departments impose on themselves, there are few formal rules governing other types of virtual searches, and those that do exist are very relaxed. A prominent reason for this state of affairs is that, until fairly recently, the courts have concluded that the United States Constitution has little or nothing to say about virtual searches if they focus on activities that occur outside the home or seek information surrendered to third parties such as banks and phone companies. That detached judicial attitude may be in the process of changing. For the time being, however, most virtual searches are not governed by the highest law in the land.

Of course, federal, state and city legislatures need not follow the courts' lead. Representative bodies have authority to impose greater limitations than those required by the federal and state constitutions. As the above discussion illustrates, however, bills that try to do something in this vein often die on the vine due to bickering between civil liberties groups and law enforcement or obstacles to ascertaining the polity's attitudes toward surveillance. The Nashville hearing in particular makes clear the difficulties in ascertaining what the "community" thinks about these issues, or even in identifying what the relevant community is and who speaks for it. Nonetheless, if legislatures rather than courts are to be the source of legal regulation for surveillance techniques, then democratic values necessitate some attempt to assess those views. This is especially the case now, in the wake of the George Floyd murder, when calls for citizen involvement in constructing rules governing police have intensified.[19]

A closely related issue is whether the legislature responsible for regulation should vary depending on the type of virtual technique at issue. It is probable that, if Congress were to pass a statute regulating a virtual search technique, such as Senator Klobuchar's genetic privacy law, it would apply across the country because of what is known as the "preemption doctrine" (which provides that federal law often supersedes state and local law when there is a conflict between the two).[20] The congressional statute requiring a warrant to intercept electronic communications, commonly known as Title III, has precisely that effect.

The more important question is whether Congress should exercise its preemption authority. Paul Schwartz argues that preemption by Congress would stymie experimentation in state and local jurisdictions and lead to ossified regulatory structures given the difficulty of amending federal legislation.[21] Patricia Bellia counters that, if Congress waits long enough to allow states to experiment, it can pick the best solution, which should establish a floor of protection below which states may not go.[22] She also rejects the idea that decentralized regulation is good for its own sake in the privacy regulation realm, because privacy harms can cross state borders and because "inconsistent regulations generat[e] compliance burdens."[23] For instance, without a uniform nationwide standard, police may have a difficult time figuring out which state rule applies when they have to track an individual from one state to the next, intercept communications that transcend state borders, or access internet images, the source of which is impossible to determine.

At the same time, some types of surveillance—including, for example, CCTV and ALPRs—are likely to be localized in their effect. And there can be advantages to legislating at that level. As the Supreme Court has said:

> [The] federal structure of joint sovereigns preserves to the people numerous advantages. It assures a decentralized government that will be more sensitive to the diverse needs of a heterogenous society; it increases opportunity for citizen involvement in democratic processes; it allows for more innovation and experimentation in government; and it makes government more responsive by putting the states in competition for a mobile citizenry.[24]

Thus, both Schwartz and Bellia make valid points. Surveillance that impinges solely on a particular locale, such as citywide ALPR and camera systems, is probably best handled through municipal ordinances such as those contemplated by the Nashville City Council. Federal legislation is most obviously preferable when dealing with national security surveillance and other surveillance technologies that routinely cross state lines. In other situations, the states should probably be dominant. However, preemption by Congress might sometimes be the best approach, if sufficient state experimentation occurs before Congress weighs in and if states are permitted to provide more protection against virtual searches if they so desire. Administrative regulations, and the administrative law jurisprudence that governs them, should play a significant role here as well, a point I develop in chapter 7.

The Goals of This Book

The primary question addressed in this book is how, consistent with the United States Constitution, federal, state, and local legislative bodies can regulate virtual searches in a way that adequately addresses the important conflicting concerns they raise. After discussing the constitutional rules that provide the general framework for regulation in this area, this book develops a five-category typology of virtual searches and uses that typology to provide a roadmap for city councils, community groups, and state and federal legislatures negotiating the potential uses of technological surveillance by law enforcement. My earlier book, *Privacy at Risk*, focused on what this book calls "suspect-driven" searches and seizures—investigatory actions aimed at an identified suspect. But police today routinely resort to two other technological and data-driven investigative techniques, specifically virtual searches that use algorithms designed to detect as-yet undiscovered or uncommitted crime (what I call "profile-driven" searches) and virtual searches that use technology to nab criminal perpetrators by matching crime scene information like DNA or cell phone location with particular individuals ("event-driven" searches). Also extremely important to modern law enforcement are the surveillance and data acquisition *systems* that enable these various types of virtual searches ("program-driven" searches). Finally, there are virtual searches undertaken by private parties rather than the government but under ambiguous circumstances that could make them government surrogates ("volunteer-driven" searches). Each of these virtual search domains deserves separate attention, and each receives its own chapter in this book.

In developing this typology, I largely sidestep the efficacy issue. The jury is still out on whether many of the techniques discussed here work; for instance, research on the usefulness of ALPRs often reaches ambiguous results.[25] Further, as discussed in chapter 5, some virtual search technologies—in particular, "predictive policing" algorithms based on local data that identify crime hot spots—work well only if backed up by considerable local research. But it is also the case that, inevitably, surveillance technology will improve. For instance, facial recognition technology, once considered to be laughably bad, is now routinely used as a passcode to open cell phones. In this book I will assume that, as one of the commentators in the Nashville meeting put it, the "dots can be connected" between virtual search techniques and law enforcement goals.

That still leaves a two-part normative question with respect to each virtual search technique: Should it be allowed and, if so, under what circumstances? This book stakes out a position between, on the one hand, the nonchalant attitude toward virtual searches taken by many courts, legislatures, and police departments and, on the other hand, calls by privacy advocates for abolition of surveillance regimes—or what often amounts to the same thing, stringent warrant and probable cause requirements. I defend two central propositions, one substantive and one procedural. Substantively, I argue that the justification for police action should not be a unitary standard of probable cause but rather should vary proportionate to the action's intrusiveness, an implementation of what I call the "proportionality principle." Procedurally, I argue that, while courts should continue their authorizing role when virtual searches focus on specific individuals, legislatures should take the lead in defining "intrusiveness" for purposes of the proportionality principle and should also be the preferred arbiter in deciding whether the executive branch may develop virtual search programs that focus on the community as a whole.

Taken together, these two guideposts protect privacy and related values without unduly restricting the police. They also ensure democratic participation in the process of defining the scope of government surveillance. With proper regulation, governments can take advantage of technological advances without undermining the values of a free society.

Constitutional Constraints

The Fourth Amendment has to be a prominent source of rules regulating virtual searches. After all, the text of the amendment states that "the people shall be secure from unreasonable searches and seizures of their persons, houses, papers and effects." It also requires that a search warrant particularly describe the items sought and where they will be found and that a judge should issue a warrant only if there is probable cause to believe those items will be there. More generally, since colonial times, the Fourth Amendment has always been seen as the ultimate bulwark against arbitrary government intrusions; in the words of James Otis, often considered the father of the Fourth Amendment, the prohibition against unreasonable searches and seizures was the Founders' response to British practices that placed "the liberty of every man in the hands of every petty officer."[1]

Yet, to date, the Fourth Amendment has rarely had any impact on virtual searches beyond the electronic eavesdropping setting. The United States Supreme Court, which is the ultimate arbiter on the meaning of the Fourth Amendment, has defined the word "search" very narrowly. And even when it has determined something to be a search, it has often been quite willing to let police proceed without a warrant. Only recently has the Court recognized that, now that we are in the Information Age, all this might have been a mistake.

The Court's struggle with what to do about virtual searches is a story worth briefly recounting, for a number of reasons. First, the Court's decisions set out the constitutional floor, below which legislatures may not go. In crafting rules governing virtual searches, policy makers need to make sure they abide by these constraints. Second, the Court's struggle exposes many of the fault lines between the often-competing goals of public safety and private security. Third, the story makes clear that the Fourth Amendment, at least as construed today, does not begin to address the many regulatory issues that virtual searches raise. Commentators' attempts to fill these holes by rejiggering Fourth Amendment analysis have also come up short.

The Definition of "Search," Phase I: From Physical Intrusion to Privacy

One might think that the word "search" in the Fourth Amendment means looking for, in, at, or through something. That is the definition found in the typical dictionary.[2] But it has never been the constitutional definition of the word.

In the beginning, a search, for Fourth Amendment purposes, meant physically intruding into one of the four "protected areas" listed in the amendment: persons, houses, papers, and effects. Thus, for instance, according to a 1924 Supreme Court decision, police forays onto private property outside the area immediately surrounding the home were not searches—even though they involved trespasses—because they did not target the "house."[3] Nor was the Court willing to hold, four years later in *Olmstead v. United States*,[4] that bugging phone wires outside a house was a search or, per *Goldman v. United States*,[5] that placing a "detectaphone" against a wall was a search (although in a later case the Court held that using a "spike mike" inserted beneath the floorboards of a house wall did trigger Fourth Amendment protection).[6]

Looking inside a home from a "lawful vantage point" like a sidewalk did not implicate the Constitution either, because "the eye cannot commit the trespass condemned by the Fourth Amendment."[7] If that is true, then clearly the observation of activities that take place in public is not a search. In short, since, by definition, virtual searches do not involve physical entry—again, envision cops sitting in their patrol cars looking at video feeds or in their offices accessing information on their computers—this intrusion-based characterization of Fourth Amendment protection, had it persisted, would have left these types of police actions unregulated by the Constitution.

Then, in 1967, came the decision in *Katz v. United States*.[8] Charlie Katz was a gambler; to elude the cops, he would saunter down to the nearby public telephone booth (remember those?) to place and receive bets. The police figured as much, but they wanted definite proof. So they rigged a very primitive listening device, consisting of two microphones and a recorder, on top of two of the three booths that Katz frequented. To make sure he used one of the bugged booths, the police got the phone company to render the third phone out of order. The recorder picked up several days' worth of conversations about bets, all of which were introduced into evidence at Katz's trial.[9]

Katz's defense team argued that the recording violated the Fourth Amendment because the police did not obtain a warrant authorizing the seizure of his conversations. But the government had a seemingly invincible rebuttal, at least if Fourth Amendment language and precedent were any guide. First, by its terms, the Fourth Amendment applies only to "persons, houses, papers and effects," and a phone booth fits into none of those categories (the only possible candidate, "effects," has traditionally been confined to items of personal property). Second, even if a phone booth *were* considered to be a "constitutionally protected area," the police did not "commit the trespass condemned by the Fourth Amendment" because the tape recorder did not intrude into the booth or the wires that carried Katz's conversations. Third, even if those two arguments somehow failed, obtaining a recording of those conversations could not trigger Fourth Amendment protection because intangible things such as conversations are not only not one of the four protected categories listed in the Fourth Amendment, they cannot be "seized" in the first instance.

As powerful as those arguments were as a formal matter, they did not persuade Justice Stewart and six of his colleagues; only Justice Black dissented from the opinion finding in favor of Katz (Justice Marshall did not participate in hearing the case). In rejecting the government's arguments and holding that the police should have obtained a warrant authorizing the recording, the Court appeared to declare that the debate over whether a phone booth is a constitutionally protected area—a person, house, paper, or effect—was irrelevant. Rather, Justice Stewart's opinion famously stated that "the Fourth Amendment protects people, not places."[10] Even more famously, Justice Harlan, in his concurring opinion, stated that, in defining the protection afforded by the Fourth Amendment, previous cases had really been focused on privacy, not trespass. As he put it, "the rule that has emerged from prior decisions is a twofold requirement, first that a person have exhibited an actual (subjective) expectation of privacy and, second, that the expectation be one that society is prepared to recognize as 'reasonable.'"[11]

The "reasonable expectation of privacy" language has since become the primary means of defining when law enforcement engages in a Fourth Amendment search. Like the pre-*Katz* definition of "search," this new formulation is still narrower than the lay definition of that word. But, given the resolution of the *Katz* case, the "expectations of privacy" language seemed to contemplate a much broader scope to Fourth Amendment protection than the trespass-oriented language found in earlier Court opinions. One might reasonably assume that *Katz*'s redirection of the Fourth Amendment toward a privacy focus would open the door to fuller protection against warrantless virtual searches.

Except that is not what happened. Instead, the Supreme Court pretty much confined the *Katz* decision, as lawyers would say, "to its facts," meaning that virtual searches that did not, like the one in *Katz*, involve an interception of communications were still left largely unregulated by the Constitution. The Court accomplished this feat through its development of four doctrines: the *knowing exposure doctrine* (we should not expect privacy with respect to anything we expose to the public); the *general public use doctrine* (we should not expect privacy from police use of technology that anyone can easily obtain, even if the technology is used to observe activity that is not exposed to the public); the *evidence-specific doctrine* (any technology, even if not in general public use, that merely discovers evidence of crime, and nothing else, does not infringe legitimate privacy interests); and the *assumption of risk doctrine* (by revealing confidences to a third party, we assume the risk they will be revealed to the government and thus should not expect they will be kept private). To illustrate the huge gaps in privacy protection these doctrines contemplated and how they have recently changed, consider a hypothetical account of a man stopped for a traffic violation.

The Definition of "Search," Phase II: From Privacy to Physical Intrusion

One day in the spring of 2022, Ahmad Abdullah is stopped for driving at an unreasonable speed by Officer Jones of the Chicago Police Department. While issuing the citation, Jones notices that Abdullah seems very nervous. (Most police accounts of people who end up being targets mention something about the individual's nervousness, even though, in my experience, nervousness is a natural state when confronted by a cop.) Given Abdullah's anxiety, Officer Jones asks to search Abdullah's car and Abdullah consents. Jones finds nothing of interest. But he still notes down Abdullah's license plate and phone number. Jones also gets out his Raytheon electronic-magnetic radiation device, which can detect bombs and other weapons. Abdullah objects at this point, but Jones scans the car anyway; again, he finds nothing and lets Abdullah go on his way.

Officer Jones remains suspicious, however. Using signals from Abdullah's cell phone and data from automatic license plate readers in the area, the police track Abdullah to his home and monitor every trip he takes over the next week. They also use closed-circuit television (CCTV) cameras to watch him when he leaves his apartment and goes for walks; this is an easy task, since Chicago trains more than 35,000 cameras, many equipped with zoom and night-viewing capacity, on its urban populace day and night—some operating openly, others covertly—and all patched into the city's multimillion-dollar operations center.[12] The camera images pick up the fact that Abdullah visits several mosques in the area. Now even more suspicious, the police deploy a drone to stalk his comings and goings. They request and obtain Abdullah's bank and phone records and pay ChoicePoint, a private data aggregator, for any information about Abdullah that the company has obtained from public and quasipublic records. Finally, they set up an observation post in a building across the way from Abdullah's apartment and use a Star-Tron, essentially a high-powered binocular device with night vision, to watch his activities inside his apartment.

By any measure, this is a fairly elaborate surveillance operation, using many different types of technology, all of which could be said to infringe Abdullah's privacy. Yet none of it is regulated by the Constitution, at least as of yet. That is because, despite *Katz*, the Supreme Court has interpreted the reasonable expectation of privacy definition of search to mean something not very different from the old intrusion-oriented test.

Knowing Exposure

Katz itself said that, while conversations over a public phone can be private for Fourth Amendment purposes, "[w]hat a person knowingly exposes to the public, even in his own home or office, is not a subject of Fourth Amendment protection."[13] The Supreme Court has confirmed this notion in several cases since. In one 1983 case (*United States v. Knotts*) it stated: "A person travelling in an automobile on public thoroughfares has no reasonable expectation of privacy in his movements from one place to another."[14] Six years later, the Court relied on the same notion in holding that police could use a plane to spy on a backyard without implicating the Fourth Amendment; after all, "any member of the public in navigable airspace" could have seen what the police saw and no physical intrusion onto property was involved.[15] In an earlier case involving a flyover of a yard surrounded by a ten-foot-high fence, Chief Justice Burger—apparently recently returned from a trip to London—had explained a similar conclusion by noting that anyone in a "double-decker bus" could have seen what the police saw from their plane![16]

So what does this knowing exposure doctrine mean for virtual searches? For one, it makes the Fourth Amendment inapplicable to the CCTV system used to monitor Abdullah because that system focuses entirely on activities that take place in public; for the same reason, the knowing exposure doctrine might well exempt from constitutional regulation satellite and drone cameras, some of which are precise enough to read license plate numbers and are now being deployed in several cities, as long as they are directed only at public activities.[17] And the doctrine means that the Fourth Amendment does not apply to cell phone tracking technology of the type used in Abdullah's case, again because it picks up only public travels. By federal law, cell phones must be capable of indicating their location within 15 feet,[18] and the police have been quick to take advantage of this tool, in recent years making millions of requests to phone companies for help with phone tracking.[19] In short, under the knowing exposure doctrine, police can monitor anything we do outside our homes without worrying about the Constitution.

In 2012, the Supreme Court took a cautious step toward rectifying this situation. In *United States v. Jones*,[20] the Court held that planting a GPS device on a car and using it to track Jones's car was a Fourth Amendment search. But the majority was careful to limit its decision to use of a GPS covertly placed on the car—what the Court termed a "trespass." Harkening back to pre-*Katz* days, that is a very narrow holding, limited to when the tracking device works a physical intrusion on private property. While a number of justices were unhappy with this limitation (as discussed below in more detail), the Court has yet to construe the Fourth Amendment in a way that governs the real-time cell phone signal tracking that occurred in Abdullah's case, because such tracking does not involve a trespass. Without infringing on Fourth Amendment interests, the government might also be able to require that every car be outfitted with a Radio Frequency Identification Device that communicates current and past routes to an Intelligent Transportation System computer.[21] No technical trespass is involved in that scenario either, because the transponder is placed in the car before the owner buys it.

General Public Use

The second doctrine construing the reach of the Fourth Amendment looks at whether any technology used by the government is "in general public use"; if so, no search occurs, even if the surveillance is of the inside of the home, as long as the surveillance takes place from a "lawful vantage point." In 1986, the Supreme Court faced a Fourth Amendment claim brought by Dow Chemical Company, arguing that use of a $22,000 mapmaking camera to spy on its manufacturing plant from the air was a Fourth Amendment search. Recognizing that the knowing exposure doctrine might spell doom for such a claim, Dow Chemical emphasized that the mapmaking camera was a specialized device that a "member of the public" was unlikely to have. But the Court demurred, declaring that such cameras are "generally available to the public" and thus police need no justification to use it.[22]

Fifteen years later, the Court appeared to rethink this idea. In *Kyllo v. United States*,[23] it held—contrary to what one might have expected from *Dow Chemical*—that a thermal imaging device costing only about $10,000 is not in general public use. Therefore, the Court concluded, relying on it to ascertain heat differentials inside a house *is* a search. But *Kyllo* is a paper tiger, for two reasons.

First, *Kyllo* did not reject the general public use doctrine. So presumably any item that is easily purchasable, including binoculars, telescopes, or night-vision devices like the Star-Tron used in Abdullah's case (which can be purchased online for between $200 and $1,000) can be used without triggering the Fourth Amendment. And it's worth noting that today, twenty years after *Kyllo*, even thermal imagers of the type at issue in that case are much cheaper these days.

The alert reader might respond that, besides the availability of the technology used, there was one other thing that distinguishes *Kyllo* from *Dow Chemical*: *Kyllo* involved surveillance of the inside of a home, whereas *Dow Chemical* involved surveillance of the outside of business property. But, according to *Kyllo*, that doesn't matter as long as the technology the police use to peer inside a house is also available to the general public. While some justices have expressed consternation about this result,[24] the lower courts have long adhered to it.[25]

And it could be even worse, at least for the privacy buff. *Kyllo* states that even sophisticated technology—devices that are *not* in general public use—can be used to look inside a home if it only detects what a cop could see with the naked eye from a lawful vantage point.[26] Taken literally, that means satellite and drone cameras can look in your picture window if all they detect is something an officer who happens to be passing by could see from the sidewalk.

Evidence-Specific

Even those parts of the home that are curtained off may not be protected from sophisticated technological surveillance if the technology is evidence-specific, meaning that it detects only items that are evidence of criminal activity. This idea—the third Supreme Court doctrine defining "reasonable expectations of privacy"—was first broached in a case involving a drug-sniffing dog, where the Court concluded that "government conduct that can reveal whether [an item is contraband] and no other arguably 'private' fact[] compromises no legitimate privacy interest."[27] Some scholars have called this a "binary search," because it tells police whether, and only whether, an item of interest is present. However, I prefer the term "evidence-specific" to convey the idea that this doctrine applies only when the items discovered by such devices are illegal or associated with crime, such as the drugs found by trained canine units.

As anyone who has visited an airport knows, scientists have developed "mechanical dogs" that can sniff out weapons and contraband. Most of these instruments, particularly if based on x-ray technology, are not evidence-specific; they expose other items as well. But if evidence-specific devices can be developed, such as the Raytheon device used against Abdullah, the logic of this doctrine would allow police to cruise the streets scanning cars, people, and homes for illicit items without infringing on Fourth Amendment interests in any way. That type of virtual search would, by definition, reveal evidence only of crimes or potential threats.

This doctrine too may be in transition, in light of the Supreme Court's 2013 decision in *Florida v. Jardines*.[28] There the Court held that a dog-sniff of a home from the sidewalk leading up to it is a search. However, as in *Jones*, the Court limited this holding to situations where there is physical intrusion on private property, here the curtilage (think of the curtilage as a skirt around the home). So if police physically detain a person for the sole purpose of using an evidence-specific device, the Fourth Amendment might be implicated, not because of the scan by the device but because of the seizure of the person. But if, as in Abdullah's case, the scan takes place in the course of an otherwise lawful traffic stop, that potential obstacle to an evidence-specific search disappears. Thus, even after *Jardines*, evidence-specific searches do not in and of themselves implicate the Fourth Amendment.

This conclusion is particularly important because of the huge increase in evidence-specific technology that is available to police today. The most prominent examples are facial recognition and license plate reader systems that match faces or plates to "most-wanted" hot lists. If these systems function as advertised, they might be classified as evidence-specific (and thus ungoverned by the Fourth Amendment), since they alert only to persons or cars that have been shown to be associated with crimes.

Assumption of Risk

While the first three doctrines are fairly capacious in their exemptions from Fourth Amendment protection, they are peanuts compared to the fourth doctrine defining when expectations of privacy are reasonable. In a series of decisions—by far the most wide-ranging and important in this technological age—the Supreme Court has held that we assume the risk that information disclosed to others will be handed over to the government and thus we cannot reasonably expect it to be private; to put this in legalese, a person (the first party) has no say about whether the government (the second party) can obtain his or her personal information when it is voluntarily surrendered to another person or entity (the third party), which explains why this rule is also often called the "third party doctrine." The most important decision in this regard is *United States v. Miller*.[29] In *Miller* the Court held that an individual "takes the risk, in revealing his affairs to another, that the information will be conveyed by that person to the government . . . even if the information is revealed on the assumption that it will be used only for a limited purpose and the confidence placed in the third party will not be betrayed."[30]

Read that language again: even if provided for a limited purpose, and even if conveyed with the understanding that the third party will not betray one's trust, information voluntarily given to a third party is not protected by the Fourth Amendment. This doctrine was first developed during the 1960s and early 1970s in cases in which the third party was a person (a friend or acquaintance) who might decide for his or her own reasons to reveal someone's secrets to others.[31] But in *Miller*, decided in 1976, the third party was a bank. The Court held that even here one assumes the risk of a breach of confidence, and therefore that depositors cannot reasonably expect that the information they convey to their banks will be protected by the Fourth Amendment. In *Smith v. Maryland*,[32] the Court held the same thing with respect to phone numbers maintained by a phone company for billing purposes, stating that because telephone users "know that they must convey numerical information of the phone company; that the phone company has facilities for recording this information; and that the phone company does in fact record this information for a variety of legitimate business purposes . . . it is too much to believe [that users] harbor any general expectation that the numbers they dial will remain secret."[33]

Note the subtle distinction between these cases and *Katz*. Katz won because neither he nor the person on the other end of the line "invited" (to use the Court's word) the government.[34] However, if instead of keeping mum about the gambling transaction Katz's fellow gambler had decided to report those conversations to the police, or had turned out to be a government informant, then that was too bad for Katz. And if the police had wanted to get the phone numbers Katz dialed from the phone company, once again Fourth Amendment protection would be absent. In both cases, according to the Supreme Court, the risk of betrayal by the third party (whether a person or a company) is something any hypothetical Katz "assumes," and thus he has no constitutional claim that his privacy was violated. Later in this book (chapter 8), I will argue that there is huge difference between human confidantes, on the one hand, and institutional informants like banks and phone companies on the other. But the Court does not see it that way, at least not yet.

The decisions in *Miller* and *Smith*, which came at the dawn of the Information Age, have enormous implications for law enforcement investigation today. The quantity of the world's recorded data has doubled every year since the mid-1990s.[35] Computing power necessary to store, access, and analyze data has also increased exponentially over the decades and at increasingly cheaper cost.[36] Virtually every aspect of our lives sits on a company's computer somewhere. Yet, without bothering with the Fourth Amendment, government can access all of it. Consider the investigation of Abdullah again: because of the assumption of risk doctrine, the police do not need a warrant or any justification for requesting the digital information they did, whether they obtain it directly or through private companies such as ChoicePoint that exist for the sole purpose of collecting and organizing data. In the old days, aggregating data from disparate sources involved considerable work and a lot of time, if it was possible at all; today it can occur at the touch of a button, with the result that private companies as well as governments excel at creating what Daniel Solove has called "digital dossiers" from public and quasiprivate records.[37]

Once again, however, there are signs that the Supreme Court is starting to realize what it has done. First, there is the revealing exchange between Chief Justice Roberts and the government's attorney in *Jones* who, before the exchange set out below, had resorted to both "knowing exposure" and "assumption of risk" language in arguing that Jones had no constitutionally recognized privacy while he drove the public thoroughfares.

CHIEF JUSTICE ROBERTS: You think there would also not be a search if you put a GPS device on all of *our* cars, monitored *our* movements for a month—you think you are entitled to that under your theory.

SOLICITOR GENERAL MICHAEL DREEBEN: Ah, the Justices of this Court?

ROBERTS: Yes.

DREEBEN: Ah . . .

[Audience laughter (very unusual during oral argument)]

DREEBEN: Under our theory and this Court's cases, the Justices of this Court when driving on public roadways have no greater expectation of privacy . . .

ROBERTS: So your answer is yes. You could tomorrow decide to put a GPS device on every one of *our* cars, follow *us* for a month; no problem under the Constitution?

DREEBEN: Yes.[38]

I emphasize the words "our" and "us" in this exchange because it makes clear that Chief Justice Roberts, and presumably the rest of the Court, recognized that virtual searches make it much easier to surveil not only those "other" people but also the justices themselves and people like them. That development, by itself, may explain some of the Court's recent willingness to rethink its Fourth Amendment precedent. When searches were physical only, police were confronted with natural impediments: not only walls and other opaque surfaces but also strained police budgets and inadequate staffing. Technology is removing those impediments. So now, even the justices and people like them have much less practical privacy from unregulated government intrusion than they did fifty years ago—unless the Court says otherwise, as it did in *Jones*.

In 2018, the Court said so again, this time in a holding that put a significant dent in the assumption of risk/third-party doctrine. *Carpenter v. United States*[39] focused entirely on historical tracking—tracking based on records—as distinguished from the real-time tracking that was the centerpiece of *Jones*. Carpenter was suspected of involvement in a series of store robberies. In a clever investigative move, police accessed over 130 days of cell-site location information (CSLI) from Carpenter's two wireless carriers to see if Carpenter was near the stores when they were robbed. It turned out that, based on close examination of seven days of his CSLI, Carpenter (or at least his phone) was in proximity to at least four of the stores on the relevant days, a discovery that helped nail down the case against him. While the police had a court order to access the CSLI data, that order was not a full-blown warrant based on probable cause. So Carpenter argued that accessing his phone records was an illegal search.

In response, the government trotted out *Miller* and *Smith*: Carpenter, the government argued, knew or should have known that his location information was maintained by his common carrier (after all, everyone knows that without that capability one could not get directions or find the nearest Italian restaurant). Therefore, Carpenter assumed the risk that the carrier would turn that information over to law enforcement. That type of argument would have won had the Court tightly adhered to the holdings in *Miller* and *Smith*. But the Court instead held that the police should have obtained a warrant. Chief Justice Roberts, who wrote the majority opinion, gave a number of reasons for the holding, but two in particular stand out: (1) "There is a world of difference between the limited types of personal information addressed in *Smith* and *Miller* and the exhaustive chronicle of location information casually collected by wireless carriers today,"[40] and (2) "Cell phone location information is not truly 'shared' as one normally understands the term [because] cell phones and the services they provide are . . . indispensable to participation in modern society."[41]

Although *Carpenter* cut against precedent, neither rationale was a complete surprise. The first rationale resonated with the opinions of five justices in *Jones*. Recall that the majority opinion in that case, written by Justice Scalia, focused on the trespass issue. But in his concurring opinion, Justice Alito, joined by three others, argued that Jones should have won even had there been no trespass, given the "prolonged" nature of the tracking that occurred (28 days).[42] In a separate concurring opinion, Justice Sotomayor, while joining the majority's trespass reasoning, likewise expressed concern about the "aggregated" data that tracking devices allow.[43] So five justices in *Jones* fastened on the government's ability to amass significant quantities of information as a reason for triggering the Fourth Amendment, an idea to which we shall return in chapter 3.

The second rationale proffered by Roberts rightly called out as a fiction the notion that we "voluntarily" transfer information to our phone companies. We do so only in the thinnest sense of the word voluntary. This side of hermits, people *must* provide information to third-party entities—ranging from phone companies to banks to internet providers—to function in modern society; thus, they should not be said to have willingly assumed the risk that their information will be revealed to the government. Scholars, litigants, and dissenting justices had been making that kind of argument as far back as *Miller*.[44] But not until 2018, 40 years later, did a majority of the Court buy it, and even then only by a 5–4 margin.[45]

The dissenters in *Carpenter* predicted that the majority's holding spelled the end of the third-party doctrine and that it would bring disastrous results. They noted that records maintained by third parties are crucial to white collar investigations, drug crime investigations, and a host of other law enforcement efforts.[46] Under pre-*Carpenter* law, these types of records could usually be obtained with a subpoena, which is much easier to obtain than a warrant, because it only requires that the evidence sought is "relevant" to an investigation, not that it will provide strong proof of the case against the suspect. But if the reasoning of *Carpenter* is carried to its logical conclusion, the dissenters warned, records of financial transactions, communications, transportation, and virtually every other type of computerized information held by third parties could be obtained only via a warrant, which could compromise and perhaps completely stymie attempts to access them.[47]

Perhaps in response to these complaints, the majority explicitly emphasized that it was limiting its decision in *Carpenter* to its facts (a common move that, as we've seen with *Katz* itself, allows the Court to minimize the impact of its holding in later cases). Thus, as of right now, all we know for sure is that a warrant is required to obtain a large amount of CSLI data and that, as far as the Court is concerned, a subpoena or even a mere request might be sufficient to get other types of personal information collected and maintained by third parties. The fact remains that *Carpenter* has thrown into disarray Fourth Amendment law as it applies to virtual searches.

The Definition of "Search," Phase III: From Physical Intrusion Back to Privacy?

Each of the four doctrines just canvassed has undergone a transformation. *Jones* indicated that some activities that are "knowingly exposed" to the public are nonetheless protected by the Fourth Amendment. That decision's indication that GPS tracking is a search also suggests that the general public use doctrine no longer has much punch, because cheap spyware that allows constant tracking of phones is currently available to, and used by, millions of people.[48] *Jardines* puts strictures on the reach of the evidence-specific doctrine. And *Carpenter*, although currently limited to its facts, could be the beginning of the end for the third party doctrine.

Because of these cases, the boundaries of the Fourth Amendment are in a state of significant flux. Many justices and commentators think this is a bad thing, and they blame it on *Katz*'s expectation-of-privacy test. While they might like the holdings of particular cases, they do not like the underlying rationale. Privacy, they assert, is an extremely amorphous concept that leaves the scope of the Fourth Amendment at the mercy of whatever a majority of justices says it is. So, they conclude, the values protected by the Fourth Amendment should be rethought in way that makes it both more easily administrable and more consistent with what the Founders had in mind when they drafted the amendment.[49]

Justice Gorsuch's dissent in *Carpenter* provides a good example of this type of reasoning. Although his opinion intimates that he thought the location data in that case was protected by the Fourth Amendment, he did not think the *Katz* test was the way to get there.

On one hand, he castigated *Miller* and *Smith* for their position that people do not reasonably expect privacy in information they surrender to third parties—"no one believes that, if they ever did."[50] He asserted that simply knowing about risk does not mean one assumes responsibility for it (otherwise, he points out, pedestrians would not be able to sue drivers who hit them on the sidewalk, given their awareness that accidents happen). Neither, he noted, do we consent to a government search of our information simply by allowing a private third party to have it.[51]

On the other hand, Gorsuch continued, the deficiencies in *Miller* and *Smith* do not mean the best solution is simply to accept the

Katz test and say that those cases got the reasonable-expectation-of-privacy analysis wrong. *Katz*, Gorsuch argued, is unmoored in the Fourth Amendment and, as a result, leads to arbitrary decisions. He noted, as many have before, that in prohibiting unreasonable searches the Fourth Amendment does not mention privacy but only persons, houses, papers, and effects; moreover, the eighteenth-century cases that triggered its inclusion in the Bill of Rights were also focused on these property interests.[52] To make matters worse, Gorsuch continued, *Katz* has created a mess. Using the majority opinion in *Carpenter* as an example, Gorsuch pointed out that, after that decision, the lower courts have no idea whether accessing less than seven days of CSLI is a search, whether accessing seven days of bank records (as opposed to seven days of CSLI) is a search, whether accessing the CSLI of dozens of people at a particular time is a search, and whether real-time cell phone tracking is a search.[53] More important, he asserted, the "expectation of privacy" test does not provide the courts with any reference point for answering these questions other than their intuition.[54]

In place of *Katz*, Gorsuch suggested that the Court link the Fourth Amendment threshold to "positive law," a phrase that refers to well-established common law rules regarding property rights and other social conventions, as well as statutes that create such rights. For instance, perhaps the act of allowing common carriers to maintain cell-site location data could be seen as a "bailment," a centuries-old property transfer concept that requires the "bailee," the person receiving the goods, to maintain or use them as the owner would but without compromising the owner's interests (think of a valet with your car keys, or an airline with your suitcase). Or statutes might give people certain concrete rights to control information, as the Health Information and Portability Act (commonly known as "HIPAA") does.[55]

A number of writers, from all points in the political spectrum, have made similar arguments against maintaining the expectation-of-privacy test as the lodestar for Fourth Amendment protection.[56] They, too, have pointed to the weak historical basis for *Katz* and the amorphous nature of privacy. Most have settled on some sort of property theme as a promising alternative, although others have argued in favor of different governing concepts, such as preservation of dignity, ensuring trust in government, or guaranteeing security from oppressive and indiscriminate surveillance.

It is not clear where the Supreme Court will ultimately end up on this point, although *Carpenter* appears to have doubled down on *Katz*. In support of that position are both negative and positive arguments. Beginning with the negative point: neither property law nor any of the other suggested Fourth Amendment thresholds are ultimately any more self-defining than "privacy." That goes without saying in connection with concepts such as dignity, trust in government, and freedom from oppression. Even "property," which has a long history of statutory and judicial treatment, turns up lacking, at least when applied to virtual searches. Contrary to Justice Scalia's assertion in *Jones*, merely attaching a device to someone's property, without interfering with that property, was probably not enough in common law to effect an actionable trespass.[57] Contrary to Gorsuch's suggestion in *Carpenter*, there is no common law basis for saying that one's location, or a record of it, is one's property that can be bailed to another. The same observation can be made with respect to many other targets of virtual searches. For instance, the records that a bank or a credit card or phone company keeps about one's transactions, or the conversations that people engage in over phones or computers, are not something one "owns."

Indeed, in their fascinating book titled *Mine!*, Michael Heller and James Salzman call into question all sorts of dogmas about property, demonstrating that, in today's world, possession is often not "nine-tenths" of the law (and is perhaps only one-tenth!), that the home is not always one's castle, and that even the content of our bodies can be up for grabs. Most relevant to this book, they point out that "[t]here is as yet no dominant principle for data ownership."[58] More generally, they state "[a]ll property conflicts exist as competing stories [and] there are no natural, correct descriptions that frame *mine* versus *mine* conflicts."[59]

That leads to a positive argument in favor of privacy as the central feature of Fourth Amendment protection. Any effort to expand the Fourth Amendment's language to cover virtual searches—say, by interpreting the definition of "papers" and "effects" to cover third-party records and communications—is likely to be persuasive only if it ties into the intuition that these situations involve intrusions into privacy. That is why *Katz* moved to the expectation-of-privacy rubric in the first place: without it, the Fourth Amendment would not have had anything to say about police eavesdropping on people's phone conversations![60] Even *Jones*, a case purporting to apply a property-based approach to the Fourth Amendment, finessed the issue. The precise holding of *Jones* was that "the Government's installation of a GPS device on a target's vehicle, *and its use of that device to monitor the vehicle's movements*, constitutes a 'search.'"[61] As the italicized language makes clear, something besides or in addition to interference with property was the real trigger of Fourth Amendment protection in that case, and that trigger was freedom from unjustified government monitoring even while in public spaces—or, in a phrase, "invasion of privacy."

Other values said to be the gravamen of a Fourth Amendment claim suffer from the same lack of fit that afflicts property-based notions. Preservation of dignity, maintenance of trust, and limiting oppressive government power can all plausibly be said to be goals of the Fourth Amendment. But the protections for speech, press, and religion found in the First Amendment, the rights accorded to criminal defendants in the Fifth and Sixth Amendments, and the prohibition on cruel and unusual punishment in the Eighth Amendment are also aimed at promoting dignity, trust between governors and the governed, and limited government power.[62] The particular way in which the Fourth Amendment does so is through requiring justification for government infringement of our reasonable expectations of *privacy*. Protection of privacy is a capacious enough concept that it can encompass all these interests while simultaneously providing a distinctive purpose for the Fourth Amendment.

A second positive argument in favor of privacy as the focus of Fourth Amendment protection—especially when compared to property, the most commonly proffered substitute for it—is distributive. Private property is not evenly distributed. Many people have very little of it. But everyone can make a plausible claim to have privacy expectations with respect to most of their daily affairs, whether they live in a tent situated on public property or in a mansion surrounded by acres; whether they travel mostly by foot or by car; whether they carry their belongings in a paper bag or in K9-resistant briefcases; and whether they disclose their personal information because they want to obtain welfare or to win tax breaks. In its original formulation by Justice Harlan, the *Katz* test contained a subjective as well as objective component—the target had to actually expect privacy as well as be reasonable in doing so.[63] But the subjective component has gradually disappeared from the Court's jurisprudence. That is a good development, for two reasons. First, subjective expectations are too easily manipulated; as Professor Amsterdam noted, the government can eliminate privacy expectations simply by announcing when and where searches will take place.[64] Second, and more important, the subjective component should be considered irrelevant because any perception among poor people that they lack privacy will often be due solely to the fact that they do not have the wealth, education, or clout to protect it. In such circumstances, concluding that they therefore ought not to have a legally recognized expectation of privacy is unfair—and unreasonable.

Anyone not immersed in Fourth Amendment jurisprudence might ask why the foregoing discussion is necessary. Rather than trying to choose between privacy and some other value as the constitutional focus, why not just define "search" the way a layperson would, so that the Fourth Amendment would be construed to cover any government effort to look for, at, into, or through a person, house, paper, or effect? Several scholars, including the one writing this book, have argued for such a definition.[65] But for the foreseeable future that move is not going to come from the Supreme Court. Moreover, even that move would not cover many types of virtual searches unless words such as "papers" and "effects" are distorted beyond recognition to include the conversations found to be protected in *Katz* or the personal data in possession of third parties held to be protected in *Carpenter*. The tendency exemplified by *Katz*, *Jones*, and *Carpenter*—which is to think of the Fourth Amendment as a bulwark against significant government intrusions into privacy—is a much better vehicle for providing constitutional protection against virtual searches.

For all these reasons, as well as a few more developed in chapter 3, the remainder of this book will assume that the core role of the Fourth Amendment with respect to virtual searches is to regulate significant privacy intrusions by the government.

The Reasonableness Inquiry

Agreement on the essential point that the Fourth Amendment's ban on unreasonable searches is meant to protect our privacy from arbitrary government intrusions is only the beginning. Fourth Amendment analysis requires two steps. The first, which we have been discussing up to this point, is the threshold question of whether the Fourth Amendment is implicated at all. The second step is determining whether a police action determined to be a search is "reasonable." Even assuming the Fourth Amendment applies, much hard work still needs to go into figuring out the extent to which privacy concerns should lead to limitations on law enforcement's use of technology.

Go back to Abdullah and assume that every use of technology in his case was a Fourth Amendment search. Do the police need probable cause to believe Abdullah is committing a crime before they can resort to these techniques, or will some lesser showing suffice? Is a court order required, or can the police decide on their own whether the requisite justification exists? Those are questions about reasonableness.

The Supreme Court's answer to the reasonableness question has been complex. The Court's cases indicate that, for many searches and seizures, a warrant issued by a judge is often required when there is time to get one. The warrant, which the Fourth Amendment states must be based on probable cause and describe with "particularity" the "place to be searched and the items to be seized," is the preeminent protection afforded against unreasonable searches and seizures. As Justice Robert Jackson put it, the warrant process ensures that the inferences that justify the search or seizure are "drawn by a neutral and detached magistrate" rather than "the officer engaged in the often competitive enterprise of ferreting out crime."[66] Studies of the warrant process find that, while magistrates sometimes merely rubber-stamp police applications, police knowledge that judges will review their applications significantly heightens their "standard of care."[67] That makes sense: when someone is looking over your shoulder, you act more carefully. Additionally, requiring police officers to justify their decision to a judge before they know what they will find (rather than after discovery of evidence of crime) reduces their ability to shape the account of why a search is justified and ensures that the judge's decision will not be tainted by hindsight bias that might arise from knowledge that a search was successful.[68]

Preparing an application for a warrant can be burdensome. But the advent of telephonic warrants, which by now have been around for decades, has substantially reduced the time and effort required,[69] with the Supreme Court recently suggesting that today a warrant can often be obtained in under a half-hour.[70] Thus, the warrant—or at least some sort of ex ante (or "before the fact") review—ought to be a major regulatory tool, and this book will treat it as one.

Even when a warrant is not required because of some exigency (for instance, hot pursuit of a fleeing felon, imminent destruction or disappearance of evidence), the Supreme Court has usually said that a search is "reasonable" only if based on probable cause. Probable cause is a "flexible, commonsense standard" that requires a "fair probability" that evidence will be found;[71] it exists where there are "sufficient . . . reasonable trustworthy" facts and circumstances that would lead a "prudent" person to believe that evidence of crime will be found in a particular location.[72] The probable cause standard requires more than a "bare suspicion" but "less than evidence [that] would justify condemnation," which requires proof beyond a reasonable doubt.[73] Thus, probable cause comes close to a more-likely-than-not showing.

While probable cause is the default standard in determining reasonableness, the Court has also recognized, in an increasing number of circumstances, that searches and seizures can take place on something less than probable cause. The justices have invented a lower justification level—"reasonable suspicion"—to govern most of these situations. Like probable cause, reasonable suspicion requires more than a bare suspicion, but unlike that standard it falls well short of the more-likely-than-not threshold. Additionally, in its "special needs" cases, the Court has recognized that when circumstances "beyond the normal need for law enforcement make the warrant and probable-cause requirements impracticable," searches and seizures may take place even when there is *no* particularized cause.[74] More is said about reasonable suspicion and special needs doctrine in later chapters.

While the Supreme Court's case law addressing when searches and seizures are reasonable has tended to favor the government, the flexibility of the reasonableness inquiry, when combined with the Court's recently demonstrated willingness to expand the scope of the Fourth Amendment, has put constitutional search and seizure law on the cusp of transformation. In particular, *Jones* and *Carpenter* have set the stage for a revolution in search and seizure doctrine both in terms of the Fourth Amendment's threshold and with respect to its reasonableness inquiry. The time is ripe to explore just how far Fourth Amendment protection should extend and how that protection should be implemented. The remainder of this book is devoted to figuring out how legislative bodies like those described in chapter 1—bodies such as the Nashville City Council, the Tennessee state legislature, and the United States Congress—might regulate virtual searches consistent with the Court's case law.

3

Proportionality Analysis

You've seen it on TV, in both crime dramas and reality police shows. Investigating a murder case, the cops zero in on a "person of interest" (POI), perhaps the husband or boyfriend of the victim. But the POI has a pretty good alibi, or at least a plausible story of innocence, and the veteran detective leading the investigation has to admit that she has only a hunch, nothing she could present to a judge. So she goes online. She finds CCTV footage that reveals that, for several weeks before the murder, the POI surreptitiously followed the victim when she left her home during the day. The detective also contacts the POI's credit card company for information about his recent purchases and finds out that, a week before the crime, he bought a gun that could be the murder weapon. She then accesses GPS data indicating that the POI was not where he claimed to be on the day of the offense.

These types of virtual searches could be crucial in nailing the POI. But if they are governed by the Fourth Amendment (as chapter 2 argued they should be), and the Fourth Amendment requires a warrant based on probable cause, the problem for the detective is apparent. She cannot legally rely on virtual searches to get the investigation off the ground. Maybe there is a more old-fashioned way of pursuing this investigation. But maybe there isn't. And, in any event, it sure would be nice if police could use the tools technology has given them.

At the same time, any leeway afforded the police in this type of investigation must proceed with caution. If the goal is to limit arbitrary privacy intrusions, permitting law enforcement to get any preliminary information it wants, simply on a hunch, sets off alarm bells. Open the door too wide for these types of inquiries and the government could, at least in theory, very easily compile digital dossiers on all of us.

This is the central dilemma posed by virtual search technology. It vastly improves law enforcement's ability to solve crime. But it also triggers anxiety about privacy intrusions.

In much of the coverage about virtual searches, the anxiety wins out. Newspaper stories tend to paint a bleak picture of technological policing, with headlines such as "Sensor Devices Threaten 'New Age of Excessive Police Surveillance'"[1] or "The Making of the US Surveillance State."[2] Many academic articles and advocacy pieces by civil liberties organizations are also of the sky-is-falling variety. The typical author describes a new surveillance technology, points out how it has or might make policing both more intrusive and more likely to affect large swaths of the population, and then calls for a warrant requirement, some version of "privacy by design" that prevents or significantly inhibits police use of the technology, or perhaps even a prohibition on whatever surveillance technique is at issue.[3] Maintenance of privacy is the main, if the not the dominant, goal. Orin Kerr has referred to this dynamic as the "equilibrium adjustment" approach to the Fourth Amendment: law enforcement must not be allowed to gain the upper hand but rather should be handcuffed to ensure a level playing field.[4] In *Carpenter v. United States*, even the Supreme Court, which traditionally has tended to favor the police side of the equation, joined the chorus. One reason the majority gave for requiring a warrant to access CSLI is that the tracking it enabled was "remarkably easy, cheap, and efficient compared to traditional tools."[5]

But consider the logic at work here. As Ric Simmons has argued, this reasoning "turns the cost-benefit analysis on its head by seeking to deter some of the most productive searches available to law enforcement."[6] Fighting crime is not one of the government's success stories. In 2019, almost 80% of all serious crimes with victims were not solved by the police, in part because many of them were not reported in the first place.[7] Even reported crimes are seldom solved; for instance, only

60% of murders are cleared.[8] In light of these statistics, preventing or severely limiting virtual searches, which can help detect and investigate unreported as well as reported crimes, may not make sense. Technology should not be shunned simply because it makes policing more efficient, unless the privacy costs are significant.

The privacy costs are there. In some cases, however, those costs are minimal. When that is the case, we should be willing to forego the traditional warrant and probable cause requirements and install a less rigorous regulatory regime. When, instead, the privacy cost is significant, a warrant (or perhaps even something more significant than a warrant) should be required. In other words, the justification the police need to be reasonable in carrying out virtual searches should be proportionate to the privacy invasion they seek.

The Rationale for the Proportionality Principle

Chapter 2 noted that the Supreme Court has been willing to forego the traditional probable cause requirement in a few limited circumstances. In the 1967 case *Camara v. Municipal Court*,[9] for instance, the Court allowed health and safety inspections of houses based simply on the age of the neighborhood and similar factors, without any showing of suspicion with respect to a particular house. And a year later, in *Terry v. Ohio*,[10] the Court allowed police to stop individuals and frisk them for weapons on reasonable suspicion "that criminal activity may be afoot,"[11] making clear that while reasonable suspicion requires more than an inchoate hunch it is not meant to amount to probable cause.[12]

Camara involved what the Court eventually came to call a "special needs" situation because it analyzed a regulatory inspection rather than "ordinary" law enforcement, while *Terry* was a typical street crime investigation. But both cases shared two essential features. First, both involved attempts to prevent harm—from health hazards and from weapons, respectively—rather than solve a crime known to have already occurred, an aspect of these cases to which we will return toward the end of this chapter and in a few other places in this book. More important as far as the Court was concerned was the fact that the police actions in both cases were relatively unintrusive. In *Camara*, the Court stated, and in *Terry* it repeated, language that has been endorsed in numerous other cases: "[T]here is no ready test for determining reasonableness other than by balancing the need to search [or seize] against the invasion which the search [or seizure] entails."[13] In *Camara*, the search involved an inspection of electrical outlets and pipes, presumably something most residents would welcome, so the Court considered the invasion to be minimal. Likewise, while a stop and frisk can be pretty intrusive, it does not amount to a full-blown arrest and a full search of the person, so once again the Court found the invasion to be, relatively speaking, minimal. As a result, the Court concluded, probable cause was not required in either setting.

In my book *Privacy at Risk* I called this "proportionality analysis."[14] Put simply, the proportionality principle states that the justification for a search or seizure should be roughly proportionate to its intrusiveness. This is a common-sense notion that is fully consistent with the Fourth Amendment's requirement that searches and seizures be "reasonable"; nowhere does the amendment mandate probable cause as the sole permissible justification for a search or seizure. Further, I noted in *Privacy at Risk*, proportionality is consistent with the intuition, reflected throughout our jurisprudence, that the government's burden should vary depending on the effect of its actions on individuals:

> The standard of proof in criminal trials is different from that in civil commitment proceedings because of the perceived differences in the deprivation of liberty that each brings. Levels of scrutiny in constitutional litigation vary depending on whether the individual right infringed by the govern is "fundamental" or not. In the entitlements context, the degree of process due before benefits can be terminated depends on the effect of the termination. Outside the constitutional setting, the same sort of thing holds true. In the tort context, for instance,

many courts require greater proof for punitive damages than for compensatory damages.[15]

In dealing with *seizures*—arrests, stops, checkpoints—the Court has pretty much made proportionality the governing principle, holding that while arrests require probable cause, stops require only reasonable suspicion, and brief detentions at checkpoints can occur on an even less demanding variety of "individualized suspicion."[16] Until recently, however, the Court has ignored this grading principle for *searches* that do not fit the special needs rubric or the *Terry* frisk doctrine, instead insisting that "[o]rdinarily, a search—even one that may permissibly be carried out without a warrant—must be based upon 'probable cause' to believe that a violation has occurred."[17] As a result, if a virtual search were said to be governed by the Fourth Amendment, it might "ordinarily" be permissible only if there is probable cause (plus a warrant in nonexigent circumstances).

In *Privacy at Risk*, I called this the "probable cause forever" take on the Fourth Amendment. It is popular among many Fourth Amendment aficionados. But, as applied to virtual searches, the unitary probable-cause-forever standard is problematic, for several reasons.

First, the standard makes policing inefficient and, in some cases, impossible. As the example that started this chapter illustrates, it prevents searches that can provide the evidence needed to establish probable cause. This investigative Catch-22 requires the police to have probable cause to develop probable cause.

The second problem with the probable-cause-forever standard is a direct result of the first: its impact on policing is so great that courts are tempted to forego regulating virtual searches altogether. Because the consequences of doing so are so serious, even liberal Supreme Court justices have been hesitant to call some types of virtual intrusions "searches." In 1983, the Court held that using a beeper to follow a car for an hour was not a search, an unsurprising decision given the knowing exposure doctrine.[18] What was surprising was that the holding was unanimous; Justices Brennan, Marshall, and Stevens, all considered left of the Court's center, agreed that "use of the information received over the airwaves" from the beeper did not implicate the Fourth Amendment, something even some conservative justices were unwilling to say three decades later, at least on the facts of the *Jones* case.[19]

Something similar happened in *Miller*. There, as one would expect, Justices Brennan and Marshall refused to join the majority in the case, instead taking the position that acquisition of bank records is a search.[20] But little noted is the fact that Brennan's dissent in *Miller* did not demand that this action be authorized by a warrant. Rather, Brennan quoted extensively from a California Supreme Court case, which he said "correctly" decided that obtaining bank records via subpoena was unconstitutional "because the subpoena was issued by a United States Attorney rather than by a court or grand jury."[21] While a subpoena issued by a court or grand jury may be harder for prosecutors to obtain than one they themselves issue, it still does not amount to a warrant based on probable cause found by a judge. In effect, Brennan was either saying that accessing *Miller*'s records was not a search or implicitly adopting a proportionality approach.

The third and most important problem with the probable-cause-forever stance is that it ignores the fact that different search techniques visit remarkably different impacts on privacy. Just as *Camara*-type inspections of houses for bad wiring are not as intrusive as ransacking homes for drugs, and just as frisks of a person are less intrusive than full searches of the person, a particular virtual search technique can vary in intrusiveness depending on the circumstances. In more recent cases, some members of the Court have begun to recognize this type of distinction and make it constitutionally significant. As chapter 2 noted, in *Jones* four justices distinguished between "prolonged" and short-term tracking;[22] in her concurring opinion in *Jones*, a fifth justice, Sotomayor, expressed particular concern about "aggregated" information.[23] In *Carpenter*, while requiring a warrant for accessing a week's worth of CSLI, the Court refused to address whether seek-

ing only a few days of CSLI should also trigger the warrant process.[24]
Riley v. California[25] is another important technological search case
that expresses a similar view. There, in the course of requiring a warrant to search a phone seized from an arrestee, the Court dismissed the
relevance of centuries-old precedent that a warrant is not required to
search an arrestee's effects (such as a wallet or purse) by asserting that
comparing those actions to search of a phone "is like saying a ride on
horseback is materially indistinguishable from a flight to the moon."[26]
Admittedly, in all three cases, the choice was still between a warrant
based on probable cause and no constitutional regulation at all, rather
than between probable cause and some lesser degree of suspicion. But
the intuition that a virtual search technique becomes more or less intrusive depending on its length or the amount of information obtained
is embedded in these opinions, just as it is in *Camara* and *Terry*.

So, in sum: The proportionality principle fits comfortably with the
Fourth Amendment's reasonableness language. It finds support in the
Court's recent virtual search cases and in other areas of the law. And it
allows courts to hold that virtual searches are governed by the Fourth
Amendment and thus subject to regulation, while still allowing the
government to carry out preliminary investigations on less than probable cause.

The proportionality principle could even be seen as consistent with
the probable-cause-forever standard *if*, as I contended in *Privacy at
Risk*, probable cause is defined as "that cause which makes probable
the reasonableness of an intrusion occasioned by a given search or
seizure."[27]

> Under a proportionality approach, the animating inquiry in setting
> levels of suspicion should be how much explanation for a given intru-
> sion is necessary to convince an innocent person subjected to it that
> the police acted reasonably. The innocent person who is arrested or the
> target of bedroom surveillance will expect a "damn good reason" for the
> inconvenience and intrusion. The innocent person who is stopped on

the street for a brief interrogation or tracked by a public camera is likely to be satisfied with a less extensive explanation for the government attention. The official excuse for a mistaken action should be adequate, but need be no more than adequate, to dissipate the umbrage the action excites. This is the central insight of the proportionality principle: the justification for a search or seizure should nullify its intrusiveness, no more and no less.[28]

The Supreme Court has insisted in many of its cases that the probable cause standard is "flexible."[29] If so, its meaning can vary depending on the type of police action involved.

In any event, regardless of whether the Fourth Amendment requires it, a proportionality principle centered around privacy makes sense as a matter of policy, as a number of prestigious policy-making bodies have recognized. The American Bar Association's Standards on Technologically-Assisted Physical Surveillance, which deal with visual observation using CCTV, tracking, aerial surveillance, and the like and were adopted in 1999, provide that law enforcement interests ought to be balanced against "the extent to which the surveillance technique invades privacy," with lesser invasions requiring less justification.[30] Similarly, the ABA's 2013 Standards on Law Enforcement Access to Third Party Records recognizes four types of information—"highly private," "moderately private," "minimally private," and "not private"—and requires descending levels of justification to access such information.[31] The American Law Institute, in its Principles of Policing adopted in May 2021, provides that, in developing policies governing "suspicion-based" policing, agencies should consider first and foremost "the intrusiveness of the technique at issue, as well as the sensitivity of the information that its use is likely to obtain."[32]

Illustrating how this analysis might play out, in Title III and the Electronic Communications Privacy Act (ECPA), Congress adopted a tiered approach to regulating police acquisition of electronic communications: Interception of email content requires a warrant; acquisition of subscriber and billing information requires a court order based on a standard akin to reasonable suspicion; and interception of phone metadata merely requires a court order based on a certification by law enforcement that the data is relevant to an investigation.[33] Although I would modify ECPA in ways described in later chapters, the statute at least recognizes that not all virtual searches are created equal.

The Role of Legislatures

If national policy-making bodies are any guide, the proportionality principle is an idea whose time has come. Nonetheless, it has at least one potential obstacle in its way. The most potent argument against the proportionality principle is that it is difficult to implement. Akin to the questions Justice Gorsuch asked in his *Carpenter* dissent, one can justifiably wonder about the extent to which, under proportionality analysis, different amounts of information (e.g., two days' worth versus two months' worth), different types of information (CSLI versus bank records), different sources of information (e.g., the target or a third party), or the recency of the information (e.g., real-time versus records acquisition) should make a difference. And, once a hierarchy of intrusiveness is established, one then has to decide what type of justification—probable cause, something short of probable cause, or perhaps something more than probable cause—is sufficient justification to act.

Even if the Fourth Amendment is interpreted to require proportionality reasoning, courts cannot be expected to answer these types of questions in detail. Courts can only decide the case before them, based on the evidence submitted by the parties. This means that they rarely have the big picture in front of them; rather, they decide cases without a good sense of how the holding will interact with and affect other types of searches. It also means that courts often lack good information about how often the technique in question will be used, its efficacy, and the extent to which it allows intrusions other than the type before the court.

Consider police use of automated license plate reader (ALPR) technology, the subject of the Nashville City Council meeting described in chapter 1. Some ALPR systems reveal the face of the driver as well as the license plate and make of the car. Some are stationary, and some are set up on police cars. Some are used only in certain neighborhoods, some are linked to hot lists, and some primarily monitor parking and traffic situations (yet might capture images that are helpful in solving crime).[34] A single judicial decision about ALPR use—say, in connection with a traffic stop—cannot and should not try to deal with all these situations. At the same time, a court decision that sticks to the facts, as it should, leaves police departments guessing about what it means in other settings. A policing agency acting in good faith might nonetheless interpret such an isolated judicial decision incorrectly, as either permission to use ALPRs in ways that should be prohibited or as a prohibition that prevents uses that should be permitted. Waiting for courts to deal with all permissible permutations of a problem (as we are now having to do in the wake of *Carpenter* with respect to the third-party doctrine) leaves both police and the citizenry in the lurch.

Legislatures—even local bodies such as the Nashville City Council—can do a better job of regulation. They have access to a wide range of information sources, including hearings, legislative staffing, reports, and law enforcement and citizen submissions. They are also much better at devising coherent regulatory schemes. As Justice Alito stated in *Jones*: "In circumstances involving dramatic technological change, the best solution to privacy concerns may be legislative. A legislative body is well situated to gauge changing public attitudes, to draw detailed lines, and to balance privacy and public safety in a comprehensive way."[35]

These are some of the reasons Orin Kerr has given in favor of prioritizing legislative regulation of surveillance over judicial regulation.[36] He contends that legislation such as ECPA is more likely to produce "a workable and sensible balance between law enforcement needs and privacy interests" by providing relatively clear rules that are, at the same time, flexible enough to cover unforeseen developments and relatively easily changed if those developments make them obsolete (as has occurred, I argue below, with ECPA).[37] He also notes that statutes are more adept at fine-tuning mechanisms for assuring accountability and compliance.[38]

The latter advantage of legislation is particularly important to recognize in the virtual search setting. The courts' primary mechanism for enforcing their rules is exclusion of illegally seized evidence in a criminal trial, which of course can be triggered only by someone who is being prosecuted. Yet many innocent people are affected by surveillance; further, the fact that most people who bring Fourth Amendment claims are trying to exclude evidence of criminal activity often makes courts reluctant to find a violation in the first place.[39] As developed in more detail in chapter 9 of this book, statutes can more easily provide for civil and administrative remedies to redress virtual searches of everyone, not just those charged with crime. They may also, as John Rappaport contends, ensure greater compliance with the law because they provide police departments with "an opportunity to participate in their own self-governance and thus feel less imposed upon by unempathetic entities, all of which should enhance allegiance to whatever rules are created."[40]

Despite the advantages of legislation as a regulatory mechanism, other scholars have been less comfortable with minimizing the judicial role. For instance, Daniel Solove questions the ability of legislators to understand technology any better than judges, especially given the availability to judges of amicus briefs and other readily accessible information about technology.[41] He points out that much of the existing legislation that is focused on virtual searches (such as ECPA and the rest of Title III, which regulates electronic surveillance of communications) came into being only after Congress was nudged by the Supreme Court.[42] He also notes that, despite ample opportunity to do so, Congress and the states have not been particularly aggressive in regulating other types of virtual searches, and he worries that, when they do consider such laws, law enforcement lobbies will often have the upper hand.[43] Peter Swire is likewise concerned about collective action deficits, noting that the Department of Justice and state law enforcement agencies have often tried to reduce restrictions on their powers and that their concentrated efforts usually trump those of privacy advocates, especially after events such as 9/11.[44] Erin Murphy confirms that law enforcement lobbying is "a clear and constant voice in the political process" and adds that the political power of the private sector (think Amazon and Google) might also push for expansive use of profit-making technologies such as GPS tracking devices and drones, as well as demand "legal safe harbors" and gag orders that minimize any public relationship damage from consumer outrage over their use.[45]

Both of these concerns—the inertia of legislatures and their dominance by law enforcement—are very legitimate worries. But they both would be substantially alleviated if, as proposed here, all virtual searches were governed by the Fourth Amendment. Then, legislatures would realize that the Constitution requires regulation of technological surveillance and that, if they do not act, the courts will make them do so. Conversely, if they do act, and do so in good faith rather than relying solely on input from law enforcement groups, then courts are more likely to defer to their decisions about what is reasonable. Finally, if it turns out that the resulting legislation is too favorable to law enforcement, constitutionalizing all virtual searches will mean that courts applying proportionality analysis can curb it, on a provision-by-provision basis, without upsetting the entire scheme. Courts would act as nudgers and backstops, but legislatures would provide the bulk of the regulation.[46]

That arrangement might well satisfy even those who worry about legislated rules. Solove, Swire, and Murphy all concede that, given the types of advantages outlined by Kerr, legislative approaches to regulation of virtual searches have benefits under certain conditions. Solove thinks that courts should be willing to defer to legislation that regulates surveillance if it conforms to fundamental Fourth Amendment principles such as "minimization" (i.e., prevention of dragnets), "particularization" (of suspicion), and "control" (meaningful oversight).[47] And Swire and Murphy advocate for what they call a "procedural approach" to defining reasonableness under the Fourth Amendment, which would focus on whether statutes and police policies provide specific rules that limit discretion.[48] That might mean, they suggest, that police could be permitted to access information based on less than probable cause if, for instance, the targets of an investigation have an opportunity to contest government access, collected records are destroyed within a short period of time, and transfer of acquired information is strictly limited.[49]

These various points of view converge on the idea that limitations on virtual searches should be proportionate to their intrusions into privacy and that legislation is probably the best mechanism for detailed implementation of this idea. From that consensus, three questions follow: First: How should legislatures measure the "intrusiveness" of a police action? Even if one agrees that the impact on privacy can vary based on the amount and type of information sought and that this variation should influence legal rules, legislatures and courts need something more to go on than seat-of-the-pants intuition. Second: What do proportionate justifications for differing levels of privacy intrusions look like? Probable cause and reasonable suspicion are two likely candidates, but there may be (and, I contend, should be) other justificatory standards both above and below these two. And third: What other considerations, besides intrusiveness, might influence the ultimate legislative scheme? While intrusiveness is the crucial variable, the nature of the crime being investigated, the extent to which a virtual search infringes First Amendment speech and assembly rights, and its potential for causing disparate racial impacts are also relevant considerations.

Intrusiveness

The big beef about *Katz*'s reasonable-expectation-of-privacy test is, again, that it is so amorphous. Those who have thought the most about privacy concede as much. Alan Westin contends that privacy is meant to encompass solitude, intimacy, anonymity, and reserve (the latter term referring to the withholding of information) and notes that all of these can be infringed by surveillance of public as well as private activity.[50] Daniel Solove divides the privacy concept into six categories: the right to be let alone; limited access to oneself; secrecy; control over personal information; personhood (in connection with, e.g., abortion rights); and intimacy.[51] David Sklansky sees privacy as "respect for a personal sphere . . . defined partly by places (especially the home and the body) and partly by activities (especially those that relate to intimacy and self-definition)," violations of which have "tangible effects . . . both on the victims' sense of security and peace of mind and, perhaps more importantly, on the habits and ways of thinking of the individuals and organizations responsible for the violations."[52] To the good, there is considerable overlap between these definitions; at the same time, they admittedly leave much up in the air.

Fortunately, there are two sources that can provide more concrete guidance on society's privacy expectations. The first, referenced in the previous chapter, is positive law—law regarding matters such as property rights and contracts, passed by legislatures or long accepted by the courts, that might be said to reveal societal privacy preferences in connection with everyday interactions and relationships. The second, even better, source, is survey data that straightforwardly asks citizens what their privacy expectations are vis-à-vis the government.

Positive Law

Positive law is an expression of what elected legislative representatives and judges (also often elected) think is worth protecting, so it can be one indication of "the expectations of privacy society is prepared to recognize as reasonable." The Supreme Court clearly thinks positive law is relevant to the Fourth Amendment inquiry. In *Jones* and *Jardines*, for instance, it referenced the common law of property in explaining its decision. And property, contract, and other common law and statutory rules often mesh nicely with privacy concerns: we expect privacy in things that we own, when we contract for it, and in relationships that the law protects, such as those between attorney–client, doctor–patient, accountant–taxpayer, and bank–depositor.

There are at least three problems with making positive law the dispositive criterion, however.[53] First, as noted in chapter 2, positive law is skewed in favor of the privileged. Property law provides little protection to the homeless. Not everyone has the wherewithal to negotiate contracts protecting their information. Few people have much say in the legislatures or courts that create the law governing private transactions.

Second, a statutory or common law rule about trespass or privilege generally tells us only whether a private party can, or cannot, legally intrude. Unlike privacy interests, which are scalar and can meaningfully be described in terms of whether they are significant or minimal, positive law at most tells us whether something is protected, not the extent to which it is protected. Thus, it provides no help with proportionality analysis.

The third reason to be reticent about making positive law the linchpin of Fourth Amendment analysis is the most important. As Richard Re points out, "government action is different—and often more deserving of regulation—than similar conduct by private parties."[54]

> The government's special capabilities derive from its tax-financed budget, its vast infrastructure and resources for conducting surveillance, and its special ability to pursue criminal prosecutions. As a political institution, the government's incentives are also distinctive, since it has an uncommon interest in investigating crime and, potentially, in suppress-

ing dissent against the incumbent regime. And the government's social role as a representative of the people means that it has special moral authority and prestige, as well as a unique capacity to inflict injury by betraying the people's trust in it.[55]

Just because private citizens or businesses are legally permitted to peer into one's backyard from a plane, monitor one's travels using GPS, or use cookies to see where you surf on the internet does not mean the government should be able to do so without any justification. Government simply has too much power to allow it to do anything private citizens or companies can do.

Stressing this last point, Re makes a good suggestion: Positive law can be relevant to Fourth Amendment analysis, but it should only provide a floor for, not dictate the ceiling of, constitutional protection.[56] Positive law could, in theory, reinforce the precept that we expect privacy not only in our homes, cars, and other tangible property but also in personal information we surrender to financial, communications, and internet companies under confidentiality agreements; perhaps it could even corroborate a privacy interest in connection with some public activities (as might occur, for instance, in jurisdictions that limit the use of Ring cameras beyond private property). But if positive law does not regulate a given situation, that should not end the constitutional inquiry. One should be able to expect privacy from government intrusion in numerous situations that positive law's regulation of private intrusions does not adequately address or does not address at all. And, as the next section makes clear, many of these situations involve virtual searches.

Surveys

A second way to get a sense of "the expectations of privacy society is prepared to recognize as reasonable," as *Katz* tells us to do, is to go out and ask society what privacy it expects. I have been doing precisely that for more than three decades, by asking large groups of individuals to rate the intrusiveness of various investigative techniques on a scale of 1 to 100.[57] Not surprisingly, the results I obtained are often inconsistent with the Supreme Court's opinions. For instance, on average my survey participants considered police perusal of bank records (with a mean score of 71 out of 100) to be as intrusive as searching a garage (which requires probable cause);[58] they found obtaining phone metadata to be as intrusive or more intrusive than a pat-down (which requires reasonable suspicion under *Terry*);[59] they concluded that using a tracking beeper is as intrusive as a pat-down;[60] and they considered flying a helicopter 400 feet above a backyard to be much more intrusive than stopping drivers at a roadblock for 15 seconds (which the Court has said is a "seizure" under the Fourth Amendment).[61] Yet the Court found, in the first-mentioned situations in each of these pairs, that the Fourth Amendment was not implicated at all!

Can these sorts of survey results be trusted? As with any survey outcomes, there are always concerns about internal and external validity. But those concerns can be addressed. The sample populations surveyed in the three studies I conducted have been diverse, both demographically and geographically. While the queries given my participants often consisted of a single sentence, and thus provided little context, they nonetheless were an accurate reflection of the Court's black-letter law, which is what governs police behavior; current constitutional rules simply tell police what they can and cannot do, without any further nuance (for example, they tell police that non-exigent intrusion into a home requires a warrant, but that examining an individual's bank records does not). And while the average ratings of intrusiveness for specific scenarios varied between studies, the hierarchy of intrusiveness has been remarkably consistent; for instance, looking through bank records has always been ranked as more intrusive than a pat-down.[62]

Most important, since I published *Privacy at Risk*, other scholars have generally replicated my results. Jeremy Blumenthal and his coauthors,[63] Henry Fradella,[64] Christine Scott-Hayward and her colleagues,[65] Bernard Chao and his coauthors,[66] and Lior Strahelivitz and Matthew Kugler[67] report similar findings, as do several others.[68] Rather than asking about "intrusiveness," as I did, some of these studies asked whether a given technique infringed "reasonable expectations of privacy," on the theory that this language better reflects the legal question.[69] I avoided that language, in part because it signals to those knowledgeable about the law the purpose of the study, but primarily because it provides an answer only to the threshold question of whether something is a "search," not how intrusive a given technique is, which is the question most relevant to proportionality analysis. Any concern that asking subjects about "intrusiveness" might not capture the relevant concept should be allayed by the fact that the Supreme Court has talked about intrusiveness or invasiveness in over 400 of its cases dealing with the Fourth Amendment (in other words, in virtually every one of its Fourth Amendment decisions).[70]

Note, too, how the survey approach improves on the positive law model's ability to ascertain societal expectations. It provides a diverse sampling of privacy expectations, not just of expectations held by the politically powerful. It gives us a hierarchy of intrusiveness, rather than simply an either/or determination of whether a police technique is governed by the Fourth Amendment. And rather than relying on perceived attitudes about intrusions perpetrated by private citizens or entities, this survey methodology specifically queries laypeople about intrusions by the *government*.

If results such as these are taken into consideration in deciding whether and the extent to which Fourth Amendment protections apply, constitutional regulation of virtual searches would look quite different. Based on a consensus among the various surveys (not just my data), police examination of online purchasing records would be a search and would be equated with a stop and frisk in terms of intrusiveness.[71] GPS tracking of a car for any length of time would be a search, and long-term tracking would require the same justification as search of a home.[72] Police attempts to obtain significant chunks of communications metadata or bank records would be equated with a search of a bedroom,[73] as would using a drone to hover over a backyard.[74]

Of course, even if these results are robust as an empirical matter, a natural question to ask is why they should require changes to current law or, for that matter, influence the courts at all. One response is that, in light of *Jones* and *Carpenter*, the Court has indicated some willingness to adjust the stance it has taken in previous cases on which privacy expectations are reasonable. But that does not mean it should rely on public opinion polls to effect that change. After all, ever since *Marbury v. Madison*[75] established the principle that courts may strike down legislative enactments, it has been clear that the scope of constitutional law is a judicial domain; it is not to be determined by canvassing the populace. Especially when construing the Bill of Rights, in which the Fourth Amendment is embedded, the courts' job is to ensure that minority interests are protected against majoritarian bias, not simply sample the most popular views. As the Supreme Court put it with respect to First Amendment rights, the freedoms of speech, press, assembly, and religion "depend on the outcome of no elections."[76] This last statement is true not only of the First Amendment but also with respect to the Fifth Amendment's protections against coerced testimony and double jeopardy and the Sixth Amendment's guarantee of the rights to counsel, jury, and confrontation; it is probably also true of the Eighth Amendment's prohibition on cruel and unusual punishment (although the Court has said this provision depends on "evolving standards of decency").[77]

However, as Robert Post has pointed out, privacy of the type at issue here is grounded "in social forms of respect that we owe each other as members of a common community" and is located "in precisely the aspects of social life that are shared and mutual."[78] Thus, "there can ultimately be no other measure of privacy than the social norms that actually exist in our civilization."[79] To discover those norms, some means of surveying society is necessary. While positive law can be helpful in this regard, surveys give us the most direct reflection of the expectations of privacy that society is prepared to recognize as reasonable.

Granted, it is simpler for judges if they are allowed to make assumptions about privacy without having to worry about evaluating the validity of empirical evidence. But ignoring good scientific findings about societal norms in making pronouncements about privacy expectations would be a blatant example of what David Faigman has called "fact-finding by fiat,"[80] the adoption of a philosopher–king role that many members of the Court purport to decry.[81] Further, if judges depart substantially from societal mores in substituting their own views about those mores, the legitimacy of the courts—not just the legitimacy of the practices they condone—could suffer. *Carpenter* seemed to recognize that possibility when it called "critical" to its decision the fact that, because "location information is continually logged for all of the 400 million devices in the United States—not just those belonging to persons who might happen to come under investigation—this newfound tracking capacity runs against everyone."[82] A decision going the other way—one that told hundreds of millions of people that the government should be able to track them at will because they are "unreasonable" in believing that their location information should be private—could easily have strained the Court's credibility.

A second objection to the survey model is that, even if one accepts the conclusion that it provides the best determinant of intrusiveness, it is likely to reveal that societal norms about privacy change and thus, if followed, could threaten the stability of the law. But that possibility should be considered a feature of the model, not a bug. As illustrated by the Court's progression recounted in chapter 2—from *Olmstead* to *Katz*, and then from *Katz* to *Jones* and *Carpenter*—privacy norms can evolve, sometimes drastically. Stare decisis is important for numerous reasons, but it should not stand in the way of recognizing the sea change in views about privacy occasioned by the huge advances in technological surveillance that have occurred since the 1970s.

A third objection to surveys is that the courts may be uncomfortable having to parse scientific survey evidence, which could require evaluating confidence intervals, measures of statistical significance, and the like. But courts routinely take on this role in other contexts; courts have resorted to survey data on topics as disparate as trademark law (in an effort to ascertain consumer confusion between brands) and obscenity (in measuring "community standards").[83] In any event, for reasons discussed earlier, legislatures should be doing most of the hard work here. Courts must set out the proportionality framework and decide specific cases. But legislatures are much better equipped to devise a comprehensive regulatory scheme. Nudged by the courts, they or the relevant agencies would commission the needed survey work or assess public views in some other way.

Other Indicia of Privacy

Survey findings, along with positive law, are the best evidence of societal expectations of privacy. But survey data may be ambiguous, conflicting, or unavailable, and positive law may also be silent on the matter or vary from jurisdiction to jurisdiction. For instance, there may be insufficiently clear input from these sources about the relative intrusiveness of law enforcement efforts to scrape information from social media accounts or to access a person's web-surfing activities. Pending more robust data, how should policy makers proceed?

In conceptualizing the degree to which particular information should be considered private, the ABA Standards on Law Enforcement Access to Third Party Records note that survey information can provide useful evidence of society's privacy expectations. But they also provide that policy makers should consider the extent to which (1) "the initial transfer of information . . . is reasonably necessary to participate meaningfully in society or in commerce, or is socially beneficial, including to freedom of speech and association"; (2) the information "is personal, including the extent to which it is intimate and likely to cause embarrassment or stigma if disclosed, and whether outside of the initial transfer . . . it is typically disclosed only within one's close social network, if at all"; and (3) the information "is accessible to and accessed by non-government persons."[84] Paul Ohm has likewise contended that privacy protection should depend on how revealing the information is, its depth, breadth, and reach, and whether exposure of personal facts is inescapable "because they relate to services one needs to use to be a functioning member of today's society."[85] These types of factors could be stand-ins when survey information and positive law are unavailing.

However, they should play that role *only* in the absence of survey information and positive law, because each of them is highly problematic. For instance, Mathew Tokson has exposed the difficulties associated with the "inescapability" idea that appears in both the ABA's scheme (in provision (1) above) and in Ohm's analysis.[86] Tokson notes that, in carrying out the inquiry into whether information transfer "is reasonably necessary to participate in society," courts will have to wrestle with numerous difficult questions. Is it relevant that relatively simple steps can be taken to avoid exposure of one's internet searches or Facebook posts, which should thus not be considered "private" absent those steps? How does a policy maker take into account the fact that ride-sharing apps and various aspects of the Internet of Things are easily dispensable for people who don't have smartphones, yet are becoming crucial to people with disabilities, and are a convenient, increasingly common (but not inescapable?) way of life for the rest of us? Is privacy protection unavailable when decisions to use technology are completely discretionary, as is the case with depositing one's DNA with Ancestry.com or buying a Ring camera? And might not a finding that use of a technology is "escapable" deter privacy-conscious people from using it, to society's overall detriment?

Similar questions can be raised about how to operationalize intimacy, stigma, and the extent to which information is "public" or accessible by others, the other factors considered important under the formulations from the ABA and Ohm. How does one define those terms and apply them in the search context? Judges and other policy makers might answer that query quite differently than the average citizen when attempting to determine societal expectations of privacy. It is the view of the average citizen that should prevail in this context, and survey information is the best way to determine what that is.

When the legislature has not already spoken on the matter and courts are thus called upon to decipher societal views, judges might perceive a requirement that they rely on such empirical reports to be an encroachment on their decision-making prerogatives. Two considerations should alleviate courts' concern about impingement on their turf, however. First, as with any information provided the courts, judges are the ultimate arbiters of what survey data mean; there is plenty of play in privacy's joints. Second, survey data should assume a prominent role only with respect to assessing privacy norms; courts will still be the arbiters of how much justification for a given police action is required under the proportionality principle. Survey research provides information only about society's view on relative intrusiveness. It does not dictate where to position the Fourth Amendment threshold or whether, assuming that threshold is crossed, probable cause, reasonable suspicion, or some other protection is warranted.

Justification

Assuming the Fourth Amendment threshold is crossed, the gold standard for ensuring that a police action is reasonable has always been the warrant, based on probable cause as found by a judge and describing with particularity the place to be searched and the items to be seized. But the courts have long recognized that the "warrant requirement" is more the exception than the rule. The knee-jerk reaction found in some scholarly commentary and court decisions (including at the Supreme Court level from time to time) that probable cause is required for anything that is a search simply does not reflect the reality of Fourth Amendment jurisprudence. Contrary to what it tells itself, the Supreme Court has allowed searches to take place on less than probable cause in numerous situations. It has also occasionally required *more* than probable cause. What follows is a description of these various justification standards, one that, given judicial precedent, is unavoidably nuanced and somewhat technical.

Relevance

The least demanding Fourth Amendment authorization is the subpoena. While a subpoena is nominally considered a "search," it merely requires a demonstration that the information sought is relevant to an investigation. Indeed, in *United States v. Morton Salt*,[87] the Supreme Court stated that a subpoena issued by a government agency is valid even if it aims merely to satisfy "official curiosity"![88] In effect, this means that a subpoena can withstand challenge as long as the information is sought for a purpose authorized by statute and the subpoena describes it with sufficient particularity that the target does not have to guess what the government wants. This is a very easy standard to meet.

It should also be recognized, however, that there are several varieties of subpoenas. As Justice Brennan suggested in *Miller*, a subpoena issued by a court or a grand jury may be at least modestly more protective than one issued by a prosecutor, given the additional layer of review. Also important is whether and by whom a subpoena may be challenged. Under federal law, some subpoenas (in particular, those issued in national security investigations) cannot be challenged by anyone,[89] and others (for instance, court orders seeking phone and email metadata) cannot be challenged by the target of the investigation but rather only by the entity holding the records.[90] Only in a small number of cases (involving medical, tax, and some financial records) are subpoenas directed at third parties challengeable by the target, and even then notice of the subpoena can be ex post (after the fact) if there is any showing that notification will compromise the investigation.[91] The relevance standard applies in all these cases. But it is likely applied more robustly in those situations where the target can raise an ex ante (before the fact) challenge in front of a judge.

Furthermore, for reasons having as much to do with the Fifth Amendment's prohibition on compelled self-incrimination as with the Fourth Amendment's protection of privacy, if the subpoena seeks information from the target rather than a third party and the target is a person rather than a corporation (which, as an impersonal entity, does not have a Fifth Amendment right[92]), the applicable standard comes much closer to probable cause. This was the import of the Supreme Court's decision in *United States v. Hubbell*,[93] which held that a subpoena demanding papers from an individual that might be self-incriminating must provide a very particular description of the evidence sought so as to avoid forcing the individual to take "the mental and physical steps necessary" to provide the information sought by the government.[94] Again, however, this higher standard applies only when an individual's information is compelled from that individual, not when the same information is compelled from a third party. Only in the first situation does the Court hold that the prohibition on compelled *self*-incrimination applies; otherwise, the relevance standard reigns in subpoena cases.

Reasonable Suspicion

Next in the justification hierarchy recognized under the Fourth Amendment is the reasonable suspicion standard of *Terry v. Ohio*.[95] The Court defined "reasonable suspicion" as "specific and articulable facts" that indicate "criminal activity is afoot." The suspicion cannot be an "inchoate and unparticularized suspicion or 'hunch'" but rather must be grounded on facts that, in light of the officer's experience, support "specific reasonable inferences" that justify the intrusion.[96]

This language sounds more demanding than *Morton Salt*'s "official curiosity" standard, and it is meant to be.

Sometimes compared to the reasonable suspicion standard is the standard found in § 2703(d) of the Electronic Communications Privacy Act, which requires that, before the government can obtain email account logs identifying the addresses of correspondents and related items, it must produce "specific and articulable facts showing that there are reasonable grounds to believe that . . . the records or other information sought are relevant and material to an ongoing criminal investigation."[97] Note, however, that 2703(d) requires only that the government be able to articulate how the information sought is "relevant" to an investigation. That language does not require a showing that the logs will provide direct evidence that "criminal activity is afoot" (such as the gun found in *Terry*). Rather, a 2703(d) order could authorize acquisition of months of email logs not only of the suspect but also of those who communicate with the suspect, because the latter information might be "relevant" even though none or very little of it would be introduced into evidence at trial.[98] Accordingly, on its face, the 2703(d) standard is probably best situated somewhere between the relevance test used for subpoenas and reasonable suspicion.

At the same time, because the 2703(d) standard is interpreted by a court rather than by an officer (as occurs under the reasonable suspicion standard in a case such as *Terry*), as implemented it places nontrivial constraints on law enforcement. In fact, some evidence suggests that, in practice, the 2703(d) standard differs only minimally from probable cause.[99] If true, that equivalency may have less to do with overly rigid interpretation of the 2703(d) standard than with the modern dilution of the probable cause standard.

Probable Cause

As noted in chapter 2, probable cause to search exists when the known facts "raise a 'fair probability,' or a 'substantial chance,' of discovering evidence of criminal activity."[100] The Court has insisted that probable cause is not meant to be "hypertechnical" but rather consists of a "flexible, common sense standard."[101] In short, probable cause is a slippery concept. But there is at least general agreement that, in theory, it falls somewhere below both the no-reasonable-doubt standard used in criminal trials and the clear-and-convincing-evidence standard used in commitment proceedings, somewhat above reasonable suspicion, and in the general vicinity of the preponderance-of-the-evidence standard used in civil courts. Probable cause for a search presumably is also usually a lower standard than probable cause to arrest, since if the police can meet the latter standard a search will often be unnecessary.

Just as with relevance and reasonable suspicion, in practice the probable cause standard can vary depending on whether it is applied by a judge rather than an officer and on whether the object of the search is evidence of crime (as the Court's definition suggests it should be) or something else. On the first point, William Stuntz has persuasively made the case that probable cause means something different when evaluated by a judge considering whether to issue a warrant (an ex ante determination) than by a judge who is considering whether police had probable cause for a search they conducted without a warrant because of exigent circumstances (an ex post determination).[102] In the ex post setting, which normally occurs at a suppression hearing at which the defendant is trying to exclude evidence on Fourth Amendment grounds, the judge knows evidence was found (otherwise there would be nothing to suppress); as Stuntz notes, under these circumstances, hindsight bias can powerfully affect the decision as to whether probable cause existed.[103] While probable cause is the standard both when a warrant is issued and at the suppression hearing, in practice it is more demanding ex ante.

Likewise, probable cause to believe *items that will aid an investigation* will be found is a lower standard than probable cause to believe *evidence of crime* will be found. For decades during the twentieth century, the Supreme Court insisted that a warrant could not authorize seizure of what it eventually called "mere evidence," that is, an item that is not contraband (e.g., drugs), the fruit of a crime (money stolen during a robbery), or an instrumentality used to commit the crime (a weapon).[104] The rationale for this triadic distinction was primarily property-based. It is illegal to possess contraband; fruits of a crime belong to the victim; and items used to commit a crime are forfeited to the government. But everything else rightfully belongs to the targets of the search and, according to the late-nineteenth and early-twentieth-century Supreme Court, could not be seized from them under *any* circumstances.[105]

However, in the 1967 decision *Warden v. Hayden*,[106] the Court abolished the mere evidence rule. Echoing *Katz*, which in the same year moved Fourth Amendment analysis toward a privacy orientation, the *Hayden* Court reasoned that "nothing in the nature of property seized as [mere] evidence renders it more private than property seized, for example, as an instrumentality."[107] As a result, the courts have held, the police can now obtain a warrant to find proof that a person owns a particular home or to search for gang insignia as easily as they can obtain a warrant to find drugs, stolen property, or weapons, as long as they demonstrate probable cause to believe that the item will help solve a crime.[108]

This move usually does not have a major impact on the scope of physical searches, since, as was true in *Hayden* (where police looking for a gun and evidence of a robbery came across discarded clothing), those types of searches usually have as a primary target contraband, fruits, or instrumentalities, with evidence of ownership and the like a secondary concern. However, elimination of the mere evidence rule has major implications for virtual searches. Translated to the virtual search context, abolition of the rule means that, assuming there is a "fair probability" that some sort of incriminating leads will be discovered, a warrant can issue to obtain data describing that person's location, records about the person's everyday transactions, and the transactions of people with whom the person deals, even if none of the information so gathered is contraband, fruit, or an instrumentality.[109]

Once the limitation imposed by that triad is gone, a search of records can be quite far-ranging.

At least when the information is sought directly from the target, *Hubbell* and the Fifth Amendment dictate that its content be identified with specificity, meaning that the government must already have a pretty good idea that the information exists and is merely looking for concrete proof of it. But, as noted above, when the information is maintained by a third party, the Fifth Amendment's protection against compelled self-incrimination disappears, as does its heightened specificity requirement. Thus, even if the third-party doctrine were abolished and probable cause were the applicable standard, a warrant authorizing search of a third party's databases for a target's emails or transactional records might well be easier to obtain than a warrant to search that same person's house for physical evidence like guns, drugs, or loot from a crime and certainly easier to procure than an order to search the contents of that person's home computer.

Probable Cause–Plus

In a few circumstances, the Court has held that a warrant based on probable cause is insufficient authorization for a search. In *Winston v. Lee*,[110] it held that forcing an individual to undergo a surgical procedure to find a bullet lodged in his shoulder required proof not only that the procedure was not dangerous but also that the bullet was necessary to "fairly and accurately" determine guilt. The Court further held that these facts had to be shown in an adversarial proceeding in open court, a requirement that in effect raises the standard of proof compared to the process by which a warrant is obtained (which is ex parte in that it occurs in the absence of a party, here the defendant).[111] Similarly, to obtain a warrant authorizing electronic surveillance, the Court's decision in *Berger v. New York*[112] stressed that a "showing of exigency" (i.e., a showing of necessity) "would appear more important in eavesdropping, with its inherent dangers, than that required when conventional procedures of search and seizure are utilized" and that any eavesdropping that occurs must avoid "indiscriminate" interception of conversations unrelated to the purpose of the warrant.[113] Title III, passed by Congress shortly after *Berger*—and clearly an attempt to implement it—limited electronic surveillance to investigations of serious crimes, required a showing that other means of obtaining evidence in the case had "been tried and failed," and mandated that interceptions "be conducted in such a way as to minimize the interception of communications not otherwise."[114]

What seems to unite *Winston*, *Berger*, and Title III is the perception that the search techniques at issue were extraordinarily intrusive (and this intuition, contrary to some of the Court's other conclusions about expectations of privacy, is consistent with survey results).[115] For most searches, there need not be any showing that less intrusive techniques will suffice. However, *Winston*, *Berger*, and Title III stand for the proposition that government resort to surveillance that amounts to mind-reading calls for a demonstration of necessity and special constraints on how the search is conducted.

Summary

In ascending order of their burden on the state (and ignoring exigencies that obviate court involvement), a hierarchy of this wide array of justification standards might go something like this:

- Unchallengeable subpoena
- Subpoena challengeable only by a third party
- Reasonable suspicion implemented by an officer in the field
- Articulable suspicion order issued by a judge (e.g., § 2703(d))
- Ex post probable cause, determined at a suppression hearing
- Subpoena directed at the target
- Ex ante probable cause, determined when a warrant is issued
- Probable cause–plus (e.g., Title III)

Whether this is the right hierarchy, whether there are real differences between adjacent justification standards, and the extent of those differences, are all highly contestable. But three much less contestable points about these standards can be made. First, the standards, and variations of them, have all been found to be permissible justifications for searches as a matter of Fourth Amendment law, depending on the circumstances. Second, they are all available to policy-making bodies figuring out how to regulate virtual searches, assuming those circumstances are met. And third, their variety enables a fine-tuned approach to proportionality analysis, one that can be adapted to different types of virtual searches.

Other Factors

To this point the assumption has been that proportionality analysis looks solely at the intrusiveness of the virtual search technique in deciding the type of justification it requires. But other considerations besides intrusiveness may, in relatively rare circumstances, play a role.

Nature of the Offense

In his *Carpenter* dissent, Justice Alito highlighted that decision's potential impact not only on corporate crime inquiries but also on investigations of "terrorism."[116] In his opinion in *Jones* he made a similar point. While agreeing that long-term tracking normally implicates the Fourth Amendment, he stated that "we . . . need not consider whether prolonged GPS monitoring in the context of investigations involving extraordinary offenses would similarly intrude on a constitutionally protected sphere of privacy."[117] Many commentators have likewise suggested that Fourth Amendment protection should vary depending on the type of crime at issue, in particular suggesting that investigations of serious crime should be less heavily regulated than investigations of minor crime.[118]

That position is insufficiently nuanced, however. The nature of the crime under investigation should never be a consideration when the issue is the definition of "search" and only rarely so when the issue is whether a search is reasonable. First, contrary to Justice Alito's insinuation in *Jones*, the Fourth Amendment's reasonableness language, while plausibly calling for balancing privacy interests against crime-detection interests, comes into play only once the police action is determined to be a search. The privacy associated with one's home, car, or data does not vary simply because the government is investigating a murder rather than marijuana possession. The fact that the suspect's alleged crime is "extraordinary," to use Justice Alito's word, does not make one's "constitutionally protected sphere of privacy" magically disappear, regardless of how desperately the government wants to resolve the case.

Even in deciding whether a search is reasonable, the seriousness of the crime should seldom play a role. In *Mincey v. Arizona*,[119] the Supreme Court rejected such an argument in holding that there is no "homicide exception" to the warrant requirement. While noting that "no one can doubt the importance" of investigating a murder, the Court pointed out that the public interest in investigating other serious crimes such as rape, robbery, and burglary is "comparable"; thus, "[n]o consideration relevant to the Fourth Amendment suggests any point of rational limitation" on a serious crime exception to the warrant requirement.[120] More important than this administrability concern was the Court's further observation that "the mere fact that law enforcement may be made more efficient can never by itself justify disregard of the Fourth Amendment."[121] In other words, the government may not dispense with a warrant requirement simply because obtaining a warrant might impede investigation of a crime considered to be grave. The contrary rule would signal to police that, if they can characterize an offense as serious, the Fourth Amendment's protections can be ignored or diluted.[122] The latter result is analogous to telling prosecutors and juries that the beyond-a-reasonable-doubt proof requirement does not apply when the alleged charges are serious, a stance that would clearly be unconstitutional.[123]

That does not mean that the nature of the offense under investigation can never be considered in evaluating reasonableness after a police action is determined to be a search. For instance, in *Welsh v. Wisconsin*,[124] the Court held that a warrant is always required to search a home for evidence of a minor crime, even if that means the evidence will disappear while the warrant is obtained (in *Welsh*, the evidence was the defendant's blood-alcohol level). The Court reasoned that the state's interest in solving these types of crimes is never significant enough to justify such an intrusion; as the Court put it, "it is difficult to conceive of a warrantless home arrest that would not be unreasonable under the Fourth Amendment when the underlying offense is extremely minor."[125] In *Lange v. California*,[126] decided in 2021, the Court relied on *Welsh* in stating that "application of the exigent-circumstances exception in the context of a home entry should rarely be sanctioned when there is probable cause to believe that only a minor offense is involved."[127] The same could easily be said for many types of virtual searches. For instance, going through one's bank or phone records to obtain evidence of a misdemeanor might always be considered unreasonable. Consistent with that view, Title III and the federal statutes regulating tracking and metadata interception limit surveillance to felonies.[128]

Conversely, crime of a serious nature might justify relaxation of the usual justification for a virtual search when the search is aimed at *preventing* it. This "danger exception" can be seen at work in the Supreme Court's decision in *Terry*, which, it will be recalled, permitted stops and frisks on the lesser, reasonable suspicion ground, in part because of the need to provide police with a mechanism both for snuffing out crime before it occurs and for protecting themselves and other members of the public. As Chief Justice Earl Warren stated for the Court: "[T]here must be a narrowly drawn authority to permit a reasonable search for weapons for the protection of the police officer, where he has reason to believe that he is dealing with an armed and dangerous individual, regardless of whether he has probable cause to arrest the individual for a crime."[129] The prevention rationale for relaxing Fourth Amendment standards can be found in a number of other Supreme Court Fourth Amendment opinions.[130] It also underlies the Court's decisions permitting preventive detention in the commitment and pretrial settings on clear and convincing evidence rather than proof beyond a reasonable doubt, despite the fact that such detentions deprive people of liberty.[131]

Consistent with *Terry* and its progeny, the danger exception as I conceive it would apply only when the threat is specific, imminent, and significant. So confined, it would permit investigations of the types of incipient terrorist acts that Justice Alito probably had in mind when writing his dissent in *Carpenter*. Thus, it might justify the National Security Agency's "two-hop" rule, which allows the agency to discover the identity of those individuals who have communicated with a "seed identifier" suspected of planning terrorist activity, as well as those individuals who have communicated with the people discovered in the first "hop."[132] But it would not allow relaxation of the Fourth Amendment in investigations of past crime, terroristic or otherwise, simply because a government official labels the crime grave or serious.

Difficulty of Discovery

A variant of Justice Alito's extraordinary crime exception is the notion that justification standards should be relaxed when the government can make a plausible argument that the usual showing would prevent its investigation from proceeding. This factor should play even less of a role in setting justification standards. At the beginning of this chapter, I noted that the probable-cause-forever stance could stymie some virtual search investigations and that a more relaxed standard would facilitate them. But this factual observation was merely meant to describe a happy by-product of proportionality reasoning, not suggest that justification requirements may be diluted any time or simply because they make a search more difficult.

Nonetheless, one sees this notion play a significant role in some of the Court's cases. For instance, in *Hale v. Henkel*,[133] an additional reason for rejecting the corporation's Fifth Amendment claim (besides the fact that corporations are not persons) was that a holding to the contrary "would practically nullify" the Sherman Antitrust Act, which could not be enforced without access to company records.[134] The Court asked: "Of what use would it be for the legislature to declare these combinations unlawful if the judicial power may close the door of access to every available source of information upon the subject?"[135] Ninety years later, the Court of Appeals for the First Circuit echoed *Hale* in pointing out the need to sometimes "hitch the horse in front of the cart":

> [T]he ability to obtain information from regulated parties and those persons in privity with them typically is vital to the success of the regulatory scheme. . . . And it is a fact of life that agencies charged with regulating economic activity often cannot articulate probable cause or even reasonable suspicion that a violation has transpired without first examining documents reflecting a party's economic activity.[136]

Note, however, that both of these cases involve regulatory investigations of impersonal entities. As discussed in more detail in chapter 4, under proportionality reasoning the difficulty-of-detection rationale is not needed to justify easy access to impersonal corporate records, precisely because those records are impersonal. The proportionality principle would require very little by way of justification for investigations of businesses, not because of the need to make the government's job easier but because of their quasipublic nature.

More surprising than the courts' reliance on the difficulty-of-detection rationale in regulatory cases is this provision in the American Bar Association's Standards on Law Enforcement Access to Third

Party Records, which are meant to govern access to individual as well as corporate records:

> If the limitation imposed by [previous provisions essentially setting out a proportionality approach] would render law enforcement unable to solve or prevent an unacceptable amount of otherwise solvable or preventable crime, such that the benefits of respecting privacy are outweighed by this social cost, a legislature may consider reducing, to the limited extent necessary to correct this imbalance, the level of protection for that type of information, so long as doing so does not violate the federal or applicable state constitution.[137]

Doing so *does* violate the Constitution when records of natural persons are involved, given the Supreme Court's aforementioned statement in *Mincey* that "the mere fact that law enforcement may be made more efficient can never by itself justify disregard of the Fourth Amendment."

First Amendment and Related Rights

Noted previously were early Supreme Court decisions suggesting that the Fourth Amendment limits or even prohibits searches of "private papers" and thus, in effect, might limit or prohibit government investigative techniques that chill expression or in some other way impinge on freedom of speech, assembly, or religion. But the elimination of the mere evidence rule, which tended to protect a wide swath of papers even when not instrumentalities of crime, undermined that possibility.[138] And in *New York v. P.J. Video*,[139] the Court held that "an application for a warrant authorizing the seizure of material presumptively protected by the First Amendment should be evaluated under the same standard of probable cause used to review warrant applications generally."[140]

The conclusion that a warrant provides sufficient protection of First Amendment as well as privacy rights does not make the First Amendment irrelevant, however. Pervasive surveillance using CCTV, drones, and the like can chill political speech and freedom of assembly, as well as undermine the "right of locomotion" and the right "to remain in a public place" recognized under the Fourteenth Amendment.[141] In recognition of these interests, a number of federal statutes that permit virtual searches on less than probable cause nonetheless require that First Amendment interests be taken into account in determining whether the search may go forward.[142]

Furthermore, even if First Amendment and related interests are not explicitly recognized in the search context, the values underlying them can be folded into Fourth Amendment analysis. Consistent with earlier discussion about the capaciousness of the privacy concept and with survey results,[143] virtual searches likely to infringe political speech or the right to assembly, or that target particularly intimate thoughts such as those expressed in diaries, might require more than the usual justification, just as Title III does for the interception of private conversations. And, if and when actual mind-reading devices are developed, their use by government would presumably be absolutely banned for reasons that resonate as much with the First Amendment's protection of freedom of thought as with the Fourth Amendment's protection of privacy.

Equal Protection

The Fourteenth Amendment to the Constitution guarantees to all persons "equal protection under the laws." Its primary purpose at the time it was ratified in 1868 was to prohibit discrimination against formerly enslaved peoples and ensure that they were treated fairly by state governments.[144] The Equal Protection Clause might seem particularly relevant to regulation of policing in light of the stubborn police penchant for disproportionately focusing on people of color. For instance, relevant to virtual searches, on its face the Equal Protection Clause could be said to provide a constitutional basis for the Breathe Act, which, as recounted in chapter 1, would "eliminat[e] surveillance tactics that are disproportionately used to target Black, Brown and Muslim communities by prohibiting predictive policing, facial recognition technologies, drones and similar tools [and] the use of electronic monitoring, including the use of ankle monitors, smartphone applications, and any other tool used to track location."[145]

However, as a matter of formal doctrine, the Equal Protection Clause is not likely to have a major impact on the regulation of virtual searches. The Supreme Court has made clear that an equal protection violation usually requires proof of racial animus,[146] which is very difficult to demonstrate in any search and seizure context.[147] In any event, given crime rates and the crime control attitudes of a majority of the population, including among people of color,[148] a ban on virtual searches like that proposed in the Breathe Act is unlikely, even assuming, as recommended later in this book, that communities affected by surveillance are given voice in the legislative process.

Instead, the subtle and pervasive effects of racism should be confronted in other ways, an effort that properly regulated virtual search can facilitate. For instance, because they do not rely on physical intrusions to detect and deter crime, cameras and other surveillance methods could foster a reduction in the number of everyday confrontations between police and citizens. Further, if, as suggested above, virtual searches for evidence of misdemeanors are prohibited, the situations in which police use of virtual search techniques can be abused would be significantly minimized. Subsequent chapters describe in more detail these and other restrictions on virtual searches that could minimize racially disparate impacts.

A Summary of Proportionality Analysis

Government investigative techniques using technology run the gamut from minimally intrusive actions, such as casual observation on the street or perusal of public records, to extremely intrusive moves, such as electronic eavesdropping or video surveillance of the home interior.

The proportionality principle posits that the more intrusive the government's action is, the more cause should be required to engage in it. This should be the governing principle in both the virtual and physical search settings, whether the rules come from the judicial, legislative, or executive branch.

If proportionality analysis were required by the Fourth Amendment, at some point along the spectrum the government's action would become a search. From that point on the Constitution would mandate commensurate justification, ranging from the relevance showing required for a subpoena to the probable cause and probable cause–plus showings required for warrants. Policy makers' job would be to use positive law and available survey information to set the Fourth Amendment's threshold and, if that threshold is crossed, determine the justification required in light of the search's intrusiveness—a determination modulated in some cases by whether the investigation involves a minor crime, seeks to prevent a serious imminent threat, impinges on First Amendment values, or implicates equal protection concerns. Table 3.1 provides, in abstract terms, a summary of the primary components of the proportionality principle outlined in this chapter.

The Supreme Court's Fourth Amendment case law has always recognized some version of this proportionality principle. Its more recent cases reinforcing *Katz*'s expectation-of-privacy test and applying it to virtual searches seem especially receptive to it. Subsequent decisions could profitably more explicitly apply proportionality analysis.

But even if the Court chooses to go a different route, the proportionality principle should inform legislative and agency deliberations about how to regulate virtual searches. Given the complex legal and empirical issues that virtual searches raise, representative bodies are better equipped than courts to devise a comprehensive set of rules governing them. Indeed, for reasons detailed in chapter 7, legislatures *must* have a role in the regulatory regime.

It remains to provide more guidance on how virtual search techniques might be matched with specific justification requirements. A

Table 3.1. Proportionality reasoning

Intrusiveness of police action (as measured through surveys and positive law)	Justification required[+]
Nonsearch	Legitimate law enforcement objective
Minimally intrusive search	Relevance (e.g., subpoena)
Moderately intrusive search*	Reasonable suspicion (e.g., § 2703(d))
Highly intrusive search*	Probable cause (warrant)
Extremely intrusive search*	Probable cause–plus (e.g., Title III warrant)

* Not permitted for low-level crimes or if aimed primarily at First Amendment activities
[+] Can be relaxed to prevent specific, imminent, serious crime

full-blown scheme will not be attempted here; again, that is a job for legislatures and law enforcement agencies, monitored by the courts. But the rest of this book fleshes out in a fair amount of detail how proportionality analysis might play out at the judicial, legislative, and executive levels.

In doing so, it distinguishes between five types of virtual searches: *suspect-driven, profile-driven, event-driven, program-driven,* and *volunteer-driven.* Some virtual searches, like most traditional searches, are aimed at getting as much information as possible about identified individuals suspected of wrongdoing. Other efforts do not start with a particular suspect but with a profile of a hypothetical suspect, purportedly depicting the characteristics of people who have committed as-yet undetected crimes or who may commit crimes in the near future. A third type of virtual search starts with neither a suspect nor a suspect profile but with an event—usually a crime—and tries to match information garnered at the crime scene with a person. Fourth, so as to have the information needed for suspect-, profile-, and event-driven operations at the ready, government might initiate data collection programs that can be used to search for suspects, witnesses, or evidence. Fifth and finally, sometimes third parties carry out their own virtual searches and decide to volunteer incriminating information they find to the government. Each of these virtual search categories requires a different regulatory scheme, laid out in chapters 4–8.

Suspect-Driven Virtual Searches

The classic search starts with a suspect. Police see a person acting suspiciously, get the name of a perpetrator from eyewitnesses, or zero in on a particular individual based on searches of the crime scene or questioning of witnesses. They then conduct further inquiry. Perhaps they search the individual's person, house, papers, or effects. They might conduct an interview of the individual. If their suspicion rises to probable cause, then an arrest, perhaps followed by interrogation and further searches, could occur.

As previous chapters illustrated with the Abdullah and "person of interest" hypotheticals, virtual searches can be a big help in these suspect-driven cases. Observation-enhancing technology allows relatively easy monitoring of the suspect, and travel, financial, and various other types of data can provide a good historical picture of the suspect's actions before and after the crime was committed. Proportionality analysis would bring most of these virtual searches within the regulatory ambit. But the justification required to carry them out might vary significantly depending on the amount and type of intrusion they visit on the suspect.

My book *Privacy at Risk* categorized suspect-driven virtual searches as either "real-time" surveillance of ongoing actions (using CCTV, drones, satellite cameras, or tracking devices) or "historical" acquisition of records about surveillance of past actions (using the government's own databases or the databases of third parties). Because of its importance in the case law, this distinction is maintained here. However, as will become clear, that distinction should not make much difference in terms of how virtual searches are regulated.

Real-Time Surveillance

The investigation of Antoine Jones—the Jones made famous in *United States v. Jones*—involved much more than the GPS tracking that was the focus of the Supreme Court's decision; in fact, in trying to prove that Jones was a high-level drug dealer, the FBI relied on almost every virtual search technique in its quiver. The agency set up a CCTV camera trained on the nightclub Jones owned. Agents also obtained a pen-register order authorizing interception of the phone numbers dialed and received on Jones's phone (an order that, under the Electronic Communications Privacy Act, *must* be issued by a court if agents certify that the phone metadata is "relevant" to an investigation).[1] Additionally, the government accessed CSLI records of three different phones associated with Jones and his accomplices—in the case of Jones's phone, the records covered a 50-day period.[2] Agents even sought a Title III warrant authorizing interception of his phone conversations, apparently based on information from three individuals who said they had purchased drugs from Jones.[3] But none of this was enough for the government. The CSLI information was not sufficiently detailed, and Jones allegedly spoke in code over the phone.

So the FBI also sought and obtained a warrant authorizing GPS tracking, which lasted 28 days and provided data about the location of Jones's car every 10 seconds over that period.[4] On several occasions, the tracking put Jones near a location in Fort Washington, Maryland, which a later search discovered was a stash house full of cocaine and $850,000 in cash.[5] The tracking information was considered an important part of the case against Jones (and was the only virtual search technique addressed by the Supreme Court in its opinion).

As a way of exploring proportionality analysis, consider the various real-time virtual searches in *Jones* one by one (we will consider the acquisition of Jones's historical CSLI later). Begin with the camera outside Jones's club. Under the Court's knowing exposure doctrine, surveillance of the outside of a business, whether technologically or through a traditional stakeout, is presumably not a search. But it is worth reconsidering that position when the surveillance is prolonged, as was true in *Jones*. Even Chief Justice Rehnquist, not the most privacy-oriented member of the Court, once opined that stationing a police car at the entrance to a bar for no reason other than to observe the comings and goings of its patrons would not be "a proper police function"; although an invasion of privacy "in any normal sense of the word" would not be involved, Rehnquist wrote, "there would be an uneasiness, and I think, a justified uneasiness, if those who patronized the bar felt that their names were being taken down and filed for future reference."[6]

In my surveys, I included several CCTV scenarios. None involved a targeted camera like the one that occurred in *Jones*. But one survey did ask about the intrusiveness of undifferentiated CCTV surveillance, that is, a CCTV surveillance system that scanned a city block 24/7, in real time. Depending on whether the cameras are covert or overt, the survey participants, on average, found this type of virtual search to be somewhat less than or about as intrusive as flying a helicopter 400 feet over a backyard, stalking a person down the street, or going through garbage cans at curbside.[7] While none of these actions is currently considered a search by the Court,[8] they were all also viewed to be more intrusive than a stop at a roadblock,[9] which is a Fourth Amendment seizure according to the Supreme Court, albeit one that requires minimal justification.[10] Based on extrapolation from these results, or a survey that provides explicit input about targeted CCTV, a court might decide that government CCTV aimed at a particular residence or business for an indefinite period of time crosses the Fourth Amendment threshold; in fact, some lower courts seem willing to do so.[11] Whether or not the courts reach a consensus on this issue, a legislature or regulatory policy attentive to societal mores might require, before this type of virtual search could occur, that the police make a relevance-level showing to a court, or at least to a prosecutor, and should require an even greater showing if the surveillance becomes prolonged.

The second real-time surveillance technique in *Jones* involved using the pen register. According to *Smith v. Maryland*,[12] accessing phone metadata with a pen register is not a search. But *Smith* was decided well before *Carpenter*, which has poked holes in the assumption of risk doctrine upon which *Smith* relied and moved the Court in the direction of proportionality analysis. Thus, while *Carpenter* refused to overturn *Smith*, it did so on the ground that the virtual search in *Carpenter* revealed an "exhaustive chronicle of location information," compared to the "limited types of personal information" obtained in *Smith*.[13] The pen-register search in *Jones* comes much closer to *Carpenter*'s facts than *Smith*'s. The pen-register interceptions in *Jones* went on for weeks, providing an "exhaustive chronicle" of every call and text Jones made during that time; in *Smith*, in contrast, the pen register obtained less than a day's worth of call information. Bolstering this analysis, my survey participants rated the intrusiveness of the *Smith* scenario about the same as a search of utility records, while giving the *Jones* scenario an intrusiveness rating between a pat-down and a search of a car.[14] Under proportionality analysis, the metadata interception in *Smith* might require a relevance showing, but the lengthy metadata interceptions in *Jones* might require probable cause or reasonable suspicion.

Consider next the interception of Jones's phone conversations. This was clearly a search, and the police in *Jones* treated it as such, obtaining a Title III warrant before conducting this especially intrusive investigative technique. In accord with proportionality analysis, the warrant should have been issued only if other, less intrusive techniques had failed (although the record is silent on this point). In other words, the probable cause–plus standard applies in this situation.

Finally, of course, there was the 28 days of real-time tracking of Jones's car, using the signals from the GPS device. In *Jones*, the Supreme Court held that this was a Fourth Amendment search. But it did not definitively conclude that a warrant and probable cause were required to carry it out. Under proportionality reasoning, probable cause probably would be required; survey data indicate that, on average, targeted tracking of this duration, whether by GPS, drone, or satellite, is very intrusive.[15] However, that data also suggest that tracking of shorter duration is viewed as less intrusive and thus might be justified on a lesser showing.[16]

As noted in chapter 3, a fortuitous by-product of proportionality analysis is that searches to obtain the information to achieve probable cause do not themselves require probable cause. For instance, in a case such as *Jones*, the information obtained through CCTV surveillance, short-term metadata searches, and short-term tracking could take place on lesser showings; if it turns out the police are on to something, the information so gleaned could then form the basis for warrants authorizing searches of residences or the probable cause–plus needed for electronic surveillance. This is analogous to the way the courts have always treated seizures. A brief encounter requires no suspicion, a stop requires reasonable suspicion, and an arrest requires probable cause. Each step builds on information gained from the preceding interaction. The same analysis should apply with searches.

Two obvious questions arise, however. First, what is the dividing line between short-term and long-term real-time surveillance? Second, once short-term surveillance has ended under what circumstances may police obtain an extension? The lower court in *Jones* tried to answer these questions with reference to what it called "mosaic theory." This theory, consistent with proportionality analysis, places few or no restrictions on short-term surveillance but requires probable cause for longer-term surveillance. As the lower court pointed out:

> Prolonged surveillance reveals types of information not revealed by short-term surveillance, such as what a person does repeatedly, what he does not do, and what he does ensemble. These types of information can each reveal more about a person than does any individual trip viewed in isolation. . . . A person who knows all of another's travels can deduce whether he is a weekly church goer, a heavy drinker, a regular at the gym, an unfaithful husband, an outpatient receiving medical treat-

ment, an associate of particular individuals or political groups—and not just one such fact about a person, but all such facts.[17]

As explained in chapter 3, this reasoning makes sense from a privacy perspective. A number of courts have refused to endorse mosaic theory, however, primarily on practical grounds.[18] They worry about how the line is to be drawn between search and nonsearch situations. Further, they worry that neither the courts nor the police can predict with certainty when something that starts out as a nonsearch will turn into a search. As one court put it: "Under the mosaic theory, . . . collection of data would become a Fourth Amendment search at some undefined point."[19] Thus, these courts adopt an either/or stance: regardless of its length, either a virtual search is a Fourth Amendment search requiring probable cause, or it is not and requires no justification. To them, nothing else works. This by now familiar complaint about replacing the probable-cause-forever stance with a graded approach to searches cannot be ignored. If proportionality analysis is to be administrable, it must take these concerns into account.

Fortunately, there is a time-tested model for doing so. Under Title III, warrants authorizing interception of phone and email communications must not only be based on probable cause–plus; they must also be renewed every 30 days.[20] That reauthorization must be based on new information—not just on what police knew before the initial authorization but also on what they've learned, or failed to discover, during the initial surveillance. As one court put it, "[a]n extension application is not complete . . . if it only duplicates the original submission."[21] In effect, renewal requires a greater showing than that required by the initial showing.

The same sort of time limitation could be imposed in other virtual search situations, with the renewal authorization requiring more justification than the initial authorization. In fact, under federal law, something similar to this already exists for tracking and metadata acquisition. The federal rule under which tracking orders are issued limits the court order to 45 days,[22] and the statute authorizing interception of phone metadata limits court orders to 60 days.[23] If the police want an extension, they have to make a new showing, which presumably cannot consist solely of the information they provided the first time around.

After *Jones*, and assuming proportionality analysis based on survey data is given credence, federal law should be amended to make clear that probable cause is required for tracking and metadata collection that is "prolonged." But if the police limit their virtual search request to a shorter period of time—say, for two days—proportionality analysis might permit a court order based on something less—say, reasonable suspicion or the § 2703(d) standard. Only at the end of that period would probable cause need to be shown. This regime would not only be proportionate; it would also allow the type of preliminary investigation that is sometimes necessary to develop probable cause. At the same time, it would prevent endless surveillance based on mere suspicion.

Of course, the precise point at which renewal is required will necessarily be somewhat arbitrary. While the 45- and 60-day periods contemplated by current law seem far too long to wait before probable cause is required, perhaps the two-day period suggested above will strike many as too short. And whatever point is chosen will undoubtedly produce over- and underinclusive searches. Depending on the target and the circumstances, a few hours of tracking in one case could be much more revealing than two weeks of tracking in another; the interception of the metadata on a couple of phone calls in a murder investigation could be more informative than a month's worth of metadata in a drug investigation.

Assuming, however, that there must be some limit to any particular authorization of a virtual search, this type of durational arbitrariness is unavoidable (a problem, it should be noted, that a probable-cause-forever approach does not avoid either, as Title III's rigid 30-day rule demonstrates). An analogous situation was at issue in *Riverside v.*

McLaughlin,[24] where the Supreme Court held that judicial review of a warrantless arrest is required to make sure the police had probable cause at the time of arrest. Depending on the person arrested and the nature of custody, the impact of postarrest detention can vary tremendously. But rather than tying the point at which judicial review is required to such imponderables, the Court created a bright-line rule: judicial review of an arrest need take place no earlier than, nor should it occur later than, 48 hours after arrest.[25] In coming to that conclusion, the Court rejected a rule that would merely require that such renewals be "prompt."[26] Rather, it recognized that more guidance was necessary, stating that "[a]lthough we hesitate to announce that the Constitution compels a specific time limit, it is important to provide some degree of certainty so that States and counties may establish procedures with confidence that they fall within constitutional bounds."[27]

That is the right approach here as well. Virtual searches should be subject to judicial review, and police and courts should be told when that review must take place. Ideally, the timeline would be set, as an initial matter, by legislatures (as it was in *Riverside*). If legislatures act first, they would establish a baseline, to which the courts might well defer (which also occurred in *Riverside*).[28]

Historical Transaction Surveillance

Time limits and renewal orders can work for real-time surveillance because, by definition, that type of virtual search is ongoing. With some modifications, that regime can also be applied to attempts to obtain historical information, such as occurred in *Jones*; there, it will be recalled, police not only tracked Jones but also collected three weeks of his CSLI. If law enforcement is seeking records covering only a short period of time—say, two days' worth—reasonable suspicion or a 2703(d) order might suffice. But acquisition of more voluminous historical information—such as the three weeks of CSLI sought in *Jones* or the four months "of all records of accounts, i.e., savings, checking, loan or otherwise," from two different banks, that agents requested in *Miller*[29]—should require a probable cause showing.

In *Carpenter*, the government tried to distinguish historical information from real-time data by relying on the assumption of risk doctrine; while real-time surveillance impinges directly on the suspect, the government noted, location records can be—and in *Carpenter* were—obtained from third parties.[30] But the majority in *Carpenter* dismissed this argument, making the obvious point that, in terms of privacy intrusions, acquiring information about a suspect's location from records is no different from tracking that location in real time. "In fact," the Court noted, "historical cell-site records present even greater privacy concerns than the GPS monitoring of a vehicle we considered in *Jones*" because CSLI location information originates from the suspect's cell phone, which, unlike a car, is virtually always near the suspect.[31] While the majority was careful to distinguish CSLI from financial and phone metadata records, the latter types of records can also be very revealing, not only about location but also about one's purchases and communicants, a fact that survey data asking about the intrusiveness of these types of virtual searches confirm.[32] Eventually, the Court will have to confront that reality.

This, in fact, was the main source of concern for the dissenters in *Carpenter*. They conjectured that *Carpenter* will lead to a warrant requirement any time police seek historical information; after all, Justice Kennedy noted, "financial records and telephone records 'reveal . . . personal affairs, opinions, habits and associations.' . . . The troves of information the Government can and does obtain using financial records and telephone records dwarfs what can be gathered from cell-site records."[33] Justice Alito, in a separate dissent, likewise warned that the decision in *Carpenter* will threaten "many legitimate and valuable investigative practices upon which law enforcement has come to rely" and asked:

> Must every grand jury subpoena duces tecum [now] be supported by probable cause? If so, investigations of terrorism, political corruption,

white-collar crime, and many other offenses will be stymied. And what about subpoenas and other document-production orders issued by administrative agencies?[34]

Justice Kennedy and Justice Alito are both right about the impact of *Carpenter*—*if* the Court adheres to the traditional probable-cause-forever standard and ignores gradations in intrusiveness. But proportionality analysis offers a compromise position, in three ways. First, as should be clear by now, that analysis would only require probable cause when voluminous records are sought, not when, for instance, government wants records of a one-time transaction or single-day transactions.

Second, as noted in chapter 3, even if probable cause is equated with a more-likely-than-not showing, now that the mere evidence limitation is a distant memory, that standard comes closer to the traditional relevance test applicable to subpoenas than many might think. Today, the effective standard requires a showing that something in the records will help move the investigation forward, not that it will produce direct proof of crime. Indeed, some commentators suggest that in many virtual search situations probable cause is relatively easy to develop for records searches.[35]

The third way proportionality analysis should alleviate the concerns of the *Carpenter* dissenters, especially those focused on the impact of *Carpenter* on white-collar crime investigations and administrative subpoenas, is that it takes into account the nature of the suspect. If the target of an investigation is an impersonal entity—a corporation or other type of business—the privacy intrusion is minimal. That fact is clearly reflected in my survey data, which ranked accessing "corporate records" as similar to accessing "criminal records" in terms of intrusiveness.[36] It is also evident in the Supreme Court's own decisions. Beginning with its very first administrative subpoena case, the Court stated that "there is a clear distinction between an individual and a corporation" in cases involving demands for production of books and papers, because a corporation "is a creature of the State . . . incorporated for the benefit of the public."[37] While this distinction was based on the notion that corporations are not "persons" entitled to Fifth Amendment protection (as compared to individuals who have a right to refuse subpoenas that might demand incriminating information), subsequent decisions focusing on the Fourth Amendment implications of subpoenas repeated the distinction. Typical is a 1946 Court decision emphasizing that its holding authorizing, over a Fourth Amendment objection, access to business records pursuant to an administrative subpoena applied "merely to the production of corporate records and papers."[38] Two years later, in its *Morton Salt* decision (the case that endorsed the official curiosity test), the Court went so far as to say that "corporations can claim no equality with individuals in the enjoyment of a right to privacy."[39]

For complicated reasons that I have described elsewhere, later Court decisions downgraded the protection afforded personal papers, in effect obliterating the distinction between personal and corporate records.[40] But *Carpenter* appears to rejuvenate it; there, the Court stated that it wanted to "prevent the subpoena doctrine from overcoming any reasonable expectation of privacy."[41] While that statement may (and should) mean that subpoenas will often be insufficient for virtual searches of information about individuals, it also means they will continue to be perfectly fine in administrative and regulatory contexts. As the *Carpenter* majority pointed out, "[a]lmost all of the examples Justice Alito cites contemplated requests implicating diminished privacy interests or a corporation's own books";[42] the majority also distinguished CSLI from "corporate tax or payroll ledgers."[43] The Court can most profitably achieve the goal of preventing subpoena doctrine from continuing to occupy the field by adhering to the well-developed corporate–individual distinction it has developed in its Fifth Amendment cases[44]—in other words, by adopting proportionality reasoning.

Encryption

Increasingly, law enforcement officials who engage in real-time or historical virtual searching of suspects are confronted with encryption. District attorneys have complained that thousands of phones housing potentially incriminating information remain inaccessible because the devices are encrypted.[45] FBI director James Comey called this phenomenon "going dark," which he analogized to a "closet that can't be opened," "a safe that can't be cracked."[46]

In fact, there are several ways the safe can be cracked. The first is to get the passcode to the phone from the owner of the device. Of course, if the owner is also the target of the investigation, resistance to that request might be raised on both Fourth and Fifth Amendment grounds. However, neither ground should necessarily prevail.

The Fourth Amendment analysis, run through the proportionality prism, is straightforward. If the government can demonstrate the justification necessary to obtain the type of information that is encrypted, the search is permissible. It is possible that the fact of encryption, by itself, would raise the perceived intrusiveness of the virtual search. But even if that is the case (as corroborated by survey data or positive law), probable cause–plus would presumably be sufficient.

The Fifth Amendment argument is based on the idea that forcing the passcode from the owner is compelling "testimony" that will incriminate.[47] However, consistent with *Hubbell*, most courts have held that, if the government can show good reason to believe it will discover incriminating information in the device and can describe with some specificity what it would be, the Fifth Amendment does not stand in the way, so long as the government does not need to rely on the identity of the source for the passcode at trial or can prove that fact without referencing how it was compelled. As one lower court put it, the Fifth Amendment "does not protect an act of production [such as producing a password] when any potentially testimonial component of the act of production—such as the existence, custody, and authenticity of evidence—is a 'foregone conclusion' that 'adds little or nothing to the sum total of the Government's information.'"[48] In such situations, once the government makes the cause and particularity showings required by the Fourth Amendment, it has satisfied the Fifth Amendment as well.

Of course, overcoming a suspect's Fourth and Fifth Amendment claims does not automatically win the government the decryption key. The target may still refuse to provide it. While the sanction a targeted person faces for refusing to comply with a decryption order is contempt of court, the penalty for contempt (repeated jailings) might pale in comparison to the penalties for some crimes.

The second way the safe might be cracked is by going to the developer of the device. That is what the FBI did in December 2015, when it asked Apple for help in decrypting the iPhone of Syed Farook, an ISIS-inspired terrorist who, along with his spouse, killed 14 people and wounded another 22 in a government benefits center in San Bernadino. The FBI was particularly interested in discovering if the phone could tell it anything about whether Farook had coconspirators and had contacted any of them prior to the shooting. Both Farook and his wife were killed in a shootout, so the owner route was foreclosed. Instead, the FBI obtained a court order requiring Apple to decrypt the phone. Apple refused, arguing, among other things, that the order would be overly burdensome, damage its business, and violate its due process rights.[49] The issue became moot when the FBI was able to get another company to decrypt the phone—the third method of defeating encryption. But the question of whether a developer can be forced to decrypt remains.[50]

Had the court order in the San Bernadino case been litigated, much of the debate would have been about the scope of the All Writs Act, a statute first passed in 1789 stating that the courts "may issue all writs necessary or appropriate in aid of their respective jurisdictions and agreeable to the usages and principles of law."[51] As interpreted by the Supreme Court, the law permits courts to compel "all information, facilities and technical assistance" necessary to execute a warrant.[52] I will not plumb the scope of the All Writs Act here. But the probable cause– plus showing that might be required by the Fourth Amendment— which would involve a demonstration that other methods of obtaining the relevant information have failed—would presumably also be sufficient to show, under the All Writs Act, that decryption is necessary to carry out the warrant.

The debate may soon be moot, however, for technological reasons. Allegedly, every Apple operating system since version 8 is inaccessible to the company.[53] And Apple recently announced that iPhone users would have the option to disable not only location tracking but also the web-surfing tracking that allows companies (and law enforcement) to learn about preferences, and that this function would be opt-in, meaning that the default is no tracking.[54] Thus, even if Apple wanted to obey a court order, it might not be able to do so.

So a fourth potential approach to encryption, periodically considered by Congress, is to require that every communications device come equipped with either a secret "backdoor" that can be activated to decrypt (with appropriate authorization), or a transparent "front door" that accomplishes the same thing (again, with the necessary court order). The most sophisticated, privacy-protective version of this approach is called "split key," with one part of the encryption key retained by the manufacturer and (to avoid collusion with the government) the other part kept by a privacy rights organization.[55] Privacy advocates have resisted even this approach because, they say, it will increase security breaches, facilitate hacking by criminals and foreign powers, and slow progress toward "ephemeral communications," which discard the encryption key after each communication.[56] Proponents of the split key approach respond that, for malicious exploitation of a key system to occur, not only would the key be needed, but the device itself would have to be in the possession of the would-be hacker.[57]

There will eventually have to be a legislative answer to the encryption dilemma. The Constitution should not prevent any of these approaches. But strong encryption may be politically popular. If so, with appropriate authorization law enforcement might still be able to take advantage of third-party workarounds, as occurred in the San Bernadino case.[58] It should also be noted that strong encryption does not prevent the government from obtaining metadata or (unless the phone owner has disabled Cloud backup) undeleted messages, contacts, account information, and photographs.[59] Furthermore, the content of texts and emails on a phone will be accessible if police can arrest the owner when the phone is unlocked.[60] Balancing these various considerations, after hearing from law enforcement agencies, the tech companies, and the public, is a paradigmatic legislative endeavor.[61]

The Future of Targeted Virtual Searches

By way of summarizing the foregoing analysis, consider three ways in which current practice might change if the tendency toward proportionality reasoning evidenced in *Jones* and *Carpenter* came to full fruition.

Long-Term Versus Short-Term Virtual Searches

Intrusive virtual searches are most likely to happen when the government has zeroed in on an individual as either a suspect or a person of interest. *Jones* is the perfect example: the police in that case went after Jones with weeks of CCTV, tracking, phone transactions, and electronic surveillance. Given their duration, each component of that investigation except the camera trained on Jones's club was more intrusive than a top-to-bottom search of a car (at least if survey results are to be believed).[62] Thus, under proportionality reasoning, at some point every investigative technique used in that case—including, as the weeks went on, even the CCTV surveillance—should have been authorized by a warrant based on probable cause.

Not all suspect-driven virtual searches are as all-encompassing, however. Consider the investigation that took place in *United States v. Knotts*.[63] This was the case, mentioned in chapter 2, where the police used a beeper to track the defendant for an hour. The minimal degree of tracking involved in *Knotts* should not require probable cause; the amount of information police could learn from an hour's worth of tracking, both in the abstract and on the facts of *Knotts*, does not come close to what the police learned about Jones, even if one focuses solely on the GPS tracking efforts in the latter case. At the same time, the Court's holding in *Knotts*, which relied on the knowing exposure doctrine in finding that no search occurred, goes too far in the other direction. That decision should be revisited now that *Jones* and *Carpenter* have poured new life into expectation-of-privacy analysis. Survey results as well as positive law (in the form of antistalking statutes) suggest that limitations should be placed even on short-term tracking. If the Constitution does not, legislation should.

Nontechnological Virtual Searches

The conclusion that some justification is required for the police action that occurred in *Knotts* raises another question: What if the tracking in that case had not relied on technology? The Supreme Court today would almost certainly conclude that the Fourth Amendment is irrelevant, even if the police followed Knotts for a much longer period of time. In *Jones*, the five members of the Court who endorsed the idea that some forms of nontrespassory tracking can be a search appeared to limit their expansion of Fourth Amendment protection to tracking that relied on some type of device. As Justice Sotomayor said in her concurring opinion in *Jones* when agreeing that a search occurred on the facts of that case, "I do not regard as dispositive the fact that the government might obtain the fruits of GPS monitoring through lawful conventional surveillance techniques."[64] The implication is that using a "conventional surveillance technique" to monitor Jones would not have been governed by the Fourth Amendment even if that technique—for instance, tailing his car, stalking him while walking, or staking out his home or nightclub—had gone on for weeks.

Yet recall also that, in coming to her conclusion in *Jones*, Justice Sotomayor emphasized the extent to which GPS tracking can record and aggregate information about people's beliefs and habits. Even "conventional" virtual surveillance can aggregate reams of information about the target if the police manage to keep it covert. And if they fail at that, so that the target knows monitoring is occurring, the surveillance becomes especially oppressive. As Rehnquist suggested with his bar example, if the police plan to stake out a building, they should have a good reason for doing so. Thus, if a court order is required for technological surveillance, I would contend that an order should also be required for targeted traditional surveillance that is meant to obtain the same type and amount of information. At the least, concern about the impact of technological surveillance should occasion a reconsideration of conventional practices as well, at a subconstitutional if not a constitutional level.

Databases and Virtual Searches

In the meantime, one cannot ignore the fact, highlighted by Justice Sotomayor in *Jones*, that technology makes virtual searching easier both to carry out and to memorialize. GPS tracking, CCTV, ALPRs, CSLI, phone metadata access, drones, and even facial recognition technologies are spreading from big cities like New York and Los Angeles to smaller burgs such as Fresno, California.[65] More important, the information collected by these technologies are much more likely to be aggregated. That development vastly facilitates what Amitai Etzioni has called "cybernation"—the use of large data sources to find out about people.[66]

A significant amount of this data is already possessed by the government. Some government databases, such as those containing criminal records, terrorist and gang watchlists, and the reports generated through street policing, house information the police and the criminal justice system create. But police might also find useful the databases maintained by other government entities, such as departments of motor vehicles, internal revenue services, and welfare agencies. And then there are government databases that combine government information with information obtained by third parties. One of the best examples of this phenomenon, discussed in more detail in chapter 7, is the fusion center, which "fuses" information from numerous different sources, both governmental and civilian.

Increasingly, law enforcement agencies are also seeking out private companies that can acquire and analyze this information for them. The scope of these programs can be voluminous. Sarah Brayne has catalogued the types of information the Los Angeles Police Department has at its fingertips through a data-mining platform developed by the private company Palantir: Crime Analysis Mapping (i.e., a summary of crime hot spots); Field Interview Cards filled out by officers about stops and other encounters they have had; traffic citations; crime alert bulletins; ALPR data; sex offender registries; tracking of offenders wearing ankle bracelets; and data about outstanding arrests and citations from Los Angeles County and surrounding jurisdictions. Palantir can also access data in the California Law Enforcement Telecommunicates System, which include criminal history from the National Crime Information System, driving history from the Department of Motor Vehicles, and records of restraining orders, as well as data about stolen vehicles, firearms possession, and missing persons.[67]

Other companies offer the police (or anyone else willing to pay for it) information that goes far beyond records associated with antisocial behavior. LexisNexis has gobbled up a number of other data companies and now facilitates access to "over 37 billion records and 10,000 disparate sources" that can include basic demographic information, income, net worth, real property holdings, social security numbers, current and previous addresses, phone numbers and fax numbers, names of neighbors, driver records, license plate and VIN numbers, bankruptcy and debtor filings, employment and business records, bank account balances and activity, stock purchases, and credit card activity, in addition to criminal records.[68] The company tells law enforcement agencies interested in learning about suspects and POIs that its technology "securely and intelligently analyzes, filters and links billions of records to provide a more complete picture of an individual."[69] Many other companies offer similar services to law enforcement,[70] and the types of information they accumulate is quite extensive.

Finally, there are also systems that combine this type of historical information with real-time surveillance. Most famous in this regard is New York's Domain Awareness System (DAS), developed with help from Microsoft and federal money, that "aggregates and analyzes existing public safety data streams" from cameras, license plate readers, cell phone tracking, radiation detectors, gun shot detectors, law enforcement databases, 911 calls, complaints to police, social media scanners, and many other sources.[71] The camera feeds can be rewound to discover historical information and can be integrated with facial recognition technology. A private entity named Fusus purports to do even more, calling itself "the first company to unify live video, data, sensor and CAD (Computer Aided Dispatch) feeds from virtually any source, creating a Real-Time Crime Center in the Cloud that enhances the situational awareness and investigative capabilities of law enforcement and public safety."[72] The company's website displays a darkened city with various locations eerily marked by encircled green camera logos, bearing descriptors such as "tips submission," "campus alert triggered," "panic alert triggered," "tactical team in position," "emergency services request," "evidence upload request," "Unit 72, 10-72 Responding," "ALPR Hotlist Hit," and "gunfire detected."[73]

Under proportionality analysis, the justification needed to deploy one of these information systems to find out more about a specific suspect should depend upon its content. In the system purportedly run by Palantir, most or all the cybernated information is "public" or generated by police observation of public activity, which, as chapter 3 reported, survey participants tend to associate with a low degree of privacy (albeit still ranked higher in intrusiveness than a brief checkpoint stop). Thus, when police use Palantir to investigate someone, they do not need probable cause. But, to prevent arbitrary intrusions, they should still have to articulate in writing, ideally to a court, reasons for initiating the investigation. And when data about a particular person are gleaned from communication or financial records through these systems, as might occur with LexisNexis or DAS, proportionality analysis dictates that more justification is needed depending on the volume of data sought. Certainly, if these systems are used to compile a "digital dossier" on all of a person's transactions and activities, probable cause, found by a court, should be required—and perhaps even probable cause–plus. If the public and private information is not siloed and instead is mixed together, police will need that level of justification from the get-go.

That much follows from the analysis of this chapter and a privacy-friendly reading of *Carpenter*. But the type of virtual searching facilitated by Palantir, LexisNexis, DAS, and Fusus—as well as the more familiar data giants such as Google, Apple, and Facebook—is not limited to an investigation of someone the police already suspect of involvement in crime. In fact, these cybernation systems can be used in four other ways. First, together with government-run databases, they assist law enforcement in generating profiles that predict who is or might be committing crime or the areas where it might be committed. Second, they respond to government efforts to identify as-yet unidentified suspects or persons of interest in connection with a crime or event under investigation. Third, they collect and maintain the information necessary to carry out these other functions. And fourth, the companies that operate these cybernation systems often take it upon themselves to investigate crime and offer the results to the government, usually with a price tag. These four other types of virtual searches are the topics of chapters 5–8. Proportionality analysis is relevant in all these situations as well, but it has different implications for each.

Profile-Driven Virtual Searches (Predictive Policing)

Police Officer Keener is cruising a heavily black neighborhood in St. Louis, in part because an algorithm from a company called HunchLab has identified the area as one in which the risk of aggravated assault is relatively high. The officer spots a Chevy Impala; its dark-tinted windows are a violation of Missouri's traffic laws. The officer stops the car, which turns out to be driven by a young black man. Because, Keener later tells a reporter riding with him, he smelled marijuana through the open window, he thoroughly searches the car and finds a gun. However, he does not find any marijuana, and the gun is legal. After letting the young man drive on, Keener tells the reporter, "He could have been going to shoot somebody. Or not."

Andrew Ferguson, who recounts this real-life example of what has come to be called "predictive policing," asks "Would Officer Keener have stopped the car without the HunchLab prediction?"[1] It is hard to know. As detailed later in this chapter, police use traffic violations as pretexts to investigate all the time, and research shows they are especially likely to do so in neighborhoods populated by people of color. But the innuendo in Professor Ferguson's question is that the HunchLab algorithm increases the chances of such encounters. In other words, predictive policing might multiply the benefits and costs already inherent in traditional policing—it might lead police to more perpetrators but also generate more false positives, that is, stops of people who are doing nothing wrong.

HunchLab (now a part of an outfit called SpotShotter Connect) is just one of many companies that use artificial intelligence to produce maps indicating "hot spots" for crime during specific times of the day, relying not only on geographic crime data but also calls for service, weather patterns, census data, population density, and the number and location of abandoned properties, schools, bars, and transportation centers, as well as upcoming events such as ball games.[2] Of course, police have long been interested in identifying those areas most in need of their presence. But the algorithms used by companies such as HunchLab and Galitica (formerly know as PredPol) appear to provide much more fine-tuned outputs about, for instance, which neighborhoods are transitioning from high gun crime to high residential burglary areas, which buildings or blocks in those areas are particularly likely to experience violence, and which streets have experienced upticks in burglaries.[3]

Increasingly combined with hot spot policing techniques is the use of big data to identify "hot people." Relying on 11 crime-related variables, as well as age and gang membership, the city of Chicago famously developed a "heat list" that assigned people with criminal records "risk scores" of from 1 to 500.[4] According to developers of the list, the higher the score, the greater the chance the person would be either the perpetrator of violence or its victim. In a similar attempt to compute "threat scores" in connection with 911 calls, Intrado, a now defunct company, introduced a program called Beware that coded people and places red, yellow, or green (with red indicating the highest threat), based on data from publicly available criminal and mental health records and trolling of social media for gang associations and violent comments.[5] Taking Intrado's place are businesses like ShadowDragon, which sucks in data from social media, dating apps, Amazon, posts on Twitter, WhatsApp, and Facebook in an effort to help police both identify trouble spots and learn more about potential suspects.[6] In addition to Chicago, Los Angeles, Kansas City, Baltimore, San Francisco, and numerous other cities have tried their hand as this type of predictive policing.[7]

In contrast to the virtual searches discussed in chapter 4, hot spot and hot people policing do not start with a suspect. Rather, they use algorithms to try to identify where crime is occurring and the type of person committing it. Hot spot policing appears to be a relatively useful way of allocating police resources. Optimally deployed (about which more in a moment), it can reduce crime without significant displacement of crime to nearby areas.[8] But the jury is still out on whether hot people policing is effective. Although the Chicago Police Department claimed that 80% of the 51 people shot over a two-day period were on its heat list, a subsequent RAND study showed the list had little predictive accuracy.[9] Further, an overview of research conducted before 2010 comparing hot spot to hot people policing asserted that "the police have to approach four times as many targets to identify the same level of overall crime when they focus on people as opposed to places."[10] A more recent comprehensive study conducted by the National Academy of Science concluded that, of the many varieties of "proactive policing"—including stop and frisk, community policing, problem-oriented policing, and "broken windows" policing (which assumes a correlation between rundown neighborhoods and crime)—the only technique that consistently reduced crime was targeting of a small area.[11]

The following discussion assumes, however, that compared to traditional techniques both hot spot and hot people policing are capable of improving the identification of places and people likely to be associated with crime. Advanced algorithms may eventually make that assumption an accurate one (or police may continue to rely on data-fed predictive policing in the false hope that they will). Even on this assumption, predictive policing—especially hot people prediction—faces several obstacles that, when added up, make it very suspect as a legal matter.

Proportionality and Predictive Policing

Proportionality analysis would have several implications for predictive policing. First, it would limit the type of data that could be inputted into predictive algorithms. Second, it would require that the algorithm perform at a fairly high level when used to justify a significant police action. And third, before any physical confrontation takes place based on an algorithm, it would mandate triggering conduct by the individual stopped by the police. The first two limitations follow directly from proportionality reasoning and would require data a demonstration that the "hit rate" associated with the algorithm is proportionate to the intrusions based on it. The third requirement, while consistent with the proportionality analysis of chapter 3, also stems from cases like *Terry v. Ohio*,[12] which stand for the proposition that searches and seizures that involve deprivations of liberty may occur only upon a determination that "criminal activity may be afoot."[13] The following discussion focuses on how these three requirements interact with stops and frisks, the setting in which profile-driven virtual searches are most likely to occur.

Hit Rates

In the traditional police setting, police and courts engage in a qualitative assessment of whether reasonable suspicion or "articulable facts" support a stop and frisk or an arrest. For instance, the police might justify a stop by saying the individual seemed conspicuously out of place, had a bulge in their pocket, or engaged in "furtive movements" (a police favorite).[14] Such subjective judgments can, of course, be biased or pretextual. The possible advantage of algorithm-based policing is that, done well, it relies on risk factors that are quantitatively shown to predict crime and are thus likely to be less prone to manipulation.

But that can be true only if the algorithm can produce a satisfactory "hit rate" (the percentage of people identified by the algorithm who are involved in crime). Further, if proportionality reasoning applies, that hit rate must be proportionate not only to the police action it purports to justify (e.g., a stop or prolonged surveillance) but also to the type of data that needs to be accessed to learn the risk associated with a place or a person. For instance, if the police want to arrest someone based on an algorithm that requires accessing financial information and social media posts, they would need a higher hit rate than if they merely want to stop and question the individual based on arrest history and gang membership or to use the latter type of information solely to identify people who might need social services or a warning about possible danger from others (as apparently sometimes occurred with Chicago's heat list).[15]

With respect to the data access issue, hot people policing is much more likely than hot spot policing to run into trouble on proportionality grounds. The hot spot algorithm developed by Hunchlab relies on population-wide statistics such as area crime reports, weather analysis, or location data that is not person-specific.[16] It then tries to predict where crime might occur, not who might commit it. Little or no intrusion into personal information is involved.

Hot person algorithms are a different story. These algorithms are constructed based on a theory of crime—say, a theory that crime is correlated with number of arrests, membership in a gang, age, and gender—or they are generated through artificial intelligence—a computer analyzing hundreds or thousands of data points and correlating them with criminal activity. To develop the necessary correlations and see if they apply to a particular person, data about specific individuals are crucial. Although data analysts and computers working with "training data" can use anonymization techniques in developing the algorithm and police can simply be fed a "threat score" that does not reveal how it was arrived at, the fact remains that actions based on a predictive algorithm will associate particular individuals with particular risk factors.

If all this information is a matter of public record, then perhaps proportionality norms are not violated. But some algorithms, such as the ones developed by Intrado and ShadowDragon, claim to include risk factors gleaned from private postings on social media. If so, in the absence of sufficient justification (about which more below) their use would violate the proportionality principle, just as a suspect-driven virtual search would if it relied on that type of information.

With respect to the second proportionality issue—the grounds needed to justify police action—hot spot and hot people algorithms are in the same boat. If police want to stop someone based on either type of algorithm, under *Terry* they need a hit rate equivalent to reasonable suspicion. If they want to arrest someone, they need a hit rate amounting to probable cause.

Given the mathematical nature of algorithms, figuring out the hit rate that justifies accessing the data used by a policing algorithm and the policing actions it permits can (and should) depend on how concepts such as probable cause, reasonable suspicion, and relevance are quantified. Fortunately, we have some information about how judges might do so. A survey of federal judges found that, on average, probable cause was associated with a 48% level of certainty and reasonable suspicion with a 30% level of certainty.[17] An opinion from the Seventh Circuit Court of Appeals suggests that a 28% hit rate might be sufficient to justify a stop.[18] These figures can provide baseline quantifications of probable cause and reasonable suspicion.

However, adjustments might be made under certain circumstances. Most prominently, consistent with the danger exception discussed in chapter 3, some might argue for a lower hit rate if the crime sought to be prevented is serious. Along these lines, Justice Scalia once speculated that a 5–10% hit rate might be permissible if the stop is based on suspicion that a driver is drunk.[19]

Yet most algorithms do not do even this well. Hot spot policing tools don't even try to identify high-risk individuals, and the typical hot person algorithm in use today is a long way off from a 10% hit rate, much less a one-in-three rate. Taking at face value the Chicago Police Department's statement that 80% of the 51 people arrested for involvement in a shooting during a particular weekend were on its heat list,[20] that amounts to a hit rate of only .014% if, as reported by the *New York Times*, the list contained over 280,000 people with a score above 250[21] (the score at which, according to a spokesperson for the department, people "come on our radar").[22] It is not difficult to compile a list that contains most of the people involved in violence if the list includes almost everyone in the jurisdiction with a violent criminal record or a gang affiliation! Had the goal of the heat list instead been to identify people who possessed weapons on the weekend in question rather than who would shoot, or be shot by, a gun, the hit rate undoubtedly would have been higher, but probably still nowhere near the 30% range that proportionality analysis might require to justify a stop based on reasonable suspicion.

This is not to say that a predictive algorithm cannot reach that goal. Using data from field interrogation cards that describe the reasons police gave for close to a half-million stops carried out by the New York Police Department during 2008–2010, a group led by Sharad Goel developed an algorithm that included the following variables: "[D]emographic information about the suspect (sex, race, age, height, weight, and build); location of the stop (precinct; inside or outside; and on public transit, in public housing, or neither); date and time of the stop (year, month, day of week, and time of day); the recorded reasons for the stop (e.g., 'furtive movements,' 'a bulge in the pocket,' or 'high crime area'); whether the stop was the result of a radio run; whether the officer was in uniform; how long the officer observed the suspect before initiating the stop; and the 'local hit rate' of stops at that location."[23] Based on regression analysis, the authors calculated the weights of each of these "risk factors"; for instance, greater weight was assigned to bulges in pockets than for furtive movements and to presence in certain locations over other locations. Using this algorithm, which I will call the "GSFA" (for Goel et al. Stop & Frisk Algorithm) and applying it to a different sample of stops and frisks taken from the years 2011–2012, the Goel team was able to differentiate weapon-discovery cases from weapon-absent cases 83% of the time.[24]

For understandable practical reasons, Goel et al. then wanted to reduce the number and types of factors considered by their algorithm, which they did by identifying the five factors (out of 18 that police identified as relevant to their stop decisions) that were positively correlated with possession of a weapon, which turned out to "suspicious object," "sights and sounds of criminal activity," "suspicious bulge," "witness report," and "ongoing investigation."[25] Those factors were then reduced to the first three because they were the most robustly predictive items, and those three were assigned points based on their relative predictiveness (with suspicious object assigned 3 points, and sights and sounds of criminal activity and suspicious bulge assigned 1 point each). Goel et al.'s analysis showed that the results produced by this "heuristic" or short-form model of the GSFA were "virtually indistinguishable" from those produced by the five-factor model or the more complicated full model. More specifically, it differentiated between people with weapons and those without weapons about 80% of the time.[26]

Note, however, that this figure is analogous to the 80% figure produced by the Chicago heat list data. It only describes the characteristics of people who were found to have weapons; it does not give us the hit rate, which tells us how many people who were stopped based on the GSFA had weapons. I asked Goel and his colleagues to calculate that rate for 10 different precincts, using the heuristic model of the GSFA and its six cutpoints (with 5 points—3 plus 1 plus 1—as the top possible score and 0 as the lowest possible score). Results varied significantly between precincts. For instance, in Precinct 32, the one person with a score of 5 had a gun, roughly 48% of those with a score of 4 had a weapon, roughly 27% who scored a 2 or 3 had a weapon, and 1% of those with 1 or 0 points had a weapon. In Precinct 23, no 5-point scores were produced, while 35% of those with a 4, 22% of those with a 2 or 3, and 2% of those with a 0 or 1 had a weapon. In Precinct 75, the percentages on all six cutpoints fell between 5% and 35%. In Precincts 40 and 101, none of the hit rates for any score rose about 25%.[27] And so on.

These results illustrate several things about hot people algorithms. First, the algorithms need to be validated on a local population, down to the precinct level; local crime rates, criminal histories, and other variables can vary from precinct to precinct, which may affect hit rates. Second, hit rates depend upon cutpoints. A very respectable hit rate can be obtained if the cutpoint authorizing a stop is set high enough (at 4 or 5 in the case of the GSFA); the trade-off, of course, is that many fewer weapons will be found because many fewer stops will be made.[28] For instance, in Precinct 23 roughly 88% of the weapons came from people who scored 0, 1, or 2 on the GSFA;[29] however, because there were so many of them, the *percentage* of people with those scores who had weapons (the hit rate) was very low (in the 1% range). A third and related point is that, as the data for Precincts 40 and 101 illustrate, if police lower the cutoff score in an effort to obtain more weapons (to, say, a score of 2 on the GSFA), they may be hard put to achieve the 20–30% hit rate demanded by proportionality reasoning.

This all adds up to a fourth and final point: Compared to seat-of-the-pants assessments by police, well-constructed algorithms can radically reduce the number of unnecessary stops (including, as discussed further below, unnecessary stops of people of color). The NYPD's hit rate for weapons discovered during the stop and frisk program found unconstitutional in *Floyd v. City of New York*[30] was well below 2%.[31] Had New York City police limited themselves to stopping only those with scores of 4 or 5 on the GFSA, their hit rate would have been much higher (in the 30% to 40% range); at the same time, they would have confronted 80% fewer people, most of whom would not have had weapons on them. The research by Goel et al. suggests that, if algorithms are validated locally, have good discriminant validity (i.e., an ability to differentiate high- and low-risk individuals or places), and are periodically updated,[32] they can significantly outperform the qualitative judgments made by the typical cop, presumably because they structure officer decision-making based on statistical analysis.

Quantification of justification standards may strike some as artificial and unresponsive to the reality of policing, which involves consideration of a host of factors that an algorithm cannot capture. Indeed, the Supreme Court has refused to equate Fourth Amendment justification with any particular numerical probability, instead emphasizing, as pointed out in previous chapters, that police and courts should rely on "commonsense judgments." But the Court has also lamented the lack of "empirical studies dealing with inferences drawn from suspicious behavior," acknowledging that "we cannot reasonably demand scientific certainty from judges or law enforcement officers where none exists."[33] With the advent of predictive algorithms, empirical studies do exist. And if they produce better results than common-sense judgments, the fact that they do not take into account every factor police believe important should not count against them. Indeed, in the absence of the requisite algorithm-defined threshold for a stop, police might be prohibited from detaining an individual unless they have probable cause to arrest, a point that leads directly to the imminence issue.

The Imminence Requirement

Even if an algorithm can achieve the proportionality-derived hit rate needed to justify data access and subsequent police actions, a Fourth Amendment seizure cannot be based on a high score alone. Allowing detention in that situation would violate the danger exception outlined in chapter 3, which in turn is based on the precept, going back to John Stuart Mill, that the government should not deprive people who have yet to commit a crime of liberty unless the risk they pose is imminent.[34] Once shown to have committed a crime, a person's long-term risk can be a legitimate consideration during sentencing.[35] But in the policing setting, before arrest and conviction for a crime, the courts—including the Supreme Court in *Terry*—have made clear that preventive deprivations of liberty must be based on *near-term* risk; as the Court noted in a later decision, in every one of its stop cases in this vein "police stopped or seized a person because they suspected he was about to commit a crime, or was committing a crime at the moment of the stop."[36] This limitation also makes good practical sense. Otherwise, an algorithm such as the Chicago heat list, which is based primarily on historical factors such as previous arrests, would authorize the police to stop anyone with a high score anytime they wanted to do so, any day and every day or multiple times a day, even though they find no weapons on any of those occasions.

An example of how failing to abide by the imminence precept can go awry comes from Pasco County, Florida.[37] In 2020, the Pasco County Sheriff's Department, relying on data from local school records as well as their own records, used profiling techniques to place juveniles in "risk" categories. Juveniles considered high risk for committing crime—a determination apparently based on their home life, grades, and intelligence as well as criminal history—were all provided "mentoring" by sheriff's deputies assigned to the juvenile's school. More problematic, deputies also "harassed" high-risk students by going to their homes, asking for consent to search, and then repeating the process on a frequent basis.[38] The proportionality principle would probably prohibit the department's access to individual school records (which are protected by federal law) as well as the attempts to conduct home searches, given the likelihood that the hit rate associated with these actions was extremely low. But even if proportionality reasoning were somehow satisfied, the imminence requirement would clearly bar these nonconsensual actions, given the absence of any triggering misconduct.

Barring an algorithm that can precisely predict when a crime will occur (which, contrary to the fantasies one sees on TV and in the movies, is not in our foreseeable future), the only way to meet the imminence requirement is to observe a suspicious act that corroborates the algorithm's prediction. The definition of "suspicious act" for these purposes is likely to be hotly contested. But, at the least, it should depend upon the outcome being predicted and the law in the jurisdiction. For instance, if the algorithm is attempting to predict possession of a weapon in a jurisdiction where carrying a concealed weapon is a crime, a bulge in the pocket might be sufficient. If the algorithm is attempting to predict illegal drug possession, a "furtive movement" involving quickly pocketing a packet of something upon seeing the police may be sufficient. In contrast, mere presence in a high crime area would not be enough to meet the imminence requirement, since there is no conduct suggesting a crime is occurring. Neither would a "furtive movement" consisting solely of failing to make eye contact or walking away from the police suffice.[39] In the latter two situations, even a high algorithmic score would not justify a stop.

In short, the imminence requirement means that stops and frisks based on predictive algorithms will require what the law has always required (at least in theory): suspicious *conduct* at the time of the stop. The added value of the algorithm, if any, is that it establishes a baseline before a stop may occur and helps identify the type of suspicious conduct that can justify a stop of a particular individual at a particular point in time. For instance, an algorithm such as the short-form GSFA significantly limits the type of conduct that can justify a stop to possession of a "suspicious item," the "sights and sounds of criminal activity," and "a suspicious bulge." Granted, these terms still leave much to the discretion of officers. But they drastically narrow the universe of reasons an officer can give for detaining someone without arresting that person on probable cause.

The imminence requirement's mandate that suspicious conduct precede an algorithm-based stop addresses a common critique of predictive policing: that because algorithms like the GFSA are constructed by analyzing the conduct of groups of people, their use violates the Supreme Court's mandate that stops and arrests be based on "particularized suspicion" (to use *Terry*'s phrase).[40] The point is sometimes illustrated by fanciful thought experiments in which it is assumed, say, that based on a study of college student habits an algorithm can tell us that 60% of the rooms in a college dorm contain contraband.[41] While the 60% hit rate would exceed the quantified version of probable cause required for search of a residence, permitting a search of every dorm room based solely on that figure, it is argued, would violate the legal requirement that searches must be based on suspicion specific to the individual.[42]

This brand of criticism, which suggests that algorithmic decision-making always violates the Fourth Amendment, is insufficiently nuanced, for two reasons.[43] First, stopping a person who has all the risk factors in an algorithm such as the GSFA *is* based on characteristics the person has (e.g., age, location, or pocket bulge). Second and more important, if stops based on nomothetic information are impermissible, then all stops are impermissible; even stops purporting to be based on "individualized" suspicion are triggered by assumptions about how people act or should act. For instance, in *Terry v. Ohio*, when Officer McFadden stopped *Terry* and his companions for walking past and peering into a store several times, he was relying on an "intuitive algorithm," based on the notion that people who engage in such behavior do not "look right," to use McFadden's words.[44] Predictive judgments about people are often based on past experiences with other people and on stereotypes about what certain behaviors mean.[45] Fred Schauer put the point this way: "[O]nce we understand that most of the ordinary differences between general and particular decisionmaking are differences of degree and not differences in kind, we become properly skeptical of a widespread but mistaken view that the particular has some sort of natural epistemological or moral primacy over the general."[46]

Nonetheless, the intuition that the hypothesized dorm room searches should be prohibited is not off base. As Schauer admits, there can be a "difference in degree" between group-based general decision-making and particularized decision-making. In the predictive policing context, that difference is noticeable, for two reasons.

Most important, predictive policing that relies solely on statistics derived from static factors, such as number of arrests, demographic features or neighborhood, violates fundamental notions of autonomy. As Richard Re has contended, stops justified by "population-based statistics" do not afford the innocent target "an opportunity to reduce the risk of being searched."[47] Along the same lines, I have argued that the principle of legality, which has long been the basis for the actus reus requirement in crimes, mandates observation of "risky conduct" before intervention on prevention grounds may occur.[48] In our college dorm room example, since none of the individuals have been observed exercising a choice to engage in wrongdoing, they should not be subject to state-sanctioned searches or seizures.

A suspicious or risky conduct requirement also protects the innocent, particularly so where profiles are involved. As Jane Bambauer has noted, adherence to the Supreme Court's notion of individualized suspicion—as operationalized through a suspicious conduct requirement—limits the number of innocent people stopped or "hassled."[49] In the dorm example, assuming 100 students in 100 rooms, the absence of a conduct requirement would permit search not only of the 60 students who are committing crime but also of the 40 who are not. Compare that outcome to the effect of the intuitive "individualized suspicion" algorithm at work in *Terry*. No one besides Terry and his colleagues met Officer McFadden's stereotyping judgment. In the dorm case, the hassle rate is 40%; in *Terry* it was zero.

Re and Bambauer make valid points. But in the predictive policing setting,[50] the requirement that the wrongdoing be imminent addresses both of their concerns. Imminence will not exist unless the target has engaged in conduct that is corroborative of wrongdoing. And although an algorithm might target some innocent people, the requirement that suspicious activity be observed at the time of the stop will minimize the hassle rate.

An added advantage of the risky conduct requirement is that it provides a more palatable explanation for the police intervention than an algorithm based solely on static factors. The procedural justice literature suggests that both the legitimacy of the police and the public's willingness to assist in their endeavors are significantly undermined when police are opaque about their motives.[51] If police can explain a stop on the ground that the person possessed a "suspicious item" or manifested the "sights and sounds of criminal activity," and can back up that conclusion with specific facts, they are likely to be perceived as acting fairly even if, at bottom, they are working from an algorithm.

This is a particularly important consequence of the imminence requirement, given the impact of preventive policing on communities of color.

Algorithms and Race

For years, people of color have wryly joked about the "offenses" of "Driving While Black" and "Walking While Latino." The tragic fact is that, in practice, these offenses do exist. In part this is because the ubiquity of our traffic, loitering, and misdemeanor laws, combined with the ease with which they can be violated, give police leeway to do pretty much what they want.[52] More importantly for present purposes, police do not always feel the need to wait until a law has been broken or articulable suspicion has developed before they move in, especially, it seems, when black people are the target. I show my students tapes of people—all young black men—stopped for waving to a "drug dealer," turning a corner "too widely," or walking away when the police approach them.[53] Police have also been known to stop black people and Latinos simply because they are in "white" neighborhoods, are thought to have an arrest record, or "don't look right," to use Officer McFadden's words.[54] And once stopped, detentions can last a long time, accompanied by frisks or full searches. Sometimes, as we see so often on nightly news, matters can escalate into the use of deadly force.

The police will say that this type of policing is an important way of keeping a handle on the neighborhood, of nipping incipient crime in the bud, of discovering people with outstanding warrants, and of occasionally serendipitously finding evidence of more serious crime. They are backed up by research suggesting that "aggressive policing" produces higher arrest rates for robbery, decreases various types of thefts and gun crimes, and increases seizures of guns.[55] Those affected by these types of police actions instead call them state-sanctioned harassment and assert that traffic and pedestrian laws are often used as pretexts to carry out racist agendas. These assertions are bolstered by studies showing that the hit rates for finding weapons or evidence during street confrontations are in the single digits and that aggressive patrolling merely displaces crimes to other neighborhoods, is visited disproportionately on people of color, and severely damages community attitudes toward the police and government generally.[56]

In theory, predictive policing algorithms could help resolve the tension between these two perspectives. They could produce better hit rates than traditional policing and, because they are data-driven, could expose in a quantified way the racial disparities associated with traditional street policing. They could also inform improved methods of reducing these disparities. As Sendhil Mullainathan has noted, "biased algorithms are easier to fix than biased people."[57] While police training programs aimed at addressing explicit and implicit bias have had, at best, mixed success,[58] tools like the GFSA and Hunchlab's algorithms can be mechanistically tweaked (in ways suggested below) to counter whatever racially improper motivations police may have. Because algorithms express in concrete terms the cost of street policing, they could even quantify the grounds for *ending* predictive policing, empirically based *or* traditional.

At the same time, if data-driven predictive policing is not ended, or it is not implemented judiciously, it could give police still another reason to stop people on the street, through an algorithm that helps "launder" racially motivated stops by making them appear to be based on neutral numbers.[59] Consider how this laundering might play out with hot people policing first. It is well documented that, in some cities, black people are stopped and arrested for minor drug crimes and misdemeanors much more often than other ethnicities, despite similar violation rates.[60] This differential treatment may exist for a number of reasons: the greater likelihood that disadvantaged communities lack private spaces and thus commit these offenses where police can more easily observe them; the greater willingness of police to accost black people than white people for such crimes; the greater concentration of police resources in certain areas of the city; or some combination of these and other factors.[61] Whatever the cause, this differential means that, when they rely on arrest records, even algorithms with well-calibrated and sufficiently high hit rates (i.e., hit rates of 30%) will pinpoint black individuals much more often than white individuals, with the result that there will be many more black false positives in absolute terms. For instance, given racially disparate arrest rates, a black person with three minor arrests on his record may be no more at risk of carrying a weapon, possessing drugs, or engaging in some other arrestable offense than a white person with one prior arrest.[62] Yet the black person will have a much higher threat score on an algorithm that uses number of arrests as a risk factor. It may also be the case that arrests of black people for minor crimes are less likely to represent solid evidence that the crime was in fact committed; that would make the algorithm doubly misleading if, as it should be, the outcome sought is identifying people who are actually involved in criminal activity.

Based on these types of "dirty data" concerns,[63] some algorithm developers do not include drug arrests or minor misdemeanors in hot people algorithms.[64] This move can mitigate the problem. However, some data indicate that arrests for people of color are inflated even for some types of violent crime.[65]

If so, another potential solution to algorithmic racial bias is to develop algorithms for each race. In effect, that would discount the impact of racially disparate arrest rates. For instance, a race-based algorithm might assign a black person with three arrests a lower relative threat score than a white person with the same arrest history because the comparison group would be other black people, not people of all races. It might be objected that explicit reliance on race as a discriminating factor violates the Supreme Court's "anti-classification" approach to the Fourteenth Amendment, which prohibits classifications based on race.[66] Clearly, the Court's jurisprudence would render impermissible the explicit use of race as a risk factor, as the initial version of the GSFA did. However, if the developers of a predictive algorithm do not use race as a risk factor but instead, as suggested here, rely on it to define the sample on which the algorithm is validated, an equal protection challenge would probably fail.[67]

Better yet, as is true with the heuristic model of the GSFA, an algorithm could rely solely on suspicious traits. That approach entirely avoids static variables (such as arrests) that could correlate with race and thus should reduce disparate racial impacts. For instance, Goel et al. found that, using their heuristic model that eschews historical information, only 49% of the 10% of stops associated with a score of 5 were of black people, compared to 61% of those stopped by police under the NYPD's actual stop and frisk program.[68]

Use of racially skewed stops and arrests in algorithms can also have a pernicious impact on hot spot policing, because of what Bernard Harcourt has called the "ratchet effect":[69] if arrest data reflects racialized policing, they will tend to identify the same hot spot areas and neighborhoods over and over again, because police will be deployed there and will witness crimes that will then be fed back into the algorithm. In the meantime, neighborhoods with equivalent crime problems may be ignored, because they are never identified by the algorithm. This potential for a vicious cycle of law enforcement has always afflicted hot spot policing, but the quantified nature of algorithms could intensify it.

As with hot people algorithms, excluding stops and arrests for minor crimes as risk factors in the algorithm is one way developers have tried to minimize this problem. Another alternative is to randomize policing efforts to some extent, as Harcourt and Tracey Meares have suggested.[70] For instance, at least initially, departments could assign enhanced patrols to half (or some other fraction) of the hot spot areas, while other patrols would be randomly assigned to other parts of the jurisdiction. This approach would mean that some areas known to be associated with above-average crime problems will receive little or no service unless there is a 911 call. But it might also generate more reliable, less racially biased, data.

A final way of avoiding any exacerbation of racialized policing that hot people and hot spot predictive algorithms might produce—one that fits nicely with the Defund the Police movement's agenda—is to use the data solely for the purpose of allocating *non*-police resources to people and places. Chicago's alternative use of its heat list as a means of offering social services to specific individuals is one possibility. Similarly, in the past few years, the St. Louis County police department, Officer Keener's outfit, has begun sending lists of high-crime areas to a nonprofit called Better Family Life, which deploys social workers and counselors to help connect residents to drug treatment and education programs. As one report noted, "[i]n theory Hunchlab could provide even more targeted areas for this organization and others to apply their model of what [Better Family Life's vice president] calls 'hot spot resources.'"[71] This use of algorithmic information, focused on long-term, community-based efforts, may well turn out to be a much more effective preventive mechanism than predictive policing.[72]

Transparency

ShotSpotter (owner of Hunchlab), Intrado (developer of Beware), ShadowDragon, and Galitica are all private companies. While Galitica is open about the factors used in its algorithms, the other three companies have not been, claiming trade secret protection. The advent of the more sophisticated versions of artificial intelligence, if applied to policing, will make these types of predictive endeavors even more opaque, because modern AI learns from experience, without explicit programming.[73] Even if the algorithm is made available for inspection, this type of machine learning can be, in the words of Andrew Selbst and Simon Barocas, both "inscrutable"—impervious to understanding—and "non-intuitive"—meaning that even if based on an understandable model it relies on "apparent statistical relationships that defy intuition."[74]

This lack of transparency should be fatal to predictive policing. Open knowledge about the risk factors used and the weights they are assigned is crucial for several reasons. First, as just explained, algorithms may not use race as a risk factor and should probably not use arrests for minor crimes as an outcome measure. Without transparency, these flaws cannot be detected.

Second, transparency is needed to improve algorithms. Hit rate studies should be replicated by an entity independent of the police. In theory, this replication process need only determine whether the algorithm performs as well in the field as with the training data; plumbing the inner workings of the algorithm is not necessary. But improvement is not possible without knowing the relevant variables and their weights. Private companies, driven by a profit motive, should not be trusted to carry out the necessary updating.

Third, transparency is needed to resolve individual cases fairly. While the determination about whether the algorithm uses appropriate variables and has an acceptable hit rate can be made by a jurisdiction-wide entity (thus avoiding relitigation of such issues in every case), targets and their attorneys should be able to discover whether the algorithm was properly applied in their particular investigations. In other words, they should be able to get an answer to the question "Did the suspect meet the algorithm's risk factors?" Even if a target turned out to have a weapon or drugs on their person, hindsight bias should not affect whether a stop was legitimate. Stopping someone who does not meet the quantified reasonable suspicion standard associated with the algorithm is just as unconstitutional as a stop based on an unarticulated hunch.

Unfortunately, the law dealing with the subject of algorithmic transparency is in a fledgling state. The case most on point is from a state court and addresses *sentencing* algorithms. In *State v. Loomis*,[75] the Wisconsin Supreme Court held that the Due Process Clause is not violated by a sentence based on a risk assessment tool protected by trade secret law. The court pointed out that, while the company that developed the algorithm refused to disclose its inner workings, Loomis was given a list of 21 questions and answers used by the evaluator in calculating the offender's risk score. Thus, the court said, Loomis had "the opportunity to verify that the questions and answers listed on the [algorithm] report were accurate."[76] However, Loomis did not know if the answers to those questions comprised all the information that went into the algorithm, whether (conversely) only some of the answers were used, or what weight was assigned to any answers that were used. For instance, the fact that Loomis was able to verify that the evaluators using the algorithm correctly calculated how many times he had been arrested (one of the algorithm's risk factors) elucidated nothing about how that information affected his sentence, thus leaving unclear whether the judge should have been foreclosed from considering his record independent of his algorithmic score. Neither did it tell him whether, if he could elaborate on his answers (by, for instance, noting that many of the previous arrests had been for misdemeanors), the risk score would change.

In making his argument that more transparency was required, Loomis relied on *Gardner v. Florida*,[77] a United States Supreme Court case holding that, in a capital sentencing proceeding, "[a] defendant has a constitutionally protected due process right to be sentenced upon accurate information."[78] But, as the Wisconsin Supreme Court pointed out, that case could be construed to mean only that the facts underlying a sentence must be verifiable by the defendant. More relevant to the policing context is *Roviaro v. United States*,[79] involving a simple drug case, where the Supreme Court held that the identity of a confidential informant must be revealed to the defendant when the informant possesses facts that are relevant to the defense. The Court was unimpressed with the argument that the officers who "ran" the informant could describe what the informant said and did with Roviaro; questioning of the officers "was hardly a substitute for an opportunity to examine the man who had been nearest to [Roviaro] and took part in the transaction."[80] Analogously, questioning the developers of the

algorithm or the police who used it about the information they inputted is not a substitute for questioning the algorithm itself. Although
Loomis, *Gardner*, and *Roviaro* were all based on the Due Process
Clause, the better constitutional hook is the Sixth Amendment's Confrontation Clause, which guarantees the right to confront one's accus-
ers. As Andrea Roth has observed in discussing government use of
technology in the criminal justice system more generally, "the state's
use of accusatory machine conveyances to prove a defendant's guilt
seems to implicate many of the same dignitary and accuracy concerns
underlying the framers' preoccupation [in drafting the Confrontation
Clause] with in-the-shadows accusations and ex parte affidavits."[81]

Roviaro establishes that even strong claims of a need for secrecy—
the confidentiality of informants is considered sacrosanct in policing
circles[82]—should not prevail when the information is crucial to the
case. While *Roviaro* has been given short shrift in more recent lower
court decisions, its central rationale has not been abandoned.[83] Some
lower courts have followed its logic in requiring that defendants be
given the facts and opinions underlying their proposed sentences.[84]
Analogously, in the predictive policing setting, independent entities
should have the ability to retest privately developed algorithms, and
attorneys for targeted individuals ought to be informed if their client
is on a hot list and the reasons why, so that misinformation can be corrected and the application of the algorithm double-checked.

A Preliminary Assessment of Predictive Policing

Whether predictive algorithms can improve policing, or instead are
simply a fancy cover for racially skewed and ultimately ineffective
police tactics, remains to be seen. Given its potential for preventing
and detecting crime in a relatively unbiased manner, predictive policing cannot be summarily dismissed. But if the foregoing limitations
arising from proportionality analysis were to apply, the fate of predictive algorithms would be in serious doubt.

This is especially so with respect to algorithms aimed at identifying hot people rather than hot spots. First, such an algorithm should only rely on data that are a matter of public record, unless the anticipated hit rate of the algorithm justifies accessing nonpublic information or steps are taken to anonymize that information from the government. Second, the algorithm's hit rates would have to justify whatever action the police claim it justifies; if that action is a stop, for instance, it might need to generate hit rates of approximately 30%, barring a serious imminent threat. Third, even then the algorithm should not be used as a basis for a stop unless, immediately prior to the stop, the police observe or obtain through witnesses evidence of suspicious conduct. Fourth, the algorithm should take into account and correct for the effects of racially disparate policing with respect to both its risk factors and its outcome variables. And fifth, independent experts should have access to the inner workings of the algorithm to access whether it meets these requirements.

Because the short-form GSFA generates fairly good hit rates, is based entirely on recent suspicious conduct (and thus does not rely on any historical information that might misleadingly correlate with race), and is statistically transparent, it might meet all of these limitations. But Chicago's heat list and the Beware algorithm, if used to justify stops or frisks, almost certainly do not. And even the GSFA can be faulted for relying on relatively vague types of triggering conduct.

Hot spot policing is not off the hook either. Good hot spot algorithms might help deploy the police in an efficient way, which in turn might enhance deterrence through timely police presence. But physically detaining an individual—even one found in a very hot spot— should still require suspicious conduct. Recall the traffic stop made by Officer Keener, described at the beginning of this chapter. The hot spot report that Keener says influenced his actions predicted a heightened risk of assault for individuals in the area. But conduct signaling that the young man he stopped was contemplating an assault was entirely lacking. To the extent a hot spot profile is proffered as a reason for such stops, it should be given no weight at all. The Supreme Court agrees, stating in *Illinois v. Wardlow* that "[a]n individual's presence in an area of expected criminal activity, standing alone, is not enough to support a reasonable, particularized suspicion that the person is committing a crime."[85]

The nature of predictive policing is likely to change as technology advances. For instance, in the not-too-distant future, camera systems may come equipped with "anomaly" detection capacity that uses machine learning to alert to behavioral patterns, emotions, or appearances that are "abnormal," such as walking back and forth or in circles, looking angry, or wearing unusual clothing.[86] The likelihood is significant that this type of system, left unregulated, would result in increased hassle of individuals, chilling of innocent activity, and racially biased interventions. Imagine, for instance, how an anomaly detector might react to a person walking up and down the street for exercise, a driver getting cut off by another driver and then following the offending car for several blocks, or a person entering a neighborhood populated mostly by people of a different race.

Police using these detectors can often point to conduct by the target, and the fact that the conduct is identified as an "anomaly" might, in at least some cases, make it suspicious in the eyes not only of the police but also of the courts. Even then, however, an anomaly, by itself, is highly unlikely to produce the hit rate for full-blown stops demanded by proportionality analysis. At most, proportionality reasoning would permit surveillance of people who trigger the device, unless further suspicion develops.

Consider also the Department of Homeland Security's (DHS) Future Attribute Screening Technology (FAST), a biometric-based algorithm that is meant to detect terrorists by measuring body and eye movements, eye blink rate and pupil variation, body heat changes, breathing patterns, voice pitch changes, alternations in vocal rhythm, and changes in intonations of speech.[87] Depending on whether it is deployed remotely or through "contact," the DHS claims FAST has a hit rate of 70–81%, well above what is needed to justify a detention for questioning on proportionality grounds, especially since the threat to be prevented is serious. Operated remotely, FAST does not require a seizure or acquire information that is not "exposed" to the public. Assuming DHS's hit rate claim can be replicated in the real world (a very significant assumption), many might conclude that, at the least, a short detention of any person who triggers the algorithm for the purpose of questioning and checking terrorist watchlists is justifiable. Yet the biometric information collected by FAST is difficult to classify as suspicious behavior and thus may be an insufficient ground for meeting the imminence requirement. And the device is likely to produce a noticeable hassle rate given the number of nervous people at airports.

It can be anticipated that science will continue to raise difficult questions about when predictive virtual searches can justifiably lead to physical confrontations. Proportionality analysis, together with the imminence requirement, provides a framework for answering those questions.

The Role of Legislatures

While courts would certainly be involved in setting the parameters of modern predictive policing, legislatures should, as with suspect-driven virtual searches, be the primary movers in this area. Representative bodies should decide, in the first instance and perhaps on a conditional basis, whether law enforcement may use such algorithms. If they do so, they should also provide funding for the necessary research, ideally independent of both government agencies and for-profit developers. This research, which is much more easily analyzed by legislatively commissioned experts than courts, would be the basis for authorizing or reauthorizing the program. Only then would it be up to the courts to decide whether the resulting hit rates and risk factors satisfy the

Constitution, an analysis that should be structured consistent with proportionality analysis, the imminence requirement, and equal protection concerns.

One of the advantages of legislative deliberations over judicial decision-making is that they are not made in a vacuum. Rather, balancing the usefulness of algorithms against their potential discriminatory impact can take place against the backdrop of other potential reforms of street policing, of which there are many. For instance, decriminalization would be one way of reducing abuses of police stop and frisk authority (two out of three arrests for felony drug possession involve a trace amount of drugs[88]). Another reform would be a prohibition on custodial arrests for misdemeanors and lower-level felonies and therefore searches incident to such arrests (roughly 90% of arrestees in the United States are taken into custody, compared to less than 5% in countries such as Germany[89]). A third reform is to shunt traffic enforcement to an auxiliary law enforcement body that would not have search or arrest authority[90] (compared to white drivers, black drivers are disproportionately stopped and searched yet are found to have contraband less often[91]). A fourth possible reform is to make damages remedies more robust when police abuse their stop and frisk authority. The current regime erects numerous obstacles to civil actions against police and police departments, which are seldom brought in any event because of the small sums involved, the unwillingness of lawyers to bring such claims, and the reluctance of juries to make police departments or officers pay money to people they claim were suspicious.[92]

Legislatures could also consider whether virtual search technology could play a role in this reform effort, in three distinct ways. First, virtual search technology could take the place of the police in certain settings. For instance, rather than allowing police or other agents to issue tickets for traffic violations, CCTV and ALPRs could be used to identify violators, who would then be sent citations.[93] The resulting reduction in police–citizen confrontations—and the potential for violence that comes with them—could be substantial.

Second, virtual search technology that discovers only weapons or evidence of crime, as hypothesized with the Raytheon device in the Abdullah case described in chapter 2, could also minimize such interactions. No longer would police who want to see if a person has a gun need to stop and frisk the person to find out. Of course, if use of this type of virtual search itself requires a seizure (for instance, to aim the device), then the usual Fourth Amendment requirements would have to be met.

Finally, virtual search technology can be used to monitor the police. The most obvious example of this reform—well underway in many jurisdictions—is the body-mounted camera.[94] But location tracking, social media posts, and other types of data can also be used to keep tabs on how police officers do their job and interact with the public.[95]

Each of these proposals about how to use virtual search capabilities has challenges. Making traffic enforcement the domain of machines will vastly increase the number of citations, which in turn will occasion community reaction, as we've seen with citizen outcries against red-light cameras. The easy availability of evidence-specific technology might lead to dragnet search programs that indiscriminately surveil the population, both suspect and nonsuspect, a prospect examined more fully in chapter 6. And virtual searching of police raises some of the same privacy concerns that afflict virtual searching of the public; furthermore, body cameras can infringe on the privacy of those the police target (and pose a host of implementation problems as well).[96] But some combination of these proposals, with or without predictive policing, could form a cohesive legislative package aimed at regulating street policing.

A final potential advantage of legislative over judicial deliberations is that representative bodies can more readily incorporate the views of the citizenry. The decision about whether to adopt a program such as hot spot or hot people policing, anomaly detection, or FAST in the first instance—or to reauthorize it after it is experienced by the citizenry—is ultimately likely to depend on how many innocent people it hassles, and the voices of those people are more likely to be heard by legislators than judges. Of course, certain voices may be louder or accorded more weight than others, to the detriment of those who lack access. Given their target populations, for instance, one might predict that hot spot policing has a better chance of surviving the legislative gauntlet than FAST, unless the latter device proves to be highly effective. The mechanism for ensuring that legislatures and policing agencies are kept honest on this score is described in chapter 7. But first we need to consider one more way in which police are using technology to investigate crime, a type of search for which hassle rates are a particularly important consideration.

Event-Driven Virtual Searches

In early 2017, a taxi driver named Nwabu Efobi was gunned down in front of the Universal Cab Company in Raleigh, North Carolina. Security camera video caught Efobi in some kind of confrontation with the shooter before the unknown man opened fire. The day before, cameras had caught the same individual walking around the same building with what appeared to be a cell phone at his ear.

Unfortunately, the camera image was too grainy to get a good fix on the man's face. But police were able to resort to another type of virtual search. On a satellite image of the area, they drew a cordon around the building and its environs. They then convinced a judge to issue a warrant ordering Google to hand over account identities on every cell phone that crossed the digital cordon during times related to the camera images and the shooting. Seven months later, police arrested Tyron Cooper for Efobi's murder. The inventory for the warrant proffered to Cooper's defense team indicated that electronic records within the cordon were in fact retrieved (although it did not make clear whether those records were instrumental in fingering Cooper).[1]

The technique used in Efobi's case is sometimes called "geofencing," at other times a "reverse warrant," because it is used to locate a suspect rather than to investigate one who has already been identified. Police department use of geofencing is quite common today. The city of Raleigh, where Efobi was killed, relied on it in at least four cases in 2017, involving two killings, an arson, and a sexual assault (helping to solve two of the crimes and coming up empty in the other two).[2] In 2018, Google reported it was receiving roughly 180 geofencing requests per week,[3] in 2019 it reported a 500% increase in such requests,[4] and in 2020 it responded to 11,554 geofence demands, over 3,000 more than in the previous year.[5]

Geofencing and virtual searches like it are very different than the two categories of virtual searches discussed in chapters 4 and 5. Geofencing is clearly not suspect-driven, because a suspect has yet to be identified. While it is a form of profiling, it differs from predictive policing profiling in significant ways. Rather than constructing a profile that tries to predict where crime will be committed or the type of person who will commit it, geofencing attempts to identify the perpetrator of, or an eyewitness to, a crime that has already occurred. Thus, it is retrospective rather than prospective and aims at solving a particular crime rather than a category or type of crime. It uses a crime as the starting place and works from there, whereas predictive policing starts with data in the hopes it will lead to discovery of crime. These differences can have significant implications both for Fourth Amendment analysis and regulation more generally.

I will call the types of virtual searches discussed in this chapter "event-driven" (they are also usually "crime-driven," but I avoid that term because they sometimes focus on non-criminal events). Event-driven virtual searches come in numerous guises. A visual analogue to geofencing is what could be called "TiVo droning," which uses camera surveillance footage from drones or planes to reverse engineer the routes of figures at a crime scene in an effort to determine where they came from and who they are. Less obviously, event-driven virtual searches also are involved when police obtain DNA from a crime scene and then seek a match in DNA data banks—here, too, police already have evidence from the crime and use it to help figure out the perpetrator. Similarly, facial recognition technology can be used to identify a perpetrator by matching a surveillance photo from a crime scene with an image database or, conversely, to discover the whereabouts of a known perpetrator by trying to match faces recorded by surveillance cameras in various locations with that person's image in a data bank.

Then there are a number of "alert systems" that fit in the event-driven category. For example, software programs can sample social media sites for images of child pornography, which can then be linked to a particular IP address. A program called Patternizr now in use by the New York Police Department compares a "seed" crime to hundreds of thousands of recorded crimes in the NYPD's database in an effort to generate a "similarity score" that quantifies the likelihood the crime fits a pattern, thus helping to determine whether a given individual committed the seed crime or previous crimes with a similar modus operandi. Each of these techniques uses evidence gathered at an event to identify the people involved in the event.

All of these virtual searches are controversial not only because, like suspect-driven and profile-driven searches, they often are covert and rely on big data but also because they are likely to cast a wide net, one that is more likely larger than the scope of the other types of virtual searches discussed to this point. Suspect-driven virtual searches are, or should be, limited to investigation of a particular person for whom police have the proportionality-mandated suspicion; profile-driven virtual searches are, or should be, limited in their scope by the hit rate and imminence requirements. Event-driven virtual searches, in contrast, cannot be suspect-limited (again, the goal is to look for a suspect, not investigate one who has already been identified) or imminence-limited (because the crime has already occurred). Further, to identify or find the suspect associated with the event, law enforcement must often obtain data about a large number of innocent people: Geofencing will collect location information about anyone near the event, DNA analysis will discover all partial matches, facial recognition systems could scan thousands of faces, pornography software could access thousands of computer files, and Patternizr will go through tens of thousands of records. To use Jane Bambauer's term again, the hassle rates of event-driven virtual searches can be quite high unless significant limitations are imposed on them.

At the same time, the amount and type of information police obtain through event-driven searches—one's location at a particular point in time, the fact that one is related to a criminal, the fact that one has engaged in crime—are often minimal. Consequently, proportionality analysis might not require much justification for these searches. The more important limitations will often come from carefully circumscribing the scope of the search (consistent with the Fourth Amendment's particularity requirement) and from applying normal Fourth Amendment constraints on what police do with the information they obtain from the event-driven virtual search.

The Supreme Court case most relevant to the event-driven inquiry is *Illinois v. Lidster*,[6] which involved a checkpoint set up one week after a hit-and-run incident, at the same hour of the day it occurred; the goal of the police was to identify eyewitnesses to, or the perpetrator of, the event. The Supreme Court held that the checkpoint did not violate the Fourth Amendment, despite the fact it resulted in the seizure (hassling) of a large number of individuals for whom the police had no individualized suspicion. In analyzing the constitutionality of such suspicionless event-driven seizures, the Court said, courts should consider "the gravity of the public concerns served by the seizure, the degree to which the seizure advances the public interest, and the severity of the interference with individual liberty."[7] Because the policing technique was aimed at finding a hit-and-run culprit, was constructed in a way that furthered the chances of finding that person while minimizing hassle rates, and involved a relatively minor seizure, the checkpoint was permissible.

Likewise, most event-driven virtual searches initially involve minor interferences with privacy and often can significantly advance the public interest, at least if limited to investigation of serious crimes. These general concepts are explored in each of the specific contexts mentioned above, beginning with geofencing.

Geofencing

Google has been hit by so many geofencing requests of the type used in the Efobi case that it has developed a procedure that it insists law enforcement use, consisting of three stages, all requiring a "warrant."[8] The first step—the initial data dump—must be authorized by a court order that defines the geographic area and time window for the location data. So, for instance, the application to the court might ask for data about any phone within 100 yards of the crime scene during a 30-minute period both before and after the crime. The second step—called "selective expansion"—allows law enforcement to ask for more location data information about the phones identified in the initial dump that are of special interest; for instance, it might ask that, for phones that lingered near the crime scene during the relevant time period, Google provide location data outside the original geographic zone and/or beyond the original time window to see where those phones came from and where they went. The final stage is the unmasking—the disclosure of account owner identity—which could include the owner of every phone within the original warrant but presumably would be narrowed down considerably if the unmasking warrant is to issue.

Some courts have readily issued the geofence warrant that starts this process.[9] Others have been more reluctant to do so, especially if the scope of the initial data dump is significant. For instance, in one case, law enforcement requested a warrant for location data within a 7.7 acre area that included dozens of residences, seven businesses, and health care providers. The judge refused to issue the warrant, stating that the "vast majority of cellular telephones likely to be identified in this geofence will have nothing whatsoever to do with the offenses under investigation."[10] The same judge also rejected a second request for a warrant for a smaller area and time frame, as well as a third request that kept those variables constant but did not ask for the unmasking step (but also reserved the right to achieve the same goal through a subpoena).[11]

If one adopts the probable-cause-forever stance, geofence warrants should rarely, if ever, issue. While the police might be able to demonstrate probable cause to believe one of the phones in the geofence zone belonged to the perpetrator, they usually will not be able to particularly describe which phone or phones belong to that person even at the second or third stages, much less the first. Thus, one magistrate concluded that execution of a geofence warrant was an unconstitutional general search unless everyone within the designated area was reasonably believed to be involved in the crime, in effect precluding such warrants in almost every case.[12]

Proportionality analysis would approach the issue differently. Whether or not a request for geofence location information implicates the Fourth Amendment (after *Carpenter*, one could make a strong argument it does, and the lower court decisions described above agree), a court order would be required. However, the order would not (and could not) be a warrant, given the Fourth Amendment's traditional probable cause requirement. Instead, it would be an order based on a finding by the judge that the police have made a good faith effort to minimize the area and time zones consistent with the known facts about the crime. Although this showing would be analogous to the particularity mandate found in the amendment, under proportionality reasoning neither probable cause nor reasonable suspicion with respect to any given individual or phone would be required, for two reasons. First, the location data are anonymous; police will not know whose location they are learning (and if they tried to de-anonymize the data by, say, going to a data broker,[13] they would be engaging in a suspect-driven virtual search that would require specific suspicion). Second, and most important, the only information learned about any particular individual after the initial data dump is where he or she was during a short period of time.

Thus, consistent with *Lidster*, a legislature might permit the first stage of geofencing if police can articulate to a judge why the requested area and time coordinates are likely to provide relevant information about the perpetrators of or eyewitnesses to a serious crime, and the judge then ensures that a geofence of smaller scope would be insufficient. If the police want to expand the geofence for particular phones, as contemplated in the second stage of Google's procedure, they would need to provide additional justification for doing so. But again, given the limited information sought, probable cause would not be required. Nor would it be required at the unmasking stage, unless, under the relevant suspect-driven rules (and as in *Carpenter*), police had acquired multiple days of location data about the individuals they seek to unmask.

Note that the hassle rate for this type of procedure is minimal. It is true that a given geofence might, at the initial data dump stage, allow police access to the location information on hundreds or even thousands of people. But none of these people—presumably whittled down to only a few individuals by the unmasking stage—will be physically hassled or even identified until that stage. And what the police do after unmasking would be governed by traditional rules. Any subsequent arrest or custodial interrogation would, of course, require probable cause. If instead the police merely want to question some or all of those who have been unmasked, they would be engaging in encounters no different than those the police have routinely conducted in traditional investigations, when they go from door to door in the neighborhood adjacent to a crime scene asking residents if they heard or saw anything.

The case of Jorge Molina, often cited as an example of how geofencing can go awry,[14] needs to be viewed with these considerations in mind. Based on a geofence investigation, police accosted Molina, stating that they knew "one hundred percent, without a doubt" that he had committed a murder. Instead of checking out Molina's explanation that he had loaned his phone to a friend (who was later found to have committed the homicide), the police immediately arrested Molina and put him in jail, where he spent six days before he was freed. The police conduct in Molina's case had little to do with geofencing and much to do with police willingness to act precipitously, without a full prearrest investigation.

AIR

Even less problematic under proportionality analysis is a visual version of geofencing operated by a company called Persistent Surveillance Systems. In Baltimore's now discontinued Aerial Investigation Research (AIR) program, the company used cameras on high-flying planes to monitor the city during the daytime.[15] If a crime was caught on camera or otherwise came to the attention of the police, the aerial recordings were used to trace the people and cars near the crime scene at the time it occurred both forward and backward in time to help identify who they were. Because any individuals picked up on the cameras appeared merely as blurry dots, facial features were not observable. The only information revealed about them was their location for a short period of time. Consistent with *Lidster*'s admonition that the "gravity" of the state's interest be factored into the analysis, Baltimore also limited the types of crimes AIR could be used to investigate. If people were identified by connecting them to certain locations, subsequent interviews, interrogations, stops, and arrests were presumably governed by traditional Fourth and Fifth Amendment law.

Perhaps because of concerns about disparate racial impact, but also based on straightforward cost-benefit calculations, Baltimore ended its program in 2021.[16] That response is, of course, the government's prerogative. But in *Leaders of a Beautiful Struggle v. City of Baltimore*,[17] the Fourth Circuit Court of Appeals took it upon itself to hold that, had the department not ended AIR, it would have found the program unconstitutional under the Fourth Amendment. Relying on *Carpenter*, the court found that the day-to-day aerial surveillance that took place under AIR was a search and required a warrant. Because a warrant is impossible to obtain until a specific crime has occurred or a suspect has been identified, that holding prohibits the precrime and citywide recordings on which AIR depended.

The Fourth Circuit appeared to be particularly concerned about the fact that the program retained recordings of the movements of everyone caught on camera for 45 days.[18] But, as noted above, those recordings were not accessed unless violent crime—a serious problem in Baltimore at the time—was caught on camera. The court failed to recognize that the issue of when AIR can be used to track down suspects is different from the predicate question of whether the system should exist in the first place. While it is the job of judicial bodies like the Fourth Circuit to determine whether AIR records are properly accessed, the decision about whether to create those records in the first instance and, if so, the length of time recordings are kept, the types of crimes they can be used to investigate, and other programmatic matters are subjects best left to the legislative and democratic process. As Judge J. Harvie Wilkinson's dissent in the case pointed out, the majority's "dictation" that the AIR program be ended regardless of how its use might be regulated "cannot be superior to federalist experimentation and giving Baltimoreans some leeway to chart their future course."[19] This case, and the important distinction it illustrates between authorization of a virtual search program—which should occur through the democratic process—and its use in particular cases—which requires case-by-base justification—is examined further in chapter 7.

DNA Matching

Law enforcements attempts to match crime-scene DNA with a profile in a DNA database are common today. All 50 states and the federal government allow collection of DNA from convicted individuals, and at least 31 states and the federal government allow collection of DNA from arrested individuals.[20] DNA profiles are also maintained both by publicly accessible databases—such as GEDmatch—and by private direct-to-consumer databases—such as Ancestry.com, 23andMe,

FamilyTreeDNA, and My Heritage—all of which cater to people looking to find relatives, learn about their ancestry, or discover health
problems. In querying these various databases, police hope for a
direct match, but increasingly they are also looking for partial "familial matches," which can often identify people to whom the perpetrator
is related and allow police to construct a family tree that they hope
includes the perpetrator.[21] The power of familial searching was dramatically illustrated by the authors of a 2019 study who calculated that,
in theory, the data bank maintained by GEDmatch (with three million
profiles) could, by itself, be used to identify well over half of the people
in the United States with European ancestry, either directly or through
a relative who had contributed to the database; the authors went on to
predict that this figure would grow to over 99% as the database grew.[22]

In the most famous recent case involving DNA, police used the familial matching process to identify and arrest Joseph DeAngelo, the
so-called Golden State Killer (GSK) responsible for dozens of sadistic
rapes and murders.[23] After decades of dead ends, an officer (posing as
a donor) got FamilyTreeDNA to produce a profile of the DNA in the
semen from one of the case's rape kits, then sought matches from both
FamilyTreeDNA's two-million-profile database and GEDmatch's even
larger database. Unfortunately, the only match was to distant cousins,
which meant there were too many individuals in the suspect pool to
provide police with useful leads. But then a civilian genealogy expert
working with police, using the My Heritage database, identified some
second cousins of the GSK who appreciably narrowed the pool, especially after females and others who could not or were unlikely to have
committed the crime were excluded. Police visited one of the second
cousins and asked for her DNA, thinking that her brother might be the
killer. While that testing cleared the brother, it indicated that the GSK
was related to women in another family tree that police were building
using Ancestry.com's database, which narrowed the pool to six male
suspects. Only one of those six had the blue eyes that fit the genealo-
gist's profile: DeAngelo, a retired police officer. Police then surrepti-

tiously collected DeAngelo's DNA, first from the door handle of his car, and later from a discarded tissue.

The fact that the DNA profiles used in the GSK case came from databases containing the profiles of people who submitted their DNA for purposes other than fighting crime bothered many people. As even a relative of one of DeAngelo's victims stated, "Any time you are using a DNA service, it should be between you and the service."[24] In the effort to track down perpetrators, human "leads" in investigations like the one that found DeAngelo are often subjected to heightened scrutiny despite being completely innocent of crime and perhaps even ignorant of the existence of their criminal relatives. Because of backlash against police use of its database to solve another case, GEDmatch now allows its users to opt out of allowing law enforcement to use their profiles (and a high percentage have done so),[25] while companies such as Ancestry.com tout their resistance to law enforcement requests.[26] Meanwhile, FamilyTreeDNA has gone the opposite direction, promoting the fact that police may use its services for crime-scene matching.[27]

Some states ban certain familial matching practices, while other states and the federal government place restrictions on them.[28] However, under current Fourth Amendment doctrine, familial matching is likely to be immune to challenge.[29] Even if the Supreme Court decided to expand *Carpenter*'s rejection of the third-party doctrine to records other than cell-site location information, DNA matching can be distinguished fairly easily. Recall that the *Carpenter* majority opinion focused on two reasons for its decision requiring a warrant for CSLI: "[T]he exhaustive chronicle of location information casually collected by wireless carriers today," and the fact that CSLI "is not truly 'shared' as one normally understands the term [because] cell phones and the services they provide are . . . indispensable to participation in modern society."[30] As is true of geofencing and Baltimore's discontinued AIR program, the personal information discovered through familial matching is minimal—a list of potential relatives—and, at least when the database accessed is maintained by a private company such as GEDmatch or Ancestry.com, it is also willingly shared (with the company), much more intentionally than one shares digitized location information with phone companies. Only if the DNA is compelled from the person, as occurs when people who are arrested or convicted, does the second rationale have any purchase, and in that setting the Court has held, over a Fourth Amendment challenge, that the state's interest in identifying arrestees and solving crimes justifies obtaining the genomic information.[31]

Proportionality analysis would arrive at the same result but under different reasoning. The Court's second rationale in *Carpenter*—having to do with the extent to which information has been "shared" with a third party—is of no relevance under proportionality reasoning, unless the sharing amounts to exposure of the information to the public at large. As this book has consistently demonstrated, people do not, and should not, lose their expectation of privacy in information vis-à-vis the government simply because they surrender it to a third party.

The first rationale, in contrast, is pertinent, because it goes to the issue of the type and amount of information that is accessible to the police. In *Carpenter*, Justice Gorsuch asked "can the government . . . secure your DNA from 23andMe without a warrant or probable cause?" and went on to suggest that, while the answer would be "yes" under *Miller* and *Smith*, application of the third-party doctrine to the DNA setting "is not only wrong, but horribly wrong."[32] Survey research that I carried out with James Hazel confirmed that view. We found that, on average, law enforcement access to public databases such as GEDmatch and direct-to-consumer companies such as Ancestry.com was perceived to be at least as intrusive as accessing the content of emails or texts and almost as intrusive as a search of one's bedroom.[33]

With that data in mind, we proposed that, when police want DNA profile data to determine whether a match or partial match exists, they should follow a reverse warrant process similar to the geofence process described above.[34] First, police would have to demonstrate probable cause to believe that the DNA sample they plan to submit for the matching procedure in fact comes from the perpetrator. Second, they must demonstrate that the database to which they plan to submit the sample is large enough that it could produce at least a partial match.

However, that is all we would require. A demonstration of probable cause to believe that submitting a DNA sample to a database *will* result in a direct or partial match —a requirement that would, as a practical matter, prevent all DNA matching until there is something approaching a national DNA database—would not be necessary. That stance can easily be justified on proportionality grounds. If a court authorizes the match query and no match is discovered, no privacy invasion of any kind has occurred; the hassle rate is zero. If, instead, a direct or partial match occurs, personal data—specifically, identification of the suspect or people related to a criminal suspect—will be revealed, but, assuming standard limitations on the matching process, no other information (about, for instance, health predispositions[35]) will be disclosed.

Furthermore, as with geofencing, subsequent police actions should be governed by the Fourth Amendment. As occurred in the GSK case, relatives might be asked for a DNA sample, but only a warrant based on probable cause could compel such a sample. Whether police can obtain a DNA sample from a suspect through covert means—as they did with DeAngelo—is a slippery Fourth Amendment issue that will not be addressed here, although most courts have answered in the affirmative.[36]

The survey that Hazel and I conducted also found that, in contrast to our results regarding publicly accessible databases and direct-to-consumer companies, government access to forensic databases maintained by the government itself was perceived to be no more intrusive than a seizure that occurs at a roadblock.[37] Nonetheless, as *Lidster* indicates, even a checkpoint should not be set up arbitrarily. Furthermore, forensic databases are likely to contain a high proportion of profiles from people of color;[38] without limitations on their use, hassle rates among that population would likely be high. At the least, law enforcement accessing forensic databases should have to make the initial probable cause showing that the sample police seek to match is believed to come from the perpetrator of a crime. As usual, a further legislative limitation could (and I would argue should) be a requirement that DNA matches be sought only in connection with violent or other serious crime.

Facial Recognition

Probably the most controversial new police technology is facial recognition. Much in the news has been a company called Clearview AI, which claims to have scraped billions of images from public records on the web and social media and used them to train an algorithm that is able to identify those faces with close to 100% accuracy when later captured on CCTV, cell phones, and police body cameras.[39] According to BuzzFeed News, Clearview "hawked free trials of its technology to seemingly anyone with an email address associated with the government or a law enforcement agency and told them to 'run wild,'" and hundreds of agencies have taken the company up on the offer, at least on a trial basis.[40]

Clearview's claim that its algorithm is accurate is highly suspect, especially with respect to identifying people of color, since its training sample contains fewer of them.[41] Civil rights groups are also concerned that Clearview's "face-prints" will be abused by police—for instance, to track down immigrants, identify protesters, and harass minority groups—and by private citizens—for example, to find domestic abuse victims. More generally, they are concerned that Clearview's services will "end privacy as we know it."[42]

Assume, as eventually is likely to be the case, that facial recognition technology (FRT) evolves to the point that accuracy claims such as Clearview's can withstand scrutiny. Under the Supreme Court's jurisprudence, a facial image on a public website or sent out over unrestricted social media would be "knowingly exposed" to the public, so scraping it would not violate the Fourth Amendment. In any event, governments already possess, in their divisions of motor vehicles and other agencies, a vast treasure trove of images. The FBI is spending more than a billion dollars expanding its Next Generation Identification system to include not only fingerprints and photos but also iris scans, palm prints, gait and voice recordings, scars, tattoos, and DNA legitimately obtained through other means.[43]

Proportionality analysis would nonetheless impose requirements on how FRT is used. As I discussed at length in *Privacy at Risk*, a person should be able to expect some degree of privacy even in public, based on what I called a "right to anonymity" (or, as others have put it, a "right to obscurity").[44] An amalgam of freedoms—freedom of association, freedom to travel, and freedom to define oneself—could be said to bolster such a right,[45] but the Fourth Amendment's prohibition on unjustifiably intrusive government actions, filtered through proportionality analysis, provides the most solid protection of this interest in public anonymity. My survey data indicated that police access to stored facial images are perceived to be at least as intrusive as a pat-down.[46] In the absence of justification, use of FRT, which relies on capturing and matching one's image, should not be permitted.

However, proportionality analysis also suggests that, with justification, FRT should not be barred as an investigative tool. If police obtain a facial image from the scene of the crime, they should be able to seek a match if—analogous to the procedure outlined in connection with DNA matching—they can demonstrate that the image is likely that of the perpetrator or a key eyewitness and that there is a nontrivial chance a match will be found. At the same time, as suggested in connection with other event-driven examples, legislation might limit use of FRT to investigations of serious crimes, with the aim of preventing harassment of people of color, protesters, or people who look "out of place."

Further, as with the previous examples of event-driven virtual searches, a match should never automatically permit a stop or arrest. For instance, the NYPD FRT policy states that, if a potential match is produced using FRT, an investigator is to make a visual comparison and perform a "detailed background check" to confirm the "reliability" of the match; further, the match is to be considered "an investigative lead only."[47] As the Supreme Court stated in *Illinois v. Gates*,[48] "[o]ur decisions applying the totality-of-the-circumstances analysis [in determining whether probable cause exists] have consistently recognized the value of corroboration of details of an informant's tip by independent police work."[49] The same should be true in this setting. In the absence of exigency, this independent corroboration should be seconded by a judge. It is too easy for officers in the field to confirm that an FRT match is in fact a match when no one is looking over their shoulder.

With these types of limitations, a ban on FRT may be an overreaction. FRT that can accurately identify faces could, if regulated as suggested, be a very useful law enforcement technique. It reportedly has helped police track down suspects in hundreds of serious criminal cases.[50] It was also used to identify people involved in the January 6, 2021, storming of the US Capitol and those who committed crimes during the post–George Floyd protests.[51]

Rather than consider regulation of FRT, however, many commentators have called for a complete ban,[52] and some jurisdictions, such as San Francisco, have obliged.[53] The discussion about FRT is particularly heated because of what is going on in China. There, FRT is being linked with big data, so that once a person's image—say, one captured by a police officer's body camera—is identified, the person's criminal history, ethnicity, religious practices, credit scores, education levels, travel logs, and even utility usage can immediately be called up. Among other uses, this surveillance regime has purportedly helped identify Uyghurs, the politically oppressed Muslim minority found largely in Xinjiang Province, who are often labeled "extremists" and sent to detention camps.[54]

While our substantive laws and First Amendment protections would presumably prevent use of FRTs for religious or ethnic persecution of this type, unbridled linkage of FRT and big data does raise the specter of totalitarian abuses. Note, however, that the Chinese scenario is not event-driven; the detentions there are not predicated on occurrence of a crime. Rather, they are meant to prevent conduct the regime does not like. Thus, the relevant proportionality analysis comes not from this chapter but from chapter 5's discussion of predictive policing. That analysis would not ban a marriage of predictive policing and cameras. But it would place substantial limitations on it. First, only the types of public information that could be used for predictive policing could be used in connection with FRT; criminal history could be accessed, but many of the other informational items relied on by the Chinese system could not be, because there is no ex ante justification for doing so. Further, unless the imminence requirement is met, stops and arrests could not occur based on whatever information is received.

Alert Systems

FRT could aid law enforcement in still another way. Police could use a CCTV system equipped with FRT to scan faces on the streets for possible matches with known at-large criminals, in effect generating self-executing "electronic wanted posters." Automated license plate readers can carry out a similar function with respect to cars; in fact, most police LPRs are tied into nationally generated hot lists of stolen cars and cars used to commit crime.[55] The reach of such alert systems could be vastly expanded by patching in private cameras, operated by both businesses and by homeowners, either through Cloud-based camera systems, such as Amazon's Ring, or independently of any such system (although for reasons developed in chapter 8, analogous to how GEDmatch is handling DNA profiles, owners would have to consent to such use).

There are many other types of alert systems using virtual searches. For instance, every computer file has a unique identifier called a "hash value," essentially a computer fingerprint. Analogous to its fingerprint database, the FBI maintains a database containing the hash value of every known computer file containing child pornography. Software can and has been developed that sifts through digital files looking for any that are associated with these values and then alerts when one is found.[56] Another very different example of an alert system is Patternizr, an automated system that compares crime modus operandi by scouring all reports within the NYPD's database, looking at method of entry, time of day, weapons used, location, and the distance between incidents and various other aspects. A human data analyst then determines which complaints should be grouped together and presents those to detectives to help winnow their investigations.[57]

A common problem with many alert systems is the potential unreliability of the predicate for the alert. Perhaps the most dramatic examples of this flaw are the federally maintained "terrorist" and "no fly" watchlists, which are infamous for including numerous innocent people (including, at one point, Senator Edward Kennedy and Assistant Attorney General James Robinson).[58] Unless the government has demonstrated probable cause to believe that the information in the database is what it purports to be (a known terrorist, a facial image of the perpetrator, a license plate on a stolen car, the hash value for a pornographic file), alert systems should be considered unconstitutional from the get-go. The following discussion assumes that this hurdle, which is not trivial, has been overcome.

On that assumption, one could justify many of these alert systems under the Supreme Court's evidence-specific doctrine. Recall from chapter 2 that this doctrine, which arose out of cases involving drug-sniffing dogs, holds that the Fourth Amendment does not apply to techniques that discover only evidence of crime. Arguably all the alert-based virtual searches described here fit that exception because, at least in theory, they are triggered only by information that is highly probative of crime—a wanted suspect, an automobile that is the fruit or instrumentality of crime, pornographic material, or idiosyncratic crime patterns. At the same time, these techniques vary significantly in the extent to which they actually alert only to criminal events or evidence. While hash value software (HVS) almost always correctly identifies pornographic images, most researchers have concluded that FRT has some way to go to approach that level of accuracy, ALPRs may be appreciably worse (even a study conducted by police produced an error rate of over 35%),[59] and advocates for the Patternizr have yet to provide any concrete evidence of its efficacy.

Yet allegations of potential error did not seem to faze the Supreme Court when analogous arguments were made against a search based on an alert by a drug-sniffing dog. As many commentators pointed out after *United States v. Place*,[60] the initial case involving such dogs, because canines can alert to trace amounts of drugs, the handler's unconscious suggestions, and even the smell of other dogs, alerts can often be erroneous.[61] Thus, dog alerts are not always responding solely to contraband; in this sense, they are not really "binary." Yet in *Florida v. Harris*,[62] the Court, per Justice Kagan, held that "[t]he question—similar to every inquiry into probable cause—is whether all the facts surrounding a dog's alert, viewed through the lens of common sense, would make a reasonably prudent person think that a search would reveal contraband or evidence of a crime."[63] Strongly hinting that a dog that has successfully completed training can be used to detect drug odors,[64] *Harris* made clear that the state need not prove that its evidence-specific technique is perfect, or even close to it.

In a proportionality regime, that conclusion is correct, but it comes with an important empirical caveat. The majority in *Harris* can be faulted for ignoring the fact that dogs that do very well during training often do much worse in the field. Depending on how closely training samples reflect base rate drug possession on the streets, even "certified" dogs may have a real-world accuracy rate below 50%. Say, for instance, dog testers parade in front of a dog a group of people, 50% of whom have drugs on their person, and the dog accurately alerts 50% of the time, which we have been assuming can be a quantified stand-in for probable cause. While, on its face, the dog's alerts may appear to satisfy *Harris*, in fact the dog is doing no better than chance. Even if the dog is correct 90% of the time during this type of training, the accuracy rate generated could well be an overestimate of what will happen in the field since, unlike the group in the test sample, most people do not carry drugs.[65] However, if dogs are instead tested under conditions that replicate the real world (e.g., only one person in 50 in the test sample has drugs on them), the success rate of a particular dog during certification is likely to carry over into the field. Dogs tested under realistic conditions that have accuracy rates over 50% should be seen as meeting *Harris*'s test, even though they do not produce truly "binary" results.

If this analysis of *Harris* applies, all four types of virtual searches at issue here are probably permissible under proportionality analysis. Take first FRT and LPR. Both have accuracy rates well above 50% under real-world conditions. More important, the hassle rates associated with them are probably very low compared, for instance, to the use of drug-sniffing dogs in airports (something courts have upheld[66]). Even a dog that alerts falsely only one out of 20 times could subject a large number of innocent people to searches of their luggage and clothing, given the crowds in the typical airport. In contrast, because they are triggered by unique identifiers (a particular face, a particular license plate number) rather than an odor that is not person-specific, FRT and LPR systems are likely to alert much less often than dogs and thus, ineluctably, will have fewer erroneous alerts.

At the same time, even one false arrest based on an FRT or LPR alert is significant hassle for the person involved. Given that fact, even if FRT identifies a person as a wanted felon, and we assume FRT is highly accurate, police should never automatically arrest; rather, as they would if an informant named someone as a perpetrator, they should first seek corroboration and, in the absence of exigency, obtain a warrant. Again, the NYPD's FRT policy noted above makes sense: Before acting on an FRT match, investigators must make a visual comparison and perform a detailed background check to confirm the reliability of the match, and until then may consider the match "an investigative lead only"; I would add that any physical confrontation based on an FRT match ought to be authorized by a court unless exigent circumstances exist. Similarly, if an LPR alerts to a car, police should double-check the license number before engaging with the driver.

The HVS technique is much closer to the airport dog scenario; it scans hundreds or perhaps thousands of files for those that are pornographic. Thus, even a very accurate HVS system could produce, over the breadth of cases, a large number of false positives and a high hassle rate. Once again, however, much depends on what law enforcement does after an HVS alert. Attempts at corroboration should be made prior to an arrest or a search of the relevant computer (presumably based on a warrant). Moreover, only the identified file should be searched, not the entire computer, unless the initial search produces probable cause to do so. Under these circumstances, the HVS alert may be permissible as well.

Finally, the Patternizer could escape major criticism, despite its questionable accuracy, for two reasons relevant to proportionality analysis. First, it mines only criminal records, not otherwise presumptively innocent personal information. Second, at most it provides an investigative lead, not grounds for arrest. Of course, any reliance on criminal justice records raises concerns about disparate racial treatment even if, as is true with Patternizr, race is not considered in the algorithm.[67] But the types of crimes that Patternizr examines—thefts and robberies[68]—tend not to be the types of crimes most prone to racialized policing.

Particularity Is the Key

When police have information about a completed crime that gives them a profile of the suspect or, better yet, an image of the perpetrator, today's technology gives them numerous ways to use virtual searches as a means of identifying or capturing that person, including geofencing, genomic sleuthing, facial recognition algorithms, and various types of alert systems. Most of these means involve querying databases about, or conducting visual surveillance of, large numbers of people. However, they usually do not require revelation of a significant amount of personal information about any identifiable individual. Often the information police already have gives them good cause for carrying out these minimally intrusive virtual searches.

Nonetheless, to ensure against arbitrary use of technology and unnecessary intrusions on innocent people, legislatures and courts should develop mechanisms for limiting both virtual hassle rates (the proportion of people whose personal information is accessed) and physical hassle rates (the proportion of people who are interviewed, stopped, interrogated, or arrested as a result of the virtual search). Most important, event-driven virtual searches should be closely tied to the event in question and be limited to investigation of serious crimes. If those steps toward particularizing the investigation are taken, and the technology is effective at what it purports to do, event-driven virtual searches may end up being the most useful, least intrusive type of virtual search.

At the same time, the virtual search systems needed to make event-driven virtual searches possible—especially government-run systems such as CCTV, AIR, and DNA, facial, and other biometric databases—are understandably controversial, because they collect information about entire populations, only a tiny percentage of which is involved in wrongdoing. These systems are also crucial in carrying out many types of suspect-driven and profile-driven virtual searches. Because these systems accumulate and store information about people before any reason to suspect them of wrongdoing can be developed, they require an entirely different regulatory regime.

Program-Driven Virtual Searches

Shortly after the intelligence debacle of September 11, 2001, the Department of Defense initiated the Total Information Awareness (TIA) program.[1] The idea was to collect information from a huge range of sources—including communications, financial, education, medical, immigration, and even veterinarian records—collate it with information already possessed by the government, and then comb the information for evidence of terrorist activity. Congress, apparently not enamored of this idea, defunded TIA in 2003 (by voice vote).[2] But, thanks in part to Edward Snowden, we know that several programs in operation today, most of them run by intelligence agencies and boasting mysterious code names like PRISM, Stellar Wind, and REVEAL, bear a close resemblance to it.[3]

The data collection phase of TIA and its progeny—as distinguished from the subsequent analysis of the data these programs obtain—is the classic example of a program-driven virtual search. This book has already noted a number of other large-scale data collection programs. For instance, the FBI's Next Generation Identification system at the federal level, and CCTV, AIR, ALPR, and FRT systems on the state and local levels, all aim to collect information for later investigative use. Domestic law enforcement agencies even have their own version of TIA, called "fusion centers." These federally supported but locally run operations—over 75 of them nationwide, some of them sporting more than 200 personnel—"fuse" for police use financial, rental, utility, vehicular, and communications data from federal, state, and local public databases, law enforcement files, and private company records.[4]

The data collection aspect of these programs is different from suspect-driven, profile-driven, and event-driven searching because it is not based on suspicion that any particular person has engaged in wrongdoing, on a suspicion-based profile, or on proof that a particular crime has occurred. Rather, these virtual searches are, in a word, "panvasive"—that is, they are aimed at large swaths of the population and possibly everyone in the jurisdiction, almost all of whom are concededly innocent and all of whom are targeted solely because their information *might turn out to be* useful to a criminal investigation. Indeed, what I am calling "program-driven" virtual searches are, in effect, closer to a seizure than a search;[5] they are engaged in seizing and recording evidence with an aim to enabling subsequent suspect-driven, profile-driven, and event-driven searches.

I will continue to describe these programs as virtual "search" systems, however, because of their impact on privacy and related values. As noted privacy scholar Julie Cohen points out, in a regime that sanctions unconstrained surveillance programs, liberal democracy can be "replaced, gradually but surely, by a different form of government," modulated "by powerful commercial and political interests" that will increasingly hamper our "ability to form and pursue meaningful agendas for human flourishing."[6] History here and in other countries abounds with examples of how the mere fact of government surveillance—even in the absence of stops or arrests based on it—can be oppressive and intimidating. The associated fear is that access rules of the type discussed in previous chapters will routinely be violated, because once the data is collected, the temptation to use it to compile digital dossiers on all of us cannot be resisted. The icon for the TIA program, which depicted an all-seeing eye looking out over the globe, accompanied by the maxim "Knowledge Is Power," is perhaps the most chilling symbol of this tendency.

There are at least five specific worries about the ways data can be misused. First, there is corrupt use of the data by government officials. Even in the predigital age, the exposés of J. Edgar Hoover's reliance on

FBI files to blackmail, discredit, and destroy his adversaries provided concrete examples of "knowledge as power";[7] more recently, virtual search systems have been used to keep tabs on peaceful protests and minority and religious groups, pursue personal vendettas, tail acquaintances, and even provide information to organized crime syndicates.[8] Second, as daily news stories remind us, any centralization of data is a lure for hackers, domestic and foreign; government databases are particularly tempting veins of information.[9] Third, the inclusion of inaccurate information in databases is a pervasive problem and has led to erroneous arrests and unfounded exclusion from work, travel, and even voting.[10] Fourth, mission creep is also a common affliction, demonstrated by the migration of fusion centers, CCTV systems, and other technologically enhanced programs that were originally designed to focus on terrorism or other serious public safety issues toward mundane domestic law enforcement.[11] Finally, as already discussed at length, databases can easily solidify racially biased policing if care is not taken about the types of data entered and how it is used.

Thus, it makes sense to keep data out of government's hands whenever possible. An example of how to do so comes from the national security setting. For many years after 9/11, the NSA ran a program that collected en masse the phone metadata of virtually everyone in the United States; although these phone numbers and email addresses were only supposed to be mined for terrorist activity, in fact they were used to investigate domestic crimes as well.[12] After the program was exposed, President Barack Obama, by executive order, prohibited government collection of the metadata. Now it remains housed with Verizon and other common carriers, which must retain the information for five years but then can destroy it. Consistent with suspect-driven rules, the NSA may obtain the data only through a court order based on a "seed identifier" number or address associated with involvement in terrorist activities.[13]

While this siloing approach can work in the metadata context, government obviously cannot be insulated from all types of information in this manner. To function effectively, federal and state agencies must maintain a wide variety of data, ranging from criminal history and biometric data to tax, real estate, driving, and welfare records. To avoid misuse, some restrictions on police access to this information may be necessary as well.

The situation is complicated by the fact that government increasingly "loans" information in its possession to private companies in the hope that they can make the data more useful to the police. Federal and state law enforcement agencies routinely contract with data brokers and data analytic companies such as Acxiom, ChoicePoint, Oracle, and Palantir to analyze the agencies' data with the goal of providing investigative leads on suspects, hot spot and hot people profiles, and the location data, DNA profiles, and faceprints needed for event-driven policing.[14] Sarah Brayne's work examining the use of data by the Los Angeles Police Department, referenced briefly in chapter 4, provides a vivid, detailed description of this type of arrangement. Documenting what she calls "data greed," she explains how officers in the LAPD are instructed to fill out field interrogation cards about every street encounter they have, even those that are not *Terry* stops, and then feed the data to Palantir, a $25 billion company that, among many other things, develops software to help police departments make use of their records.[15] The information transferred to Palantir is not checked for accuracy. It comes primarily from minority neighborhoods. It is used in every type of investigation, down to the lowest misdemeanor. And it is maintained indefinitely.[16]

In light of all this, the temptation might be strong to prohibit or severely limit many law enforcement–run data programs. That could well be wise policy in many instances. But the central point made in this chapter is that, if such steps are to be taken, they should usually come from the legislature and the administrative rulemaking process, not the courts. Unlike suspect, profile, and event-driven virtual searches, panvasive program-driven virtual searches affect the entire population or very significant subsets of it. Thus, the proportionality principle, which evaluates the intrusiveness of a search on specific individuals, is no longer apposite. Rather, program-driven virtual searches should be regulated by the collective through their representatives. So long as the citizenry affected by the program is involved in the decision-making process, courts should be deferential toward panvasive programs and should find "unreasonable" only those that are clearly irrational.

At the same time, if the legislative process has not authorized a virtual search program, policing agencies should not be permitted to carry it out on their own. Further, contrary to current practice, I contend that traditional administrative law principles ought to apply to police departments, just as they do to other administrative agencies. That would mean, among other things, that legislatures must provide a sufficient outline of how police are to implement a virtual search program; that police departments must promulgate, subject to community input, regulations governing how the program will operate; and that courts should ensure these regulations are rational and applied even-handedly.

Before explaining this regulatory regime in more detail, an illustration of the institutional dynamics involved will help explain why the legislative and executive branches ought to be the first movers when it comes to controlling program-driven virtual searches.

Courts versus Legislatures: *Leaders of a Beautiful Struggle v. Baltimore*

"I have no problem if the AIR program is discontinued. I have a big problem, however, if this court and not the citizens of Baltimore are the ones to terminate it."[17]
—Judge J. Harvie Wilkinson, dissenting, in *Leaders of a Beautiful Struggle*

Mentioned in chapter 6 was the Fourth Circuit's decision in *Leaders of a Beautiful Struggle v. Baltimore Police Department*,[18] in which a 15-member court declared, 8–7, that Baltimore's AIR program was unconstitutional. The decision was particularly controversial because the city had already ended the program a few months before the Fourth Circuit considered it, thus making that court's decision to take the case procedurally problematic. But for present purposes, the case is important because it illustrates why virtual search programs should usually be regulated through a democratic, not a judicial, process.

The major flaw in *Leaders of a Beautiful Struggle* is its conceptualization of the problem. The majority opinion described AIR as a program that was aimed at "capturing everyone's movements outside during the daytime for 45 days" (purportedly the period for which images were retained by the police department).[19] Citing *Carpenter*, it then channeled proportionality analysis in declaring that "prolonged tracking that can reveal intimate details through habits and patterns . . . invades the reasonable expectation of privacy that individuals have in the whole of their movements and therefore requires a warrant."[20] But that type of reasoning applies only to long-term tracking of identified individuals, as occurred in *Carpenter*. The issue before the court was not the constitutionality of such suspect-driven virtual searches but rather the constitutionality of a virtual search program that collected the information used for such searches.

This confusion between the legitimacy of collecting data and the legitimacy of its use permeated the majority's opinion. The district court had noted, as one ground for refusing to grant a preliminary injunction against the program, that AIR images show only "a series of anonymous dots traversing a map of Baltimore."[21] In rebuking the lower court for relying on this fact, the Fourth Circuit correctly observed that the habitual behavior of those "dots" (such as starting and ending the day at home), when "analyzed with other available information, will often be enough for law enforcement to deduce the people behind the pixels."[22] But that use of AIR was not before the court; had it been, the court could rightly have demanded a Fourth Amendment justification (although, under proportionality analysis, a warrant might not be required if the event-driven rules in the previous chapter applied). In another passage the majority, once again conflating collection with use, asserted that "[t]he AIR program is like a 21st century general search, enabling the police to collect all movements, both innocent and suspected, without any burden to 'articulate an adequate reason to search for specific items related to specific crimes.'"[23] But AIR's day-to-day collection of pixels was not seeking, nor did it find, information about any specific items, crimes, or people. And its "general" nature made it a perfect candidate for jurisdiction-wide legislative regulation rather than case-specific judicial determinations.

That was the gist of Judge Wilkinson's dissenting opinion, captured in the quote set out above. He began by contending that the majority had extended *Carpenter* "beyond recognition to bar all warrantless tracking of public movements."[24] While this may be an exaggeration, one does wonder how the majority would distinguish AIR from CCTV, ALPR, and other citywide systems that can record the activities of large numbers of people; perhaps it wouldn't. More to the present point, Judge Wilkinson noted that AIR had been established on an experimental basis, after obtaining endorsements from the governor of Maryland, the mayor of Baltimore, the Baltimore City Chamber of Commerce, and a number of other high-profile groups, including community leaders in East and West Baltimore, the Greater Baltimore Committee ("the region's premier organization of business and civic leaders"), the presidents of local universities, and religious leaders from the United Baptist Missionary Convention, representing 100 churches across the state.[25] The reason for this wide-ranging support, reminiscent of some of the comments made at the Nashville ALPR meeting recounted in chapter 1, was summarized by the local head of Neighborhoods United: "We have to do something. The murders are doing a lot of disruption to our city, especially in the black population."[26] Pointing to this community support, Judge Wilkinson concluded: "The people most affected by a problem are denied by this court a say in ameliorating it."[27]

In short, the Fourth Circuit had no business ending the program on the ground it did. At the same time, the judiciary was not the only branch of government that overreached in connection with the AIR program. The Baltimore Police Department was also too dominant in the decision-making process. Despite the widespread support for AIR, the Baltimore City Council never formally authorized it, even on a test basis, and the police department's guidelines under which it operated were not subject to community input. The type of democratic process normally associated with the initiation of citywide programs was only tangentially involved in vetting AIR.

The aptly named *Leaders of a Beautiful Struggle* is a harbinger of cases to come as law enforcement continues to experiment with new technologies. If the Fourth Circuit reached the right result in *Leaders*, it was for the wrong reason. AIR does not violate *Carpenter*, *Jones*, or any of the other Fourth Amendment cases that focus on the constitutionality of specific searches. Rather, the city of Baltimore and its police department erred because proper democratic and administrative processes were not followed.

In critiquing the majority's ruling, Judge Wilkinson quoted a statement from the concurring opinion of Justice Alito in *Jones* (joined by Justices Ginsburg, Breyer, and Kagan) that we have seen before: "A legislative body is well situated to gauge changing public attitudes, to draw detailed lines, and to balance privacy and public safety in a comprehensive way."[28] That call for legislative involvement in regulating virtual searches resonates with a primary theme of this book and is particularly apt when it comes to program-driven virtual searches. Assuming so, there remain the two crucial tasks of drawing the "detailed lines" to which Justice Alito refers and figuring out how to cajole legislatures and police agencies into promulgating them.

Substantive Rules: The American Law Institute's Principles of Policing

There are two broad issues raised by programmatic virtual searches. The first, of course, is whether a particular program should be authorized. For what purposes (suspect-, profile- or event-driven) may a jurisdiction establish an AIR, CCTV, ALPR, DNA, or FRT system, and what types of information may these systems collect? The second issue, assuming the program is authorized, has to do with how long the information it collects may be retained and under what conditions. May the data collected be maintained indefinitely, or should it be destroyed after a finite period of time, and how can the accuracy and security of the data be assured?

A helpful conceptualization of how data collection and retention might be regulated comes from the American Law Institute (ALI), which recently completed its Principles of Policing Project after six years of deliberation. The 14 chapters of the principles—which cover every aspect of the policing endeavor—were officially adopted by the full membership of the ALI in May 2022, after vetting by both an advisory committee (composed of judges and lawyers who work in the criminal justice system and police and advocacy organizations from both the left and right) and the ALI Council (composed of a select group of the full ALI membership).[29] As an associate reporter for the project, I was principally responsible for two of the principles' chapters: "Policing in the Absence of Individualized Suspicion" and "Policing Databases." Respectively, these two chapters provide principles that could govern the collection and retention issues raised by programmatic virtual searches.

"Policing in the absence of individualized suspicion" is defined by the ALI principles as policing "conducted in the absence of cause to believe that the particular individual, place, or item subject [the policing action] is involved in unlawful conduct."[30] It should be clear from previous discussion that program-driven virtual searches fit within this definition; because they are panvasive, they are designed to obtain information before any individualized suspicion develops. In this, they are like many types of physical search programs—such as checkpoints, health and safety inspections, and drug-testing programs—that operate in the absence of individual suspicion.

The ALI chapter on this type of policing provides that "legislatures and agencies should authorize suspicionless policing activities only when there is a sound basis for believing that they will accomplish an important law-enforcement or regulatory objective, and when achieving that objective outweighs their infringement on individual interests such as privacy, dignity, property, and liberty."[31] If a suspicionless program is authorized, written policies should identify, among other things, "(a) the specific harm sought to be detected or prevented; (b) the permissible scope of the suspicionless policing activity; [and] (c) the persons, entities, or activities subject to the policing activity."[32] The principles also state that any suspicionless policing activity so approved "should be conducted in a manner that ensures agency discretion is guided by neutral criteria that are applied evenhandedly and developed in advance," which must be accomplished by applying the procedure to every person within the target group, "a subset of that group that is selected on a random or neutral basis," or "a subset of that group that there is a sound basis for believing is more likely to be engaged in unlawful conduct or pose a greater risk of harm than the rest of the target group."[33] There are several more detailed principles in the chapter, but these three capture its gist: Suspicionless searches and seizures should occur only when (1) there is a strong rational basis for the program after considering its impact on collective and individual interests; (2) policies explicitly identify is purpose and scope; and (3) the program is applied in a neutral, evenhanded fashion.

The primary rationale for these principles is straightforward: "In the absence of warrants and individualized suspicion, it is essential that there be alternative mechanisms in place to ensure that search and seizures and other policing activities are justified, are not directed at individuals or groups in an arbitrary or discriminatory fashion, and are limited in scope consistent with their justification."[34] The "sound basis" requirement for surveillance legislation is admittedly vague, but inevitably so. It calls for the kind of multifactor judgment that is best made initially by legislatures. The requirement that the purpose and scope of the program be explicitly identified ensures that these matters receive due deliberation by the appropriate decision-making bodies. The neutral criteria and evenhanded application requirements minimize discretion and increase the likelihood that the program will be viewed by the public as both more legitimate and less intrusive (think, for instance, of TSA checkpoints at airports). These latter two requirements also make it likely that the program will affect those with political power, which acts as a brake on overly aggressive programs. As Justice Jackson stated in another context: "There is no more effective practical guaranty against arbitrary and unreasonable government than to require that the principles of law which officials would impose upon a minority must be imposed generally."[35]

The gist of the ALI chapter on policing databases can also be succinctly stated. It provides that "a policing database [defined to include a database such as Palantir's that is maintained by a third party] should be created only if necessary to facilitate a legitimate policing objective" and continues:

Any policing database that contains information about identified or identifiable individuals should be governed by written policy or policies that specify: (1) the purpose of the data collection, including the criteria for inclusion in the database; (2) the scope of data to be collected, including the types of individuals, locations or records that will be the focus of the database, and (3) the limits on data retention, the procedures for ensuing the accuracy and security of the data, the circumstances under which the data can be accessed, and mechanisms for ensuring compliance with these rules.[36]

The first two principles overlap with provisions in the chapter on suspicionless policing requiring delineation of the purpose and scope of search and seizure programs. The third principle, governing data retention and related issues, is given more detailed treatment in the database chapter's subsequent provisions, which focus on:

—purging databases of irrelevant information, by requiring, whenever feasible, destruction of files after a finite time period;[37]

—assuring data accuracy, through standardized procedures for entering data; training and supervision of those who enter data; periodic audits for accuracy; and a procedure that allows correction of erroneous entries by data subjects (who are entitled to notification of their inclusion in a database anytime it is the basis for an "adverse action");[38]

—maintaining security, through limiting access (under rules like those laid out in chapters 4 through 6 of this book) to those officers who are specifically authorized access; identifying an officer responsible for security; and monitoring the database for breaches;[39] and

—assuring accountability, through an unalterable record of every instance of access (detailing when it occurred, by whom, and for what purpose, as well as by what method, e.g., via algorithm); and by making available to the public "statistics about the purposes and use of policing databases, the numbers of people in each database, and the extent to which the databases have been accessed, including any violations of access rules."[40]

These two sets of ALI principles, which are consistent with suggestions made by other entities and scholars,[41] provide guardrails for thinking about data collection and retention. But they are aspirational and expressed at a high level of generality. How can legislatures and policing agencies be pushed toward adopting something like them and then fleshing out the details in connection with specific virtual search programs? Supreme Court case law has provided very little impetus in this direction, and legislative inertia or resistance has led, at best, to piecemeal statutory regulation. After documenting those assertions, this chapter argues that another source of rules—administrative law—must play a central role in this regulatory framework. If the well-established administrative law principles that govern virtually all other government agencies are made applicable to policing agencies as well, they can *force* the legislative and executive branches to produce reasonable regulations of virtual search programs.[42]

Current Regulation of Virtual Search Programs

Fourth Amendment jurisprudence to date has pretty much ignored both the data collection and data retention issues. While legislatures have been more active on this score, some types of virtual search programs today are not subject to any statutory constraints and those that are often only loosely so.

Contrary to the Fourth Circuit's assertion in *Leaders of a Beautiful Struggle*, the Supreme Court's decision in *Carpenter v. United States* provides no help on the issue of when a virtual search program may be authorized; as made clear in previous discussion, *Carpenter* involved a suspect-driven search, not a panvasive one. Of course, *Carpenter* does not exhaust the Fourth Amendment's potential. As David Gray has argued, for instance, the Fourth Amendment's language guaranteeing "the right of the people" to be secure from unreasonable searches and seizures could form the basis for protecting the collective interests of the citizens against indiscriminate, arbitrary surveillance and voracious and insecure databases.[43] Neil Richards has contended that the First Amendment's protection against chilling speech and assembly could fulfil much the same function.[44] While no Supreme Court case has endorsed these precise themes, scattered dicta hint that there may be constitutional limits on data greed. In *United States v. Knotts*,[45] the Court suggested that "different constitutional principles" might apply to "twenty-four hour surveillance of any citizen of this country . . . without judicial knowledge or supervision."[46] And in *Whalen v. Roe*,[47] it recognized "the threat to privacy implicit in the accumulation of vast amounts of personal information in computerized data banks or other massive government files."[48] It remains the case, however, that the Court has yet put any meat on these bones or even identify the specific constitutional provision that might do so.

The one existing Fourth Amendment doctrine that could potentially lead to something more comes from a convoluted series of decisions that govern situations involving "exceptional circumstances in which special needs, beyond the normal need for law enforcement, make the warrant and probable-cause requirements impracticable."[49] In some of these so-called "special needs" cases, particularly those involving inspections and checkpoints conducted in the absence of individualized suspicion, the Court has appeared to endorse something akin to the ALI Principles' requirements that search and seizure programs have a rational basis and a defined scope and be governed by a neutral plan that is administered even-handedly. For instance, in *Donovan v. Dewey*,[50] after noting the many dangers associated with operating coal mines, the Court upheld a mine inspection program because the statute

> requires inspection of all mines and specifically defines the frequency of inspection. . . . [T]he standards with which a mine operator is required to comply are all specifically set forth in the [Mine Safety] Act or in . . . the Code of Federal Regulations. . . . [R]ather than leaving the frequency and purpose of inspections to the unchecked discretion of Government officers, the [program] establishes a predictable and guided federal regulatory presence.[51]

The Court made the same type of point in a case involving a checkpoint designed to catch illegal immigrants near the border with Mexico. In upholding the checkpoint, the Court emphasized that it was set up by higher-level authorities and that everyone who came to the checkpoint was subject to initial seizure.[52] In another case, while finding unconstitutional random license checks made on the whim of individual officers, the Court noted that statutorily authorized license checkpoints that stop everyone (or every third or fifth person) would pass constitutional muster.[53]These cases resonate with the ALI's principles governing suspicionless searches and seizures. As I have detailed elsewhere,[54] however, many of the Court's other special needs cases ignore these types of strictures, with the result that, at best, the Court's message in this area is muddled.

The Court has been similarly circumspect about what the Constitution has to say concerning data retention, accuracy, and security rules. For instance, in *Herring v. United States*,[55] it suggested, without holding, that evidence found during an arrest based on an expired warrant would require exclusion if the defendant could demonstrate "routine" and "widespread" systemic errors in the arrest warrant database."[56] In *Whalen*, it noted with favor the fact that a state statute governing collection of prescription drug information prohibited unwarranted disclosures to the public, a protection it said "arguably has its roots in the Constitution" in some circumstances;[57] in later cases, it "assumed, without deciding, that the Constitution protects a privacy right of the sort mentioned in *Whalen* . . .".[58] Similarly, in *Maryland v. King*,[59] which upheld a statute permitting collection of DNA samples from arrestees, it emphasized that the state was prohibited from using the samples for any purpose other than identifying arrestees. But none of these cases straightforwardly endorse a constitutional cause of action if personal information in government-run databases is inaccurate, retained indefinitely for no reason, or gratuitously disclosed to the public.

Legislatures have been more engaged in regulating the content and use of databases. Most prominently, the federal Privacy Act and similar state statutes permit agencies to obtain and keep information only if it is "relevant and necessary to accomplish a purpose [the agency is authorized to accomplish]," and they also prohibit public disclosure of personally identifiable information that has been collected without consent.[60] Various other federal and state statutes require the destruction of information after a limited period of time (or at least the creation of policies that dictate how long that period should be) and call for procedures for assuring accuracy and security.[61]

But these statutes can be remarkably lax when it comes to law enforcement. For example, the federal Privacy Act exempts from its strictures any agency "which performs as its principal function any activity pertaining to the enforcement of criminal laws" and specifically permits police agencies to retain any "investigatory material compiled for law enforcement purposes."[62] Neither the federal government nor most states have developed statutes that specify what "investigatory material" is, or whether there are limits on the types of investigatory material that may be collected.

Of course, there are specialized statutes that deal with specific types of virtual searches. For instance, at both the state and federal levels, one finds statutes regulating electronic surveillance, drone surveillance, ALPR, and various types of records searches, including communications, tax, and video records. But with the exception of electronic surveillance laws, these statutes usually are extremely vague with respect to the types of information that may be collected, the purposes for which the information may be used, and how long the information collected may be retained, among other important issues. More significantly, for some types of virtual searches there is no authorizing statute at all; any rules that exist come solely from individual police departments.

This is where administrative law principles can change the game.

The Crucial Role of Administrative Law

Even if Fourth Amendment jurisprudence in this area remains moribund, well-worn principles of administrative law applied to program-driven virtual searches could require both legislatures and police departments to provide more substantive regulation about data collection and use, in four ways. First, it is well established under administrative procedure acts that whenever an agency plans to engage in programmatic actions it must engage in a rule-making process. Second, that process also calls for and encourages public participation. Third, under commonly accepted administrative law jurisprudence, agencies can be required to justify the rules they create to a court through what is known as "hard look" review, to ensure both that the rules have a rational basis and that they are implemented even-handedly. Finally, before any of this can happen, the relevant legislature must enact a statute that sets out an intelligible principle for the agency to follow, a requirement that forces at least some democratic consideration about whether the agency should be engaging in the practice at all.

These points are developed in turn, using, for illustrative purposes, New York City's Domain Awareness System (DAS) and the fusion center phenomenon. The DAS, in operation since 2012, endeavors to collate and provide officers in the field information gleaned from thousands of surveillance cameras, geospatial data that reveals crime "hot spots," feeds from license plate recognition systems, and GPS signals that permit real-time and historical tracking of cars.[63] As such, the program is representative of numerous other types of physical monitoring systems, including persistent aerial surveillance like AIR and camera systems equipped with FRT or anomaly detection capabilities.[64] Fusion centers, in contrast, rely on the collection of transaction information. In essence junior versions of the NSA's- metadata program and similar federal record-collection efforts, they lasso in financial, rental, utility, vehicle, and communications data from federal, state, and local public databases, law enforcement files, and private companies, with the goals of aiding in the identification of suspicious individuals and providing information on already-identified suspects.[65]

Why Law Enforcement Entities Must Develop Rules

Most government agencies—at the federal level ranging from the Food and Drug Administration to the Commerce Department, at the state level from environmental agencies to health services—are governed by administrative procedure acts (APAs). Some municipalities also have enacted such statutes, applicable to their departments; for instance, New York City, the home of the DAS, has one.[66] These acts control how government agencies make decisions and promulgate rules. Of most relevance here is the stipulation found in the typical administrative procedure act, including the federal APA upon which most other APAs are modeled, that an agency must follow certain procedures whenever it develops a policy that is a "statement of general or particular applicability and future effect"[67] and that affects "the rights and obligations" of the citizenry.[68] These procedures include providing notice to the public of any proposed policy and an opportunity for interested parties to comment on the rule. Case law has also established that such policies must be justified in writing, implemented evenhandedly, and stay within the bounds of the relevant legislative authorization.

Even though police departments are administrative agencies and even though most APAs do not specifically exempt them from their provisions, police agencies generally have not had to follow these types of rulemaking procedures. A typical pronouncement one finds in administrative law treatises is that "administrative law includes the entire range of action by government with respect to the citizen or by the citizen with respect to the government, *except* for those matters dealt with by the criminal law."[69] One its face, this is a puzzling statement. The federal APA requires that agencies abide by its rulemaking dictates when they deal with such matters as workplace ergonomics, the height of a fence around animals, and the precise manner in which farm yields are reported.[70] A regime that requires the relevant agency to submit to administrative law constraints in these situations, but not when police want citizens to acquiesce to constant visual surveillance or collection of personal data (not to mention physical search and seizure programs), is seriously askew.

The likely reason for this anomaly is the notion that police search and seizure rules are already governed by the criminal law or the

Fourth Amendment; thus, they need not be subject to the process agencies must follow when they promulgate rules interpreting statutes that apply to and regulate the law-abiding public. While this rationale may exempt from administrative law oversight those rules that tell police when to conduct a stop, arrest, or search based on reasonable suspicion or probable cause, rules governing data collection and retention programs are altogether different. The policies that established the DAS, fusion centers, or AIR are not interpreting a criminal statute or a judicial search and seizure decision about who may be subject to police action but rather authorize suspicionless actions against the entire populace. As is true with the rules of other agencies that must abide by rulemaking procedures, these policies have "general and future effect" on the "rights" of citizens because their panvasive nature has a direct impact on thousands of concededly innocent people, who must either submit to surveillance or modify their legitimate behavior if they want to avoid police intrusion.

A second possible reason for the de facto exemption of police agencies from the law of agencies is that much policing is local, carried out by municipal police, not federal or state agents, and so is thought to be outside the purview of federal and state APAs. But that would not explain why federal and state police agencies are considered to be outside the scope of their respective APAs, or why exemptions are accorded the police departments in the nine states that consider municipal departments to be agencies of the state or the departments in those cities that have their own APA (such as New York).[71] Furthermore, every municipality, not just those directly governed by APAs, is engaged in enforcing state or federal criminal laws; at least to that extent, they should be covered by state and federal APAs. Additionally, many data collection programs, such as those undertaken by fusion centers, have a much broader scope than a purely municipal program and are often funded by federal and state governments.

A third reason one might consider exempting police agencies from the rulemaking process is that they have neither the wherewithal nor the expertise to develop rules. But, in fact, big police departments develop detailed rules governing things such as use of force, stop and frisk, and surveillance techniques all the time. Smaller departments can piggyback on this work and on the recommendations made by various organizations, ranging from the International Association of Police Chiefs to the ACLU, for specific guidance.

It is also worth noting that, while the Supreme Court's special needs jurisprudence does not explicitly reference administrative procedure acts, there are a few older Supreme Court decisions suggesting that the Fourth Amendment requires some sort of rulemaking in situations where its warrant and probable cause requirements do not apply. For instance, a largely unnoticed aspect of the Court's business inspection cases is that many reference administrative law principles and appear to incorporate them as Fourth Amendment requirements. *Dewey*'s reference to the Code of Federal Regulations in upholding warrantless inspections of coal mines has already been noted. Similarly, in *Marshall v. Barlow's, Inc.*,[72] the Court stated that, to protect business owners from the "unbridled discretion [of] executive and administrative officers," the judiciary must ensure that there are "reasonable legislative or administrative standards for conducting an inspection . . . with respect to a particular [establishment]."[73] Even in *Colonnade Catering Corp. v. United States*,[74] perhaps the least fulsome opinion in this category of cases, the Court said, in the course of authorizing warrantless inspections of liquor stores: "Where Congress has authorized inspection but made no rules governing the procedure that inspectors must follow, the Fourth Amendment and its various restrictive rules apply."[75] Conversely, the Court seemed to be saying, if the Fourth Amendment does not apply, Congress or its agency delegee must act.

These various statements indicate that administrative law can perform the Constitution's regulatory function if the legislature or agency promulgates constraining rules. They also suggest that, if such rules are developed, they establish a safe harbor from aggressive judicial intervention. Most important, they can be read to hold that, in the absence of warrant and probable cause or similar authority, the Fourth Amendment *requires* formal rulemaking by the police before a search or seizure may take place.

A key advantage of subjecting police agencies to the administrative law principles that all other agencies must follow, however, is that they apply regardless of whether the Fourth Amendment does. Administrative procedure acts require a rulemaking process whenever agencies take actions that have general and future effect on the rights of citizens. Further, because they require public participation, written reasons, evenhanded implementation, and legislative authorization, these principles are a particularly useful means of ensuring that program-driven virtual searches carried out by law enforcement agencies will be closely regulated.

Notice and Comment

Under the federal APA, if an agency engages in rulemaking it must issue a generally available notice of "either the terms or substance of the proposed rule or a description of the subjects and issues involved."[76] The goal is to permit public comment on the proposed rule or rule change and thereby improve the agency's decision-making process and enhance political legitimacy. Case law establishes that if the agency fails to pinpoint critical issues covered by the proposed rule—issues that are often surfaced during public comment—any regulation that results can be challenged in court and nullified.[77]

Application of this aspect of administrative procedure would have a dramatic impact on the usually cloistered police policy-making process. For instance, despite numerous news stories about the DAS and fusion centers, the public still does not know the extent to which New York City is keeping tabs on its citizens. Nor has it been told the precise types of records that fusion centers are compiling; as one fusion center trainer said: "If people knew what we were looking at, they'd throw a fit."[78] Requiring some sort of notice-and-comment period would mandate transparency about these types of issues and provide at least a patina of democratic participation in the decision-making process. Disclosing the details of what the policing agency plans to do also accomplishes other useful goals: It educates the public about the problem law enforcement is trying to address; allows citizens to tell police whether they think there is a problem worth addressing (and, if so, what can be done about it); and endorses a consultative approach that could increase legitimacy and avoid the hostile reaction that is likely if a program is sprung on the populace without notice.

The notice-and-comment process normally associated with federal regulations has been criticized on the ground that it tends to favor well-organized, powerful groups over individual comments. The analogous fear in the virtual search context might be that victims' rights groups and other law enforcement–oriented parties will dominate. However, that seems unlikely in today's environment. There are several advocacy groups—among them the ACLU and the Electronic Frontier Foundation—that can very competently represent the privacy point of view. In the case of AIR, for instance, the ACLU was heavily involved in the push to end the program.[79]

Even so, to minimize collective action problems, local sentiment on virtual search technology not only should be welcomed but also actively solicited, as occurred in Nashville on the subject of ALPRs. While the Nashville process recounted in chapter 1 was somewhat ad hoc, widespread community involvement could become part of the procedural infrastructure, as envisioned by the ACLU's Community Control Over Police Surveillance initiative, the principal goal of which is to encourage local communities to oversee police use of surveillance technology. The ACLU has even drafted model legislation that would require city councils both to solicit community input before approving the purchase and deployment of surveillance technology and to issue reports on its usage. About 30 cities and counties have passed or are considering this legislation.[80]

There are many other models for ensuring that community sentiments are integrated with law enforcement needs. In Oakland, for example, a domain-type system such as New York's was at first approved
unanimously by the City Council's Public Safety Committee. But
then, after a few overflowing council meetings packed by concerned
citizens, considerably more thought was put into whether the government should have eyes all over the city and what the police would be
able to do with the data collected. Eventually, the entire project was
ditched. As a result of that experience, the Council passed an ordinance that created a permanent Privacy Advisory Commission. Composed of one person from each of the city's council districts, as well
as an individual appointed by the mayor and an at-large member, the
Privacy Advisory Commission is supposed to advise the city on how
to protect citizens' "in connection with the city's purchase and use of
surveillance equipment," draft model legislation "relevant to privacy
and data protection," submit annual reports describing how the city
used surveillance technology, and recommend whether the city needs
to amend its usage and data retention policies.[81] One of the primary
advantages of this process is that it can put a brake on the police department's eagerness to buy the latest shiny technology without thinking through the consequences—not only the privacy and fiscal costs of
the technology but also whether it will really benefit the community.
Administrative law can be a way of institutionalizing this process in cities that do not have Oakland's foresight or activist background.

A perennial concern of the police, and one reason their policy-
making is so secretive, is that knowledge of their tactics will undermine crime detection efforts. That apparently was the reason, for
instance, that the FBI insisted that police departments sign nondisclo-
sure agreements about their purchase of so-called Stingrays—portable
devices that can access phone metadata by tricking phones into thinking they are cell towers.[82] But the federal APA and most state APAs
accommodate this concern by providing that police need not disclose

"techniques and procedures for law enforcement investigations or prosecutions[] or . . . guidelines for law enforcement investigations or prosecutions if such disclosure could reasonably be expected to risk circumvention of the law."[83]

In any event, fear that public notification will compromise criminal investigations is highly exaggerated. First, of course, the primary aim of much surveillance involving technology such as DAS cameras is often deterrence, which publicity can only enhance. Second, matters of specific implementation need not be revealed to the public. For instance, if camera surveillance is meant to be covert, the fact of such surveillance should be disclosed, but camera locations obviously need not be. At the same time, trying to prevent all public awareness about particular technology, such as the Stringray, is likely impossible in the long haul and, in any event, probably an overestimate of the extent to which disclosures about specific surveillance techniques add to what the typical criminal already knows or suspects.

The most important reason that investigative "techniques and procedures" generally need to be disclosed to the public, however, is the one most directly related to the notice-and-comment requirement: police should have to accept the fact that they function in a democracy.[84] That was certainly the message judges meant to send when, upon finally discovering the existence of Stingrays years after they were first used, they first lambasted the police for pretending to have instead relied on other investigative means (a process law enforcement agents coyly call "parallel construction"[85]) and then excluded the evidence thereby obtained.[86] Democratic accountability—a key value sought to be implemented by administrative law—requires that the public be told not only what surveillance capacities police have but also how those capacities will be used.

Explanation of the Program

A much-discussed issue in administrative law circles is the extent to which an agency must take public comments into consideration and, when it does not follow the route suggested by a comment, explain why it failed to do so. The APA does not require a response to every comment; demanding that an agency answer all submissions it receives, regardless of coherence or number, would be inefficient and unproductive.[87] At the same time, the APA does state that agency rules and their underlying findings may not be "arbitrary and capricious."[88]

In construing the reach of the federal APA, the Supreme Court's solution to this dilemma has been to require a written rationale for rules that are promulgated[89] and to require as well that the rationale link the agency's evidence, policies, and actions in a cogent way.[90] Thus, courts are entitled to ensure that agencies have taken a "hard look" at the rules they generate. As Kevin Stack explains (quoting from the relevant case law):

> Under the leading formulation of [the hard look] doctrine, "the agency must examine the relevant data and articulate a satisfactory explanation for its action including a 'rational connection between the facts found and the choices made.'" The court "consider[s] whether the decision was based on a consideration of the relevant factors and whether there has been a clear error of judgment." In addition, the agency may not "entirely fail[] to consider an important aspect of the problem," may not "offer[] an explanation for its decision that runs counter to the evidence before the agency," nor offer an explanation that is "so implausible that it could not be ascribed to a difference in view or the product of agency expertise." The agency must also relate the factual findings and expected effects of the regulation to the purposes or goals the agency must consider under the statute as well as respond to salient criticisms of the agency's reasoning.[91]

Application of the hard-look doctrine to domain awareness and fusion programs would require the relevant agencies to produce written rules. Further, courts would be empowered to assess the proffered rationales for those rules. Given the fact that the rules come from an administrative agency rather than a democratically elected legislature, Stack notes, that assessment generally applies a standard somewhere between the "strict scrutiny" and "rational basis" tests used in cases involving judicial review of legislation.[92] In other words, the APA demands more exacting judicial scrutiny than the Supreme Court's Fourth Amendment or equal protection jurisprudence does.

Even under this heightened standard, the two virtual search programs that are the focus here would probably pass, at least based on what we know. The DAS is touted as a more efficient way of facilitating communication of crime-relevant information to police in real time and also as a means of enhancing police safety by alerting officers to the location and history of suspects.[93] Fusion center repositories likewise make information access and collation more efficient.[94] The fact remains that, had they been subjected to the ordinary administrative law regimen, the agencies would have had to provide written explanations of why they wanted to collect the data they planned to collect and how they proposed to use it; in Stack's words, they would have needed "to relate the factual findings and expected effects of the regulation to the purposes or goals the agency must consider under the statute." For instance, it might be the case that some of the virtual searching undertaken by the DAS and fusion centers is simply not rationally related to their respective missions. Or those programs might not have policies specifying how the information collected will be siloed, kept secure, screened for accuracy, and accessed; if so, they fail, again using Stack's words, "to consider an important aspect of the problem."

Moreover, the judicial hard look would not end with such abstract assessments of program rationales. Just as important is an evaluation of whether the program, as implemented, is rationally achieving its objectives. For instance, some applications of domain awareness are meant to focus police presence in hot zones that are thought to be particularly prone to crime but that also may tend to be heavily populated by people of color.[95] Fusion centers might be focused on collecting records of people belonging to disfavored groups. In such situations, hard-look review leads to a third inquiry, which can help uncover biased, capricious, or pretextual programs.

Implementation of the Program

Once a rule is promulgated, the federal APA says nothing about how it should be carried out, apparently because implementation is considered to be a form of informal adjudication or enforcement, for which the APA has not developed standards. Here, however, the logic of administrative law, consistent with the Supreme Court's inspection and checkpoint jurisprudence and the ALI's evenhandedness principles, dictates that regulations be implemented in a "regularized" fashion, and does so with much more gusto than the vague references found in the Court's Fourth Amendment and equal protection opinions. As formulated by one commentary: "It is firmly established that an agency's unjustified discriminatory treatment of similarly situated parties constitutes arbitrary and capricious agency action."[96] Thus, courts have held that, unless the rationale for the rule signals a different result, all potential targets of a program should be treated in the same manner.For instance, courts have declared agency rules invalid because the agency invoked them "inconsistently," did not treat "similar cases similarly," did not apply its policies "in an evenhanded way," and applied them in a way that "lack[ed] rationality."[97] In effect, this aspect of hard-look analysis mimics disparate treatment doctrine of the type found in equal protection jurisprudence but without requiring the usual predicate of race or religion.

Thus, for instance, if it turns out that a hot zone targeted by the DAS is not really hot, or that groups whose records are accessed by fusion centers are not more crime-prone, then the administrative policy begins to look irrational. To avoid the potential for rejection under the hard-look standard, the differences in crime rates in these various scenarios should be noticeable. Otherwise, as recommended by the ALI's Policing Principles, the agency would be well advised to apply the program either across the board or on some other neutral basis, such as focusing the virtual search program on more serious crimes in an effort to avoid skewed surveillance priorities. As noted in chapter 5, data acquisition solely from areas known to be high in crime can create a self-fulfilling prophecy; thus, random deployment of surveillance technology to neighborhoods that are not considered hot spots might also be indicated, if it is part of a neutral plan designed to minimize disparate treatment.

In short, the hard-look doctrine requires that, when carrying out surveillance, police agencies provide a rationale for any distinctions they make between places or groups of people. This requirement would force recognition of the fact that policing is redistributive. Police do not execute surveillance in a vacuum; they choose where, when, and how they will carry out their investigations and, as a result, affect some localities and types of people more than others. Today, these choices occur with little or no oversight. The result, many allege, is that some communities unfairly bear the brunt of police activity more than others.[98] Administrative law principles give the courts the authority to make sure that is not the case.

Legislative Authorization

The fundamental predicate to administrative rulemaking is that legislation must authorize the agency action about which rules are being made.[99] Sometimes the authorizing legislation directly mandates the action. Most commonly, however, the statute sets out a general directive—about, for instance, protecting the environment, avoiding discrimination against people with a disability, or disbursing welfare benefits—that the agency must interpret and attempt to implement through its own policies.

Some legislatures have done this in connection with the collection and use of data through virtual search techniques. For instance, California has enacted a statute authorizing ALPRs that requires each department to "implement a usage and privacy policy in order to ensure that the collection, use, maintenance, sharing, and dissemination of ALPR information is consistent with respect for individuals' privacy and civil liberties." The statute also provides that the police must, "at a minimum" set out, among other things, "the authorized purposes for using the ALPR system and collecting ALPR information," "the employees and independent contractors who are authorized to use or access the ALPR system, or to collect ALPR information," "a description of how the ALPR system will be monitored to ensure the security of the information and compliance with applicable privacy laws," and rules governing the sharing, accuracy, and retention of information obtained.[100]

However, in many states, and with respect to most types of program-driven virtual searches, such legislation is hard to find. For instance, New York's Domain Awareness System is, at best, grounded on an omnibus statutory delegation of law enforcement powers, which states that police shall "preserve the peace, prevent crime, detect and arrest offenders . . . protect the rights of persons and property . . . preserve order . . . enforce and prevent the violation of all laws and ordinances," and so on.[101] Similarly, fusion centers often operate without any explicit statutory authority.[102] Thus, there is no legislative directive as to the types of information they can collect, the length of time they can maintain the information, or the types of wrongdoing they can attempt to detect; as a result, for most fusion centers, the original counterterrorism focus has transformed into an "all-hazards" or "all-crimes" mission without any explicit statutory authorization.[103] Facial recognition technology is a third example of legislative failure.

For instance, there is no federal legislation governing FRT, despite findings by the Government Accountability Office that 13 of the 14 of the agencies that used private FRT services do not know which FRT techniques are being used or how they are employed.[104]

If administrative law principles were adhered to, this legislative and executive nonchalance could be a major problem for program-driven virtual searches. As a leading treatise puts it: "If an agency act is within the statutory limits (or vires), its action is valid; if it is outside them (or ultra vires), it is invalid."[105] A virtual search program that is not authorized by statute should be considered void. Further, even if a statute can be said to authorize such a program in broad sense, courts operating in an administrative paradigm might well conclude that a more specific legislative mandate is required when government action is so significant in scope and involves such sensitive information.

It is true that, at the federal level, the Supreme Court has indicated that authorizing legislation need only set out a vague "intelligible principle" to guide agencies.[106] But if the only relevant legislative pronouncement is "to enforce the criminal law"—as is in effect the case in New York—even that vacuous mandate might not be met. It is also worth noting that the nondelegation doctrine—which is the genesis of the intelligible-principle requirement—is much more robust in the states than it is at the federal level.[107] Thus, for instance, one state court has held that the nondelegation doctrine "requires that the legislature, in delegating its authority, provide sufficient identification of the following: (1) the persons and activities potentially subject to regulation; (2) the harm sought to be prevented; and (3) the general means intended to be available to the administrator to prevent the identified harm."[108]

As this language suggests, taken seriously, the nondelegation doctrine would force the relevant legislature to be specific in authorizing surveillance programs, at least as specific as California's ALPR legislation, and arguably more so, since even that law says nothing about the appropriate uses of ALPRs. Certainly legislation simply mandating that police "enforce the law" would not authorize a domain awareness system or a fusion center program. Rather, legislatures would have to specifically endorse the use of zoom cameras and license plate recognition technology necessary to carry out a domain awareness system and authorize the collection of information from financial and communications entities that occurs with fusion centers.

Mandating that these types of issues be debated at the highest policy level ensures democratic accountability. When legislators are forced to consider whether they are willing to authorize a system that tracks people 24/7 or that collects so much information it would lead many of their constituents to "throw a fit," a more rational system is likely to result. It was the absence of this debate at the legislative level that was most problematic in the *Leaders of a Beautiful Struggle* case.

Just as important, if and when such systems are authorized, the specific legislative directive about the "persons or activities" sought to be regulated, the "harm" to be prevented, and the "means" of prevention would provide crucial guidance for law enforcement agencies implementing panvasive surveillance. If, for instance, a municipal legislature authorized camera surveillance solely for the purpose of detecting and deterring violent crime, camera footage of minor incidents could not be retained and could not be the basis for further police action. Such a prohibition would alleviate concerns about pretextual actions and net-widening that often arises when new surveillance technology is introduced.

The Need to Disaggregate Legislative, Judicial, and Executive Functions

Given the ubiquity of George Orwell's *1984*, no one needs to be told about the dangers of unrestricted data collection and retention by the government. But our regulatory regime has not responded well to the exponential growth in law enforcement accumulation of information that has occurred over decades of surveillance. In many jurisdictions, new virtual search programs that gather data about vast swaths of the population are springing up seemingly overnight, with very little input from the legislature or the citizenry at large.[109]

At a minimum, rules governing the type of data that law enforcement may collect or acquire, the purposes for which it may be used, and retention, accuracy, access, and accountability issues should be set forth in legislation and administrative rules transparently and democratically passed and promulgated. Data acquisition methods should be universal, random, or statistically justifiable. Courts should enforce these rules through the Fourth Amendment or the administrative hard-look doctrine.

Some commentators believe courts should do much more, perhaps even declaring unconstitutional duly enacted virtual search programs, out of fear that legislatures will not take sufficient account of minority views. Admittedly, the phrase "democratically passed and promulgated" in the previous paragraph can hide a multitude of sins. Legislatures and administrative agencies, perhaps egged on by a majority of the populace, may not always be attentive to the privacy, autonomy, and antidiscrimination values that should be considered in setting up virtual search programs. Courts should stand ready to strike down clearly irrational programs, programs that are not statutorily authorized, and programs that are not administered in an evenhanded fashion. But they should not, as the Fourth Circuit did in *Leaders of a Beautiful Struggle*, dismiss virtual search programs using Fourth Amendment doctrines better suited to analyzing individual searches.

As John Hart Ely forcefully argued,[110] when construing how general constitutional commands such as the Fourth Amendment's reasonableness mandate govern duly enacted statutes, the judicial role should generally be one of deference to well-functioning legislative and administrative pronouncements. Under Ely's political process theory, the primary goal of the judiciary is to ensure that the political process is working properly rather than to second-guess its outcomes.[111] When the scope of a virtual search program is made clear on the face of the authorizing legislation and is meant to be evenly applied across the polity as required by administrative law principles, the political process should usually work. A program that has panvasive effects will create coalitions that can push back against law enforcement interests. As illustrated by Congress's defunding of the Total Information Awareness program and President Obama's executive order requiring that phone metadata be maintained by common carriers rather than the NSA, under these conditions such pushback can occur even where national security is concerned; this book has also noted several examples of local governments ending surveillance programs. If, in addition, a community-friendly notice-and-comment procedure is put in place, concerns about relying on the democratic process as the primary means of regulating program-driven virtual searches should be significantly allayed.

Administrative law provides a practical and well-established vehicle for translating the vestigial neutral plan and evenhandedness constraints found in Fourth Amendment jurisprudence to the virtual search setting. It can meld together legislatures, agencies, and courts into a coherent decision-making structure that should enhance democratic accountability, rational decision-making, and attention to civil liberties.

Volunteer-Driven Virtual Searches

Consider the following scenarios. The local police department asks everyone in its jurisdiction to make their Ring camera footage available to police upon request and offers a reward for images that help solve a crime. Should there be any impediment to police use of any images thereby obtained as evidence? What if, instead, Clearview, the company that is pioneering law enforcement use of facial recognition technology, provides as part of its pitch to police not only a free trial of its technology but also, as proof of its efficacy, the location of a local wanted criminal that it has discovered using FRT? Does the fact that Clearview is a private company looking for police business distinguish it from individual citizens who want to help the police? Or imagine that a Verizon employee, bothered by a recent spate of home robberies in his neighborhood that the police department has publicized on TV, dives into company records and discovers that a certain phone has been near the scene of every robbery at the time it happened, and now wants to send his discovery to the police. Should it matter that the employee probably would not have acted but for the televised police request for help?

Probably none of these actions implicates the Fourth Amendment as currently construed, even if, as argued in this book, a right to public anonymity is enforced and the third-party doctrine is repudiated. For an intrusion to trigger Fourth Amendment protection it must not only be a "search" or a "seizure"; it must also involve "state action." That is because the Fourth Amendment (and the other rights in the Bill of Rights) regulate actions only of the government, not of private individuals. If your privacy is invaded by another citizen, you may have a claim in tort, but you cannot make a constitutional claim unless the private party is, in the Supreme Court's words, "an agent or an instrument of the Government."[1]

At the same time, the private party does not have to be acting under explicit police orders to be considered a state actor. Indeed, the Supreme Court has found state action even when there is no direction by the government at all. *Skinner v. Railway Association*[2] involved the implications of a federal law governing drug testing by private railway companies. The law required testing of railway workers involved in a "major train accident" but permitted the companies to decide, in their discretion, whether to test workers who were involved in a "reportable accident or incident" and those who violated speeding or other safety rules. While the government paid for the toxicological analysis, the railways paid for the process of extracting blood and urine samples and shipping the sample to the government. Nonetheless, the Court held that the Fourth Amendment applied to the entire drug-testing program. The Court pointed out that the relevant regulations provided that the testing was for the purpose of "promoting the public safety" and that railways could not act in a way that was inconsistent with that purpose by, for instance, foregoing testing on the basis of a collective bargaining agreement.[3] Furthermore, the regulations made clear that the Federal Railroad Administration was entitled to the results of any tests administered. Thus, the Court stated, the government had "removed all legal barriers to testing" and "made plain not only its strong preference for testing, but its desire to share the fruits of such intrusions," factors that the Court considered "clear indices of the Government's encouragement, endorsement and participation, and suffic[ient] to implicate the Fourth Amendment."[4]

Replace the word "testing" in the previous sentence with the phrase "virtual searches" and apply it to the Ring, Clearview, and Verizon hypotheticals at the beginning of this chapter. In any of those cases, did the government express a "strong preference" for the surveillance and

its results? Are there "clear indices" of the government's "encouragement, endorsement, and participation"? The meaning of this language
is the topic of this chapter.

In upcoming years, this may well be the most important topic addressed in this book. If the government can obtain personal information simply by announcing it is willing to pay for any data or images
about wrongdoing that nongovernmental actors can access, it could
well do an end-run around all the restrictions described in previous
chapters, unless such an announcement is considered to be a "strong
preference" for and "encouragement" of surveillance. The usefulness
of this potential workaround is much greater than it was 50 or even 20
years ago, because technology has both greatly enhanced the potential for every citizen to become an investigator of crime and enabled
private companies to acquire a mountain of information about each
of us and monetize it—indeed, many companies are set up solely with
that goal in mind.[5] If private entities are allowed to engage in virtual
searches with the aim of discovering criminal activity that government
itself cannot conduct without justification, the Fourth Amendment
could become a nullity. In fact, the more restrictions placed on the
government's searches, the fewer compunctions it might have about
relying on the private market to do its work.

That should not mean that every private action that is meant to
help the government nab criminals is governed by the Constitution.
Private citizens should not be discouraged from bringing to the government evidence of crime they come upon; as the Supreme Court
has stated, "it is no part of the policy underlying the Fourth and Fourteenth Amendments to discourage citizens from aiding to the utmost
of their ability in the apprehension of criminals."[6] But there should be
disincentives to pry into people's lives for tangible private gain. And
private action that is intrusive should be subject to tort claims in situations akin to those that the Fourth Amendment regulates. These tenets
can be illustrated by looking at a number of scenarios, which also help
flesh out points made in earlier chapters.

Surveillance Abettors: Communications Providers

Some private companies, while not ordered to facilitate the government's surveillance efforts, willingly do so. The experience of common carriers—companies that maintain communications networks—provides a particularly interesting story in this regard. At one time these companies enthusiastically abetted law enforcement efforts. Today, they are much leerier of government requests for aid.

Shortly after the assaults on 9/11, President George W. Bush issued a "highly classified presidential authorization" finding that the attacks constituted an "extraordinary emergency" that justified allowing the National Security Agency to collect, without a warrant, the content and metadata of a wide range of communications between people outside and inside the country and between people inside the country who were not US citizens. Through Stellar Wind, the resulting program, the government cajoled AT&T, Verizon, and BellSouth—and eventually other companies as well—into forwarding routing information about the phone and email communications of their customers to the NSA.[7] In 2011, AT&T alone was sending metadata about 1.1 billion domestic call records per day to the NSA, supposedly after sifting through them to make sure they met the presidential guidelines (although the Office of the Inspector General later found they were simply surrendered in bulk).[8]

Under Fourth Amendment jurisprudence at the time, the argument was strong that, despite its scope, this collection of metadata was not a search.[9] But after *Carpenter*, and following the analysis of this book, it should be considered one today. The fact that the metadata was held by third parties should not diminish the expectation that one's communication information is private.

However, that conclusion by itself is not enough to bring Stellar Wind within the ambit of the Fourth Amendment. It must also be established that AT&T and the other companies involved in Stellar Wind were state actors. There is certainly an argument that they were not. According to a *New York Times* article in 2015, for instance, the companies "voluntarily" provided foreign-to-foreign metadata, and even metadata involving a domestic party was proffered through a "partnership" arrangement that was "collaborative."[10]

That language notwithstanding, however, the telecom providers should have been considered agents of the state. The presidential authorization for Stellar Wind made clear the government wanted metadata and specified the type of metadata it wanted. Further, the government paid the companies handsomely for it. Here, in the words of *Skinner*, there was clearly a "strong preference" expressed by the government that went beyond "encouragement."

If Stellar Wind were determined to involve state action, the implications would be significant. Under the dictates of chapter 7, the kind of suspicionless data collection involved in that program, if carried out by a domestic law enforcement agency investigating ordinary crime, would require explicit legislative authorization, regulations developed subject to notice and comment, and a judicial hard-look review of any regulations produced. There is no reason to treat national security surveillance abetted by private companies any differently. Congress should have authorized Stellar Wind's metadata program, and either a statute or regulation should have identified the type of information sought, its legitimate uses, and how long it could be retained. Disclosure of specific techniques that might help terrorists and others evade detection would not have to be revealed, but there should have been democratic debate about the scope and purpose of the program.

In fact, that is what happened in 2015, 14 years too late, when Congress passed the USA FREEDOM Act.[11] Rather than endorse the NSA's bulk collection program, the statute ended it, replacing it with a system that required that the records be maintained by the common carriers. Today, the government may access only those records that satisfy a "specific selection term" that "specifically identifies a person, account, address, or personal device" and that limits, "to the greatest extent reasonably practicable, the scope of tangible things sought."[12]

The NSA must convince the Foreign Intelligence Surveillance Court that there are reasonable grounds to believe the proposed search will obtain information relevant to an investigation authorized by a high-level official and that there is a reasonable articulable suspicion that the specific selection term is associated with a foreign agent involved in international terrorism.[13] Because it permits access to the content of communications on less than probable cause, the USA FREEDOM Act does not adhere to the tenets of the proportionality principle. But it is a decided improvement over the previous regulatory regime.

If there is one explanation for why Congress finally saw the light, it was Edward Snowden. In 2013, Snowden's release of classified documents revealed the scope of the bulk collection program, as well as of other national security programs such as PRISM, which compelled common carriers to send the NSA any communications sent to or from a specified selector such as an email address.[14] Had his disclosures and the ensuing public uproar not occurred, the USA FREEDOM Act likely would never have been passed.

Although Congress did eventually act, it failed to do so in a timely fashion. The USA FREEDOM Act should have *preceded* initiation of the metadata program, not the other way around. Ironically, according to press reports about Snowden's motivations, had the NSA asked for and received congressional approval before it started its program, Snowden never would have felt the need to make his revelations, the scope of which were much more damaging to national security than any inferences about government surveillance techniques that can be drawn from reading the USA FREEDOM Act.[15]

As it is, the Snowden disclosures, and the reaction of an outraged public (outrage that was as much the result of the coverup as it was of concern about the program), has changed the nature of government–private sector "collaboration." No longer are communications companies, concerned about the financial bottom line, as eager to assist the government in its investigative endeavors, and other types of data companies have become equally circumspect.[16] As recounted in previous chapters, these days companies such as Google, Apple, and Ancestry.com are likely to resist law enforcement requests for information.

Moreover, their insistence that the government seek court orders to obtain records in individual cases is merely the tip of the resistance by these companies. Alan Rozenshtein has documented how communications enterprises are now more likely to engage in class action litigation about surveillance, publish "transparency reports" about the number of surveillance requests they receive, construct privacy-enhancing architecture (such as end-to-end encryption), lobby the government for more surveillance restrictions (as occurred with the FREEDOM Act), and lobby other government agencies such as the Federal Communications Commission and the Federal Trade Commission to battle their law enforcement counterparts over issues such as Department of Justice access to accounts held by privacy-conscious foreigners.[17] The type of voluntary private cooperation between communications providers and the government that existed immediately after 9/11—and that characterized pre-9/11 programs such as SHAMROCK (which for decades until its exposure in the mid-1970s provided the government with all international telegraph communications[18])— may be a thing of the past, at least until the next 9/11.

That does not mean, however, that there are not plenty of companies willing to lend a helping hand to law enforcement—if it pays.

Surveillance Surrogates: Data Brokers

The information government obtains from communications providers such as Google and AT&T is already collected by those companies as part of their business model; it is surrendered to the government only upon request (ideally, backed up by a court order). In contrast, the business models of many other companies aim, at least in part, to acquire information for the precise purpose of selling it to law enforcement. For instance, the now-defunct company Geofeedia, using information it obtained from scraping Instagram, Facebook, and

Twitter posts and the locations from which they originated, claimed to help over 500 law enforcement departments predict and monitor "events" ranging from gang activities to political and union protests.[19] After this surveillance was exposed by the ACLU in 2016, Instagram and Facebook purportedly stopped proving Geofeedia their content.[20] But other companies such as Palantir, Dataminr, ShadowDragon, Fusus, Intrado, and Hunchlab (most of which were discussed in chapter 5) claim to provide similar types of information about hot spots, hot people, or hot events. Dataminr, for instance, relayed tweets about the George Floyd and Black Lives Matter protests to the police.[21]

What these companies do with social media and police records, companies such as Acxiom, LexisNexis, and Oracle simulate with a much wider array of public and quasiprivate records, including data generated from retail purchases, internet surfing, and financial transactions, as well as from "smart" devices in cars, medical apps, and home appliances that are sometimes referred to as the "Internet of Things." Acxiom, for instance, claims to have acquired, on each of more than 700 million people, over 1,500 data points, which can provide "insight into your psychological makeup to fit you into hundreds of refined consumer categories, estimating, for example, how likely you are to pay cash for a new Korean vehicle."[22] Information this granular can be very useful to law enforcement, which is why companies like Acxiom have contracts with the U.S. government estimated to be worth $56 million in 2016.[23] Even way back in 2001, ChoicePoint, now owned by LexisNexis, had contracts with 35 government agencies and was feeding the United States Marshals Service alone the results of between 14,000 and 40,000 queries a month.[24]

As Andrew Ferguson has detailed,[25] the twenty-first century has seen a huge increase in government reliance on these data sources, a reliance that brings several attendant dangers. Police departments can become increasingly dependent on private companies to do their jobs, which in turn can mean the companies will come to dominate decisions about the types of information to collect and the way it is inputted, organized, analyzed, and corrected.[26] Concomitantly, departments might have great difficulty changing vendors once they invest money and organizational resources integrating them into departmental decision-making. Unless oversight is extensive, data error, data bias, and data incompatibility with existing government databases could become more difficult to correct.[27]

Ferguson also points out that, although the Federal Trade Commission has made some effort to restrict some aspects of private data collection, no overarching statutory scheme provides a basis for regulating this situation. As he summarizes it, "federal laws targeting the national problem of data collection, aggregation and use remain weak. . . . The current reality is wide-scale, growing big data collection without commensurate legal regulation."[28] And there is even less law regarding law enforcement use of collected information; as noted in chapter 7, most of the relevant federal statutes exempt law enforcement, and state statutes regulating collection and use are few and far between.[29]

Here the state-action requirement becomes especially important. If police collect personal data themselves, they would be engaging in virtual searches subject to restrictions on programmatic actions, and if they access the data they collect they would be subject to the rules governing suspect-, profile-, and event-driven virtual searches. But if police can purchase the same information from a private company without abiding by those rules, they could engage in what has been called "data laundering."[30] Essentially, data brokers become a "fourth party" that can collect and aggregate information from third parties and deliver it to law enforcement without concern about the Fourth Amendment.

That would be the wrong result. The fact that government pays for the data that data brokers provide should, by itself, be evidence of law enforcement's strong preference for the information and its desire to encourage its collection. This situation differs markedly from government offers of a reward for turning in a suspect or providing evidence of a crime, which normally would not be considered a sufficient basis for finding state action. As Kiel Brennan-Marquez has noted, data brokers are repeat players, their existence depends in large part on government largesse, and their technological capabilities enable them to access the information easily.[31] Further, given the monetary incentives, they may be tempted to engage in intrusions that a government agent would not be authorized to undertake.

The implications of the conclusion that government use of data broker information constitutes state action are even more significant than in the common carrier setting. It requires not only that, before acquiring information from these companies, the government have the requisite justification for accessing the type of information it wants (based on whether it is suspect-, profile- or event-driven). It also requires that the data collection *by the data broker* meet the same legislative authorization, notice-and-comment, and judicial review requirements that should be imposed on government-run programs. Specifically, before government can access the data of these private companies, a statute would have to identify the types of data they can collect, specify the purposes for which law enforcement can use it, and set out guidelines for retention and security; further, regulations would have to be promulgated implementing the statute. This regime is necessary because, unlike the common carriers that helped the government post-9/11, data brokers are collecting the information as government surrogates; they are collecting information from those very common carriers, as well as from other private and public databases. To the extent Acxiom conducts its business as an agent of the government, it should be treated like the government. If it does not want to be subject to this type of regulation, it has the option of dropping the government as a client.

Application of program-driven regulatory requirements companies paid by and routinely relied upon by law enforcement could also help address the dangers of technological monopolization. As Elizabeth Joh and Thomas Joo have noted,[32] once police departments have decided

to buy body cameras, license plate readers, and predictive crime software from a private company, they tend to stick with the company
because of the sunk costs. For obvious commercial reasons, but also to
ensure compatibility, competing companies are each trying to control
the market in these areas. Joh and Joo point out that "if a single company should come to dominate the market for [a policing] platform . . .
[it will] effectively control the design, access, and availability of multiple police surveillance technologies" and thus "gain enormous power
over basic questions in democratic policing."[33] Requiring legislative,
departmental, and community input through statutory, regulation,
and notice-and-comment procedures, as well as continual monitoring
of authorized virtual search regimes, can temper that power.

Informants: Individual Versus Institutional

Data broker scenarios involve companies organized in part for the
purpose of making money from law enforcement. What if, instead,
government makes a request of a private individual for his or her Ring
footage? Today this is a common occurrence. In 2020, a daytime burglary occurred in my neighborhood. I was asked by Nashville police if
they could see my Ring camera feed of the street in front of my house
for the hour before the burglary occurred. In fact, unlike many of my
neighbors, I did not have a Ring camera, but if I had (I do now), I
would have agreed to do so. According to the *New York Times*, more
than 500 police departments have partnered with Amazon to gain
access to the "Neighbors Portal," which at the time of my experience
allowed police to request video footage directly from Ring users.[34]
(Today, Amazon requires the police to publicly post a "Request for
Assistance" rather than approach customers.[35]) Some police departments have even offered citizens discounted prices on Ring cameras
to facilitate this use of technology.[36]

Assuming a citizen's consent to a police request (whether directly
or via a Request for Assistance) is voluntary, it should be sufficient to

obtain camera footage of the consenter's own property; that is bed-rock law. But in my case the police also wanted footage of the public street. Despite my ownership of the camera, consent to disclosure of that footage is not mine to give. Thus, before police can obtain Ring footage of public areas or of the property of someone other than the camera owner, they should have the requisite justification. Granted, given the fact that, in my case, the camera picked up only a small por-tion of the public street, that justification could be minimal. But in my case, there should have at least been a showing that a burglary had occurred in the area and that my Ring might have picked up the per-petrators. Furthermore, if the police had gone directly to Amazon, bypassing me entirely, they might need even more; at least if this type of police request were a common practice (which at one time it was), Amazon would be a surveillance surrogate, subject to the same rules that govern police access to data brokers.

What if instead there is no request by the police? If I notice a drug transaction on my camera and want to forward the video to the police unsolicited, I should be able to do so without triggering any Fourth Amendment issue, since this is truly private action; even if the pos-sibility of a reward is the primary motivation for sending the video, it is not what triggered my decision to set up the camera or monitor it. The more interesting question is whether the Fourth Amendment is implicated if Amazon, noticing the same drug transaction, forwards it to the police. Once again, there is no police request for the information and thus no direct encouragement. Nonetheless, under some circum-stances, there should be a different result.

To understand why, it helps to revisit the origins of the third-party doctrine discussed in chapter 2, which interacts with the state action requirement in interesting ways. One of the first Supreme Court cases to recognize the third-party exception to the Fourth Amendment involved Jimmy Hoffa (the famed labor leader) and an acquaintance of his named Edward Partin, who agreed to pass on to the govern-ment any information about jury tampering that came to his attention, which he subsequently did.[37] Hoffa challenged the admission of Partin's testimony on the ground that Partin betrayed his confidence when he posed as an ally. The Court rejected that argument because Partin "was not a surreptitious eavesdropper" and was privy to Hoffa's statements "by invitation."[38] Other informant cases before and after *Hoffa v. United States* repeated this reasoning.[39] It was this line of cases on which the Supreme Court relied in *Miller* and *Smith*, the decisions that held that the Fourth Amendment does not apply to government requests for information from banks and phone companies. Like Hoffa, the Court reasoned, defendants Miller and Smith assumed the risk that the information they surrendered to a third party would end up in the government's hands.[40]

This book has argued that *Miller* and *Smith* are wrong and that requests aimed at third-party institutions such as banks and phone companies should be made via court order. There is much to be said for arriving at the same result when the government's source is an individual like Partin, at least when the individual is asked to inform.[41] But even if one believes that Partin was not an agent of the government and instead was voluntarily acting out of civic duty, there are at least three differences between Partin on the one hand and, on the other, the bank in *Miller* and phone company in *Smith*.

The first has to do with autonomy. Establishing a rule that the government must ignore unsolicited disclosures from individual citizens such as Partin denigrates their autonomous choice to make the disclosures.[42] In contrast, as chapter 3 made clear, corporations such as those involved in *Miller* and *Smith* have historically not been granted the same rights as natural persons in the Fourth and Fifth Amendment settings; no autonomy interest is insulted by a government refusal to accept volunteered information from an impersonal corporation.[43]

Second, precisely because companies are commercial entities, even their "volunteered" disclosures could well be driven by the hope of cultivating government favor, in all sorts of ways, ranging from beneficial regulatory decisions to direct sales.[44] Reinforcing these incentives could lead to surreptitious surrogate surveillance—for instance, the development of algorithms to detect criminal activity—that ought to be regulated programmatically but cannot be because it is undiscovered.

Third, and most important, unlike human confidantes, commercial institutions can be said to owe either formal or quasiformal fiduciary duties to their customers. Unlike the human volunteer, companies are only able to obtain personal facts because they purport to provide a particular service.[45] In that sense, they are like lawyers and doctors, who normally must maintain confidentiality.

All of this suggests that even if the Fourth Amendment does not govern individual informants like Partin, *institutional* vigilantes like the Verizon employee described at the beginning of this chapter should be discouraged. The way the Electronic Communications Privacy Act accomplishes this is through prohibiting common carriers from disclosing information to police unless its discovery was "inadvertent."[46] This prohibition should usually be rigorously enforced, either through the Fourth Amendment or, as suggested in the next section, tort law.

At the same time, even well-established fiduciary obligations do not always trump concerns about public safety. For instance, both the medical and legal professions recognize a duty to reveal information that would prevent a serious violent crime.[47] Explicitly applied to the virtual search setting, that norm might permit third-party institutions to disclose "advertently" discovered information that a serious felony is occurring or is about to occur (as distinguished from information about a completed crime).

Another well-accepted exception to a lawyer's fiduciary duties arises when confidentiality would prevent discovery of crimes involving use of the lawyer's services.[48] By analogy, if a company-created algorithm discovered that the company's services were being deployed to defraud others it should be able to report that crime to the authorities—

likewise if an employee was caught defrauding customers. Finally, a duly enacted statute requiring disclosures about a customer's transactions—as Congress has done with its "anti-Smurf" legislation requiring banks to report deposits of more than $10,000[49]—could override fiduciary obligations.

Arguably, however, this should be the extent to which the law bows to the volunteer notion where thirty-party institutions that are essential to living in the modern world are involved. Traditional fiduciary rules permit disclosure for emergencies and for self-protection but otherwise prohibit it. That prohibition is presumably based on the recognition that people should be able to trust that institutions on which they depend for the basics of life are not conduits to the government.

Crowdsourcing: Web Sleuthing and Tort Law

Still left unresolved is when, if ever, individuals who "voluntarily" help the police (like Partin?) should be governed by the Fourth Amendment. That question has become particularly germane now that the digital age has, as with everything else, dramatically changed the scope of what has come to be called "crowdsourcing." Police have always used wanted posters and televised requests for help. But today there is a website, Websleuths, that asks "[o]dinary people from all walks to life [to] come together . . . to dissect clues to crimes and unravel real-life mysteries.[50] A Georgia police department has a mobile app that allows community members, through Facebook and Twitter, to learn about and assist in investigations.[51] Vizsafe offers digital blockchain rewards for providing tips and video about "incidents," a private enterprise that could easily be converted to law enforcement use.[52] And, as discussed earlier, Ring has developed a Request for Assistance app that police can use.

While these steps could be said to express a preference for, and encourage private pursuit of, particular information, concluding that any citizen response to them is state action would make crowdsourcing almost useless. That would be unfortunate; as Wayne Logan notes, crowdsourcing "[has] promise as an investigative force multiplier for governments."[53] The lower courts have added some gloss to *Skinner*'s language that can help in this situation. For instance, the First Circuit Court of Appeals has held that whether a private actor becomes a state actor depends on "(1) the extent of the government's role in instigating or participating in the search; (2) its intent and the degree of control it exercises over the search and the private party; (3) the extent to which the private party aims primarily to help the government or to serve its own interests."[54] Under this test, providing the public with detailed information about a crime, or a crime problem, and asking for help—as occurs with Websleuths, for instance—would not trigger the Constitution.

At the same time, vigilantism can be carried too far. One can imagine over-eager sleuths, acting on a hunch or triggered by a law enforcement bulletin, hacking into computers, stalking "suspects" with cell phone cameras, and attempting amateur online stings. Without some sort of specific police direction, none of this implicates the Fourth Amendment. But it could still have repercussions for the vigilante.

In *Burdeau v. McDowell*,[55] the first Supreme Court decision to consider the state-action requirement in a Fourth Amendment case, the Court found that, given the absence of police direction, the Constitution was not applicable even though the private individuals from whom the government received the defendant's papers committed a burglary to get them. However, the Court also stated: "We assume that the petitioner has an unquestionable right of redress against those who illegally and wrongfully took his private property."[56] The common law has long recognized a tort of intrusion, which, as the *Second Restatement of Torts* describes it, occurs when a person "intentionally intrudes . . . upon the . . . seclusion of another [and] the intrusion would be highly offensive to a reasonable person."[57] In effect, this tort prohibits private individuals from engaging in the same type of conduct the Fourth Amendment forbids police and police agents to undertake in the absence of adequate authorization.

Much rides, of course, on the definition of "offensive." But here Fourth Amendment law can be useful, if only analogically. For instance, survey information of the type that should inform analysis of the Fourth Amendment's threshold might also be the best way to determine when an intrusion "would be highly offensive to a reasonable person." If so, civil liability should result.

Finetuning the State-Action Requirement

There can be a very fine line between government encouragement that amounts to state action and government importuning that does not. Given the often-close financial relationship between governments and corporations, the fiduciary duties of the companies that seek and obtain our personal information, and their lack of a strong autonomy interest, that line should be drawn in a different place depending on whether the "volunteer" is an entity or an individual. In the virtual search world, private entities can easily become willing government appendages and will often need to be treated as such for constitutional purposes; in particular, if their business model contemplates collecting data for the government, they should be regulated as if they were the government. While individual volunteers are not likely to be the same type of financially dependent repeat players and thus usually should not be considered state agents, they still should be liable in tort if they obtain their incriminating information through egregious privacy invasions.

Making It Happen

Much like every other institution in today's world, law enforcement is avidly adapting technology to its purposes. If left entirely up to the police—and if the police were given an unlimited budget—constant government surveillance might quickly become the norm. Every street could be monitored by high-resolution cameras with zoom and night-vision capacities. Planes, drones, and satellites could be flying overhead, recording all public movements. License plate readers and facial recognition technology could provide alerts on any matches to cars and people involved in crime. Records of all our financial, communication, travel, and other everyday activities could be stored for subsequent access. With the help of data brokers, internet service providers, and phone companies, governments could compile dossiers on suspects, construct algorithms meant to predict hot spots and hot people, and use cell tower dumps and other location tracking techniques to investigate crime scenes. As this book has documented, much of this is already happening in various jurisdictions around the country.

One reaction to this potential reality is to adopt an abolitionist position. In the recent past, pleas for a complete reworking of our criminal justice system, previously confined primarily to the halls of academia, have found their way into public fora. Advocates have called for razing prisons, defunding the police, replacing district attorneys with private prosecutions, and reimagining forensic science.[1] Easily fitting within this agenda are demands to put a stop to technological surveillance.

Citizen-powered initiatives, such as the Movement for Black Lives, have called for precisely that. An understandable concern, given our racialized history, is that the negative impacts of a surveillance society—identification errors, overreliance on criminal histories, concentrated monitoring—are likely to fall most heavily on people of color. Beyond that, there is fear that government will misuse its modern panopticon for political and social ends that have little or nothing to do with fighting crime. The dystopian vision today is not so much George Orwell's *1984* as it is modern China, where people are assigned "social credit scores" based on data-driven assessments of their law-abidingness, their work habits, and their respectability.[2]

The pushback to the abolitionist stance goes beyond simply asserting that "we are not China" or claims that the abolitionist agenda is politically unrealistic, a hopeless fight against "technological determinism," or pure Luddism. Wrongdoers are increasingly using technology to their advantage. The Tor browser that anonymizes internet traffic facilitates child exploitation.[3] End-to-end encryption hides the transactions of drug cartels, fraud conspiracies, ransomware crooks, and the planning and networks of terrorists.[4] Privacy-by-design features that allow users to exert total control over their social media entries and browsing history can stymie the development of investigative leads that are otherwise unattainable.[5] Police, it is argued, need to fight fire with fire.

The pushback might go even further. Technological surveillance is not just a way of keeping the police in the arms-race game. It can also give them an advantage over criminals and thereby improve government's ability to protect citizens. CCTV, ALPR, FRT, geofencing, DNA sleuthing, algorithmic profiling, and records searches can all, at least in theory, vastly enhance government's ability to solve crime and locate criminals. That should not automatically be considered a bad thing, especially when, as is often the case, they visit minimal impact on privacy and autonomy.

The Middle Ground

These competing points of view are difficult to reconcile. Ultimately, this book has argued, any such reconciliation is a job for the democratic process. By enforcing the Fourth Amendment and administrative law principles and, to a lesser extent, the First Amendment and the Equal Protection Clause, courts can establish guardrails. But the legislative branch, which can and should include grass-roots community input, is the entity best equipped to work through whether specific types of virtual searches and search programs should be permitted and, if so, precisely how they should be regulated.

Legislatures sometimes might adopt the abolitionist position. For instance, San Francisco and several other cities have banned facial recognition technology for all or most purposes.[6] Oakland rolled back its version of New York's Domain Awareness System.[7] Various cities have ended their drone programs.[8] Sometimes these decisions were based largely on utilitarian grounds: the programs were simply too expensive, not effective enough, or both. Sometimes they were more heavily influenced by the program's insult to privacy and liberty or its disparate racial impact.[9] Either way, those types of decisions are best made by representative bodies within limits set by the Constitution.

To the extent abolition is not the choice, however, the proportionality principle advanced in this book can inform both judicial oversight of the regulatory regime and the democratic process that produces it. The proportionality analysis developed in these pages can easily be derived from Fourth Amendment case law, in particular decisions such as *Terry, Jones,* and *Carpenter*. But even if the Supreme Court ultimately rejects the broad definition of "search" adopted here and fails to make more explicit the proportionality rationale that underlies many of its Fourth Amendment decisions, proportionality analysis can help representative bodies resolve the tension between the "right of the people to be secure" from government overreach and the fundamental goal of any legitimate government, which is to keep its people secure from harm. More specifically, the proportionality principle addresses that tension by requiring that every government attempt to monitor its citizens be justified—by legislation, an ex ante judicial order, or, in exigent circumstances, ex post judicial analysis—but also by recognizing that this justification should be modulated by the degree of intrusion—as measured through positive law and popular sentiment—that the monitoring occasions. The principle that the level of intrusion determines the level of justification conforms with other fundamental legal principles, such as those underlying our differing standards of proof for criminal, administrative, and civil matters, at the same time it avoids the impractical stance that every digital investigation requires probable cause even before it gets started.

The impact of the proportionality principle varies depending on the type of virtual search at issue. When a policing agency is focused on an identified person as a suspect, the justification required for a virtual search would depend on factors such as the duration of the surveillance, the amount of data sought, and the locus of the search. Casual observation on the street or access to public records should require no more than a legitimate investigatory motive. But targeted surveillance and access to records held by third-party institutions would require a court order based on articulable suspicion, usually at the probable cause level if more than a few days of observation or transactions are sought. However, legislation might vary these requirements based on the types of records at issue, perhaps distinguishing between financial and communications records, on the one hand, and utility and shopping records on the other.

If a policing agency instead wants to access data for the purpose of developing a profile that will help identify places where crime is likely to occur or people who are at risk for committing crime, it should have to show that the profile's hit rate proportionately justifies both the data access necessary to operationalize the profile and any subsequent physical search or seizure that takes place. Additionally, any physical search or seizure based on a quantified prediction should only occur if the police observe conduct that corroborates the crime being predicted. Policing algorithms should be evaluated by an independent entity or a court to ensure they are properly validated and do not rely on obviously biased risk factors. To avoid algorithms that, in effect, merely repeat a history of racialized policing, the development of race-based algorithms or algorithms that avoid using as an outcome measure arrests or convictions for minor crime should be considered. Additionally, police departments should routinely deploy their resources outside of designated hot spots and incorporate data thereby generated into an updated algorithm.

Increasingly, policing agencies are using technology to find perpetrators or eyewitnesses by looking for matches with known characteristics of the crime or the criminal. In such cases, the virtual search should be strictly limited by the time and place of the crime to minimize ensnaring people who are innocent of wrongdoing. Because, so limited, the intrusion is relatively minimal, proportionality analysis would not require police to have probable cause with respect to every individual affected; however, it would require a probable cause showing that the images, biometric information, or other details used in seeking a match are associated with a serious crime. Further, subsequent stops and arrests of those who are a match would be governed by traditional Fourth Amendment doctrine.

If a policing agency seeks to collect data in an effort to carry out the foregoing functions, the resulting databases should be authorized by specific legislation that makes clear the types of data that may be collected and the purpose for which they may be used. Policing agencies implementing this legislation must develop rational policies informed by a notice-and-comment process that encourages community participation. The intrusion associated with mere collection, absent access by a government official, is relatively minimal. However, to avoid both the fact and the appearance of inequity and to minimize abuse, data-acquisition methods should be universal, random, or statistically justifiable, and courts should enforce these rules either through the administrative hard-look doctrine or equal protection analysis. Databases should also be accurate, secure, periodically purged of irrelevant information, and audited to ensure that access occurs only when justified under the foregoing rules.

The rules regarding data collection should also apply to any private entity that the government encourages, through financial or other incentives, to gather information for law enforcement purposes. Even in the absence of such encouragement, private institutions should not disclose incriminating information about those to whom they owe a de facto fiduciary duty unless it is discovered inadvertently or they have good reason to believe it would prevent an ongoing or future serious felony or protect their customers. Private citizens who volunteer information would not be governed by these rules but should be liable in tort if they obtained it through an intrusion that would be offensive to a reasonable person.

The justification required by the intrusion the government seeks should never be lowered simply because the crime being investigated is serious; that would violate proportionality norms. But if the goal is *prevention* of a serious, imminent crime, the usual justification required by proportionality analysis might be relaxed. Conversely, if the crime is minor, virtual searches might be prohibited even if justified on proportionality grounds, both because the degree of intrusion may not be worth the potential impact on privacy, autonomy, and First Amendment values and because of the danger that this authority will be directed unfairly at people of color and people who are disadvantaged.

Holding Police Accountable

These prescriptions are stricter than most of those in existence today. Yet, when I presented a version of them to a large group at a meeting of the Privacy Law Scholars Conference, which is attended largely by privacy devotees, the reaction was mostly negative. Most of these scholars appear to subscribe to abolitionism or the probable-cause-forever position. Perhaps their greatest concern is this book's premise that government is capable of using technology responsibly and that our society is capable of holding government accountable when it does not do so.[10]

That concern must be addressed directly. Without robust enforcement mechanisms, no set of rules is likely to work. Some jurisdictions are already adopting restrictions similar to those proposed here, promulgated by either legislatures or police agencies themselves. But accountability and enforcement have generally been weak. The National Security Agency has frequently violated statutory and regulatory mandates governing national security surveillance.[11] Fusion centers have resisted congressional oversight even while routinely violating civil liberties in collecting information on individuals and groups.[12] Local agencies are often no better. In Baltimore, ALPR records are supposed to be destroyed within 45 days, but often they are not.[13] The Los Angeles Police Department is remarkably lax about its use of public and private data in carrying out its predictive policing program.[14]

This governmental indifference to legal dictates is not due solely to police recalcitrance. It also arises from the fact that virtual searches are covert. Unlike people subjected to physical searches and seizures, the targets of virtual searches may never be aware they have occurred and thus will be unable to challenge them. Further, even if the covert surveillance is discovered, when those affected are innocent and thus not subject to prosecution, seeking redress may not be a priority.

It must also be admitted that, even when sought, the remedies available today often do not have much of a punitive or deterrent effect. If the police violate the Fourth Amendment, the usual sanction has been exclusion of evidence. But even if the Fourth Amendment is construed broadly, exclusion can be sought only by those charged with crime. Many people affected by virtual searches are completely innocent of crime or are never charged. Further, exclusion of evidence does not always have a significant deterrent effect on law enforcement agents;

its impact is felt most directly by prosecutors and only indirectly by police.[15] Damages may be available in some cases, but valuing a privacy insult can be difficult, and under current law both governments and officials have potent defenses to such suits.[16] Injunctions seeking to stop government action are also difficult to obtain unless it can be shown that the action will likely occur repeatedly.[17] Criminal penalties are likewise rare, because an intent to violate the law must be shown beyond a reasonable doubt by prosecutors who are already reluctant to bring cases against law enforcement officials.[18]

Nonetheless, a combination of these remedies, fine-tuned to ensure they work in the virtual search setting,[19] together with notification requirements that keep the public informed and thus enhance democratic oversight, could provide effective accountability. Title III's protective rules governing electronic surveillance are enforced by exclusion, civil and criminal sanctions, and private and public notice requirements.[20] That regime has been effective at preventing widespread abuse of electronic eavesdropping. The same should be possible with other types of covert searches.

The potency of particular accountability mechanisms might vary depending on the type of virtual search at issue. If the virtual search violates the Fourth Amendment, which is most likely to occur with suspect-driven searches, exclusion would of course be an option and would provide at least a modicum of deterrence, over and above the ex ante court order requirement. But because exclusion is available only to those charged with crime, any target of a suspect-driven search, even those targets who are innocent, should also receive notice of the search, as occurs under Title III.[21] That would enable a civil or criminal action to be brought under appropriate circumstances.

Profile-driven searches might be handled somewhat differently. First, anyone who is physically searched or seized should be told if the police action was due, in whole or in part, to a profile, as the ALI's Policing Principles provide.[22] This notice requirement ensures not only that the basis for the stop can be challenged but also that any erroneous information about a particular person fed into the profile can be corrected. Additionally, it ensures that the public finds out about the existence of the profile system. Although all policing algorithms ought to be validated and analyzed for bias in the ways set out in this book, notice to anyone adversely affected by them will provide a backstop against covert use of profiles. If it is discovered that appropriate validation has not occurred, an injunction against its use should be forthcoming.

In contrast to predictive policing, event-driven virtual searches are crime-specific. Thus, in addition to notice about the use of technology to those who are charged based on an event-driven search (who could also avail themselves of the usual Fourth Amendment remedies), notice should be provided to anyone else who is identified during the process. While an alert-based search would require notice about the alert technology only to the persons or persons who were the subject of the alert, every person who is identified through geofencing, partial DNA matching, or use of crime-scene images should be notified of the virtual search. The notice should explain why the search occurred and, for those not arrested, that they are not a suspect; this type of information would provide an impetus to end or limit event-driven techniques that are too wide-ranging. The notification requirement should also influence police when deliberating on the appropriate scope of their event-driven search; in a geofence scenario, for instance, knowing that everyone whose phone is unmasked will be told what the police were up to should deter overbroad law enforcement requests.

The remedies for violation of program-driven virtual searches are different still. An injunction is probably the best method of ending virtual search programs that are not authorized by specific legislation, that are not guided by regulations subject to notice and comment, or that are not implemented evenhandedly. Databases that fail to meet proper accuracy and security requirements might the subject of injunctive relief as well, especially if the Supreme Court follows through on its intimation, recounted in chapter 7, that states must ensure information they gather on their citizens is accurate, not misused, and kept secure. The Court has also signaled that, if database errors are shown to be "routine and widespread," exclusion of evidence in a criminal case could be required.[23] That sanction should apply not only to evidence from databases in the control of the police but also to evidence obtained from databases maintained by surveillance surrogates. Turning technology on the police, a well-functioning audit system could also provide alerts any time a system is accessed by a person without adequate authorization, with penalties assessed if an alert occurs.

The remedy for improper volunteer-driven virtual searches would depend on how independent the searcher is from the government. Many putatively "private" searches are in fact state-encouraged (and the foregoing remedies apply). If not, the tort of intrusion is available, against both individual and institutional vigilantes.

A final "remedy" aimed at promoting transparency, and thus democratic consideration of virtual searches, is to provide the public with statistics on the overall scope of the government's engagement in technological policing. Title III requires annual reports about the number of wiretap orders requested and granted, the number of warrant extensions, the number of people whose conversations were intercepted under each warrant, the proportion of those conversations that disclose incriminating information, and the number of people arrested and convicted in a case in which a Title III warrant was issued.[24] The average cost of each interception is also reported.[25] Similar types of statistics could be reported with respect to suspect-driven virtual searches that require a court order, as well as stops that are based on profiles. With respect to event-driven virtual searches, the average number of people initially subject to each search could be divulged. Finally, consistent with the ALI's Policing Principles, all virtual search program legislation, including legislation approving the use of surveillance surrogates, should require periodic disclosure of the purposes and use of police databases, the number of people in each database, and the extent to which the databases have been accessed, including any violations of access rules.[26]

For those who are not sure government is up to the task of obeying complex surveillance rules even when confronted with exclusion, damages actions, and injunctions, these steps aimed at publicizing virtual searching should provide reassurance. To some extent, ensuring policing accountability is our job, not just the job of courts and other entities. As David Brin, author of *The Transparent Society*, has argued, historically the government has been held accountable "not by blinding the mighty but by insisting that everyone gets to see what they are doing, when citizens demand the power to know."[27] These types of disclosures about virtual searches should give us that power without undermining the ability of the government to see what it needs to see to protect the public effectively.

* * *

On April 24, 2021, three months after the meetings on automated license plate readers recounted in chapter 1, and just hours after the conviction of Derek Chauvin for the murder of George Floyd, the Nashville City Council engaged in what the local paper termed a "fierce" debate over two updated proposals.[28] The narrow proposal allowed ALPRs only on police cars and would permit their use only to recover stolen cars, help in cases involving missing or endangered people, and find people with felony warrants; further, it prohibited retention of ALPR recordings beyond 24 hours unless needed in a criminal case. The more expansive proposal permitted the use of both mobile ALPRs on squad cars and "equitably distributed" ALPRs in fixed locations, which could be used to investigate "any" criminal offense other than infractions associated with driver's licenses, license plates, and car insurance. It also permitted retention of recordings for 30 days, which could be extended if the recordings were relevant to a crime.[29]

The dynamics of the meeting were similar to those observed in the meeting reported in chapter 1. While council members who were against the more expansive proposal were particularly worried about racial profiling, some members of the minority caucus continued to support it. The sponsor of the narrow bill declared that LPRs are "the most powerful [surveillance tool] we've ever considered deploying in Nashville" and that any move in that direction should be done "very cautiously, very carefully, and in a way that leave our options open moving forward." The city's Public Safety chair responded that, if the narrow bill were adopted, "We might as well just say, Nashville's not ready for LPRs."

In the course of the debate, three changes—all accepted by the sponsor—were made to the more expansive bill. First, the city would be prohibited from equipping cameras with facial recognition capacity. Second, ALPR images would be retained for only 10 days, down from a month. And third, access to the ALPR data would be limited to 10 city employees and routinely audited by the Council.[30]

After hours of discourse, the Council decided to vote solely on whether to replace the amended expansive bill with the narrower version. The vote failed, 20–19. And on February 1, 2022, after several other meetings, the Council voted 22–14 to adopt the more expansive version on a pilot basis—a fitting outcome for the kind of difficult issue that should be resolved only through democratic debate.[31]

Notes

Preface

1 University of Chicago Press (2007).

2 Mariana Oliver & Matthew Kugler, *Surveying Surveillance: A National Survey of Police Department Surveillance Technologies*, 54 Ariz. St. L.J. (2022) (surveying 432 departments of all sizes).

1. The Legislative Struggle over Virtual Searches

1 A recording of this meeting is available from the author.

2 Nashville City Ordinance No. BL2020–491.

3 Website, Neighbor to Neighbor, www.n2n.org.

4 Adam Friedman, *Nashville Police Oversight Board Urges Council to Ditch License Plate Reader Bills*, The Tennessean, Dec. 21, 2021.

5 Tenn. Code § 39-13-609 (2019).

6 Brian Haas, *Privacy Advocates Worry About Police Use of Drone Flights*, Tennessean, May 3, 2012, at 3B.

7 Associated Press, *Shelby County Sheriff Wants Two Drone Helicopters*, Tennessean, May 5, 2012, at 2B.

8 2021 Tennessee Laws Pub. Ch. 462 (S.B. 258).

9 The Movement for Black Lives, The Breathe Act (January 25, 2019), https://breatheact.org.

10 S.847—116th Congress (2019–2020): Commercial Facial Recognition Privacy Act of 2019, §§ 3(b) (consent requirement) and e(2) (exempting "security applications"), March 19, 2019, at www.congress.gov.

11 S. 1214—116th Congress (2019–2020): Privacy Bill of Rights Act, April 11, 2019, at www.congress.gov.

12 Section 4(e)(1).

13 U.S. Senator Amy Klobuchar News Releases, *Klobuchar, Murkowski Introduce Legislation to Protect Consumers' Private Health Data* (June 14, 2019), at www.klobuchar.senate.gov.

14 Id.

15 See S. 1842–116th Congress (2019–2020): Protecting Personal Health Data Act, June 13, 2019, § 4(2)(D), at www.congress.gov.

16 Preeti Tuli & Priyanka Sahu, *System Monitoring and Security Using Keylogger*, 2 Int'l J. Computer Sci. & Mobile Computing 106, 107 (2013).

17 Grant Clauser, *Amazon's Alexa Never Stops Listening to You. Should You Worry?*, N.Y. Times: Wirecutter, Aug. 8, 2019, at www.nytimes.com.

18 See 18 U.S.C. § 2581(3)(4)(5) (providing that interception of electronic surveillance requires a warrant; is limited to investigation of certain felonies; must be based not only on a finding of probable cause but also that "normal investigative procedures" have failed; and requiring that the surveillance "shall be conducted in such a way as to minimize the interception of communications not otherwise subject to interception").

19 See Monica C. Bell, *Police Reform and the Dismantling of Legal Estrangement*, 126 Yale L.J. 2054 (2017).

20 U.S. Const. art. 6, cl. 2; *Pacific Gas and Elec. Co. v. State Energy Resources Conservation & Development Comm'n*, 461 U.S. 190, 203–204 (1983).

21 Paul Schwartz, *Preemption and Privacy*, 118 Yale L.J. 902, 913 (2009).

22 Patricia L. Bellia, *Federalization in Information Privacy Law*, 118 Yale L.J. 868, 900 (2009) ("Strong preemption is unproblematic if the resulting regulation strikes the right privacy balance; the real concern is that federal law will be broadly preemptive and will underregulate.").

23 Id. at 894.

24 *Gregory v. Ashcroft*, 501 U.S. 452, 458 (1991) (citations omitted).

25 See Cynthia Lum & Christopher S. Koper, *Evidence-Based Policing: Translating Research into Practice*, 120–124 (2017).

2. Constitutional Constraints

1 See Thomas M. Cooley, *A Treatise on the Constitutional Limitations Which Rest Upon the Legislative Power of the States of the American Union* 303 (1868).

2 *Merriam-Webster Dictionary* (2021) (defining "search" to mean, inter alia, "to look into or over carefully or thoroughly in an effort to find or discover something; to examine in seeking something; to examine a public record or register for information; to look at as if to discover or penetrate intention or nature; to uncover, find, or come to know by inquiry or scrutiny").

3 *Hester v. United States*, 265 U.S. 457 (1924).

4 277 U.S. 432 (1928).

5 316 U.S. 129 (1942).

6 *Silverman v. United States*, 365 U.S. 505 (1961).

7 *McDonald v. United States*, 335 U.S. 451, 454 (1948).

8 389 U.S. 347 (1967).

9 Pet. Br. in *Katz*, at 4–5.

10 *Katz*, 389 U.S. at 351.

11 Id. at 361 (Harlan, J., concurring).

12 See Elizabeth Matthews, *Vast Network of Surveillance Cameras Help Chicago Police Track Subjects*, Fox 32 Chicago (Nov. 12, 2019), at www.fox32chicago.com; Dahleen Glanton, *Being Watched Could be a Good Thing, Even if Done Unequally*, Chicago Tribune (Feb. 26, 2019), at C2.

13 389 U.S. at 351.

14 *United States v. Knotts*, 460 U.S. 276, 281 (1983).

15 *Dow Chemical v. United States*, 476 U.S. 227, 231 (1986) ("Any person with an airplane and an aerial camera could readily duplicate [the EPA's search].")

16 *California v. Ciraolo*, 476 U.S. 207, 211 (1986) ("Yet a 10-foot fence might not shield these plants from the eyes of a citizen or a policeman perched on the top of a truck or a two-level bus.").

17 Jake LaPeruque & David Janovsky, *Project on Government Oversight, These Police Drones Are Watching You* (Sept. 25, 2018), at www.pogo.org.

18 Judge Herbert B. Dixon Jr., *Your Cell Phone Is A Spy!*, American Bar Association, July 29, 2020, at www.americanbar.org.

19 Kashmir Hill, *This Is How Often Your Phone Company Hands Data Over To Law Enforcement*, Forbes, Dec. 10, 2013, at www.forbes.com.

20 565 U.S. 400 (2012).

21 See Federal Trade Commission, *Radio Frequency Identification: Applications and Implications for Consumers* (March 2005), 3, 5; Smithsonian National Air and Space Museum, *How Does GPS Work?*, www.nasm.si.edu.

22 476 U.S. at 238.

23 533 U.S. 27, 40 (2001).

24 See *Florida v. Jardines*, 569 U.S. 1, 12 (2013) (Kagan J., concurring with two others) (opining that using "high-powered binoculars" to look into the home from the front stoop would be a search).

25 *Kitzmiller v. State*, 548 A.2d 140 (Md. 1988); *United States v. Whaley*, 779 F.2d 585 (11th Cir. 1986); *People v. Ferguson*, 365 N.E.2d 77 (Ill. App. Ct. 1977); *People v. Hicks*, 364 N.E.2d 440 (Ill. App. Ct. 1977); *State v. Littleton*, 407 So.2d 1208 (La. 1981); *State v. Thompson*, 241 N.W.2d 511 (Neb. 1976); *State v. Louis*, 672 P.2d 708 (Or. 1983).

26 533 U.S. at 36.

27 *Illinois v. Caballes*, 543 U.S. 405, 408 (2005) (citing *United States v. Jacobsen*, 466 U.S. 109, 123 (1984)).

28 569 U.S. 1, 11–12 (2013).

29 425 U.S. 435 (1976).

30 Id. at 443 (citations omitted).

31 See *Lewis v. United States*, 385 U.S. 206 (1966) (Fourth Amendment not implicated when undercover agent posed as a potential buyer of marijuana and was admitted into Lewis's home to consummate the deal); *Hoffa v. United States*, 385 U.S. 293 (1966) (Fourth Amendment not implicated when business

colleague of Hoffa was asked by agents to report any statements Hoffa made about jury tampering).

32 442 U.S. 735 (1979).

33 Id. at 743.

34 389 U.S. at 511 (noting that Katz was seeking to exclude information obtained by the "uninvited ear")

35 Arne Holst, *Amount of Data Created, Consumed, and Stored, 2010–2025*, Statista, June 7, 2021, at www.statista.com.

36 Jeffrey W. Seifert, *Data Mining and Homeland Security: An Overview*, Congressional Research Service, Jan. 18, 2007, at www.fas.org.

37 See Daniel J. Solove, *Digital Dossiers and the Dissipation of Fourth Amendment Privacy*, 75 S.Cal. L. Rev. 1083 (2003).

38 Tr. of Oral Arg. in *United States v. Jones*, No. 10–1259, p. 9–10 (emphasis in original).

39 138 S.Ct. 2206 (2018).

40 Id. at 2219.

41 Id. at 2220.

42 *United States v. Jones*, 565 U.S. 400, 431 (2012) (Alito, J., concurring).

43 Id. at 416 (Sotomayor, J., concurring).

44 See *United States v. Miller*, 425 U.S. 435 (1976) (Brennan, J., dissenting) (citing *Burrows v. Superior Court*, 13 Cal.3d 238 (1974)).

45 Although Justice Gorsuch, in his one-person dissent, did suggest that Carpenter could have won on an "involuntary bailment" theory if he had raised it, *Carpenter*, 138 S.Ct. at 2270 (Gorsuch, J., dissenting), a point discussed further below.

46 Id. at 2229 (Kennedy, J., dissenting).

47 Id. at 2247 (Alito, J., dissenting) ("Unless it is somehow restricted to the particular situation in the present case, the Court's move will cause upheaval. Must every grand jury subpoena duces tecum be supported by probable cause? If so, investigations of terrorism, political corruption, white-collar crime, and many other offenses will be stymied.").

48 *How to Track a Cell Phone Location Without Them Knowing*, Spyic, June 30, 2019, at https://spyic.com.

49 For a sampling on the scholarship, see Christopher Slobogin, *A Defense of Privacy as the Central Value Protected by the Fourth Amendment's Prohibition on Unreasonable Searches*, 48 Texas Tech L. Rev. 153, 148–157 (2015).

50 *Carpenter*, 138 S.Ct. at 2262 (Gorsuch, J., dissenting).

51 Id. at 2263.

52 Id. at 2264.

53 Id. at 2267.

54 Id. at 2264.

55 Id. at 2257.

56 See Slobogin, *Defense of Privacy*, supra note 49.

57 *Jones*, 565 U.S. at 424–425 (Alito, J., concurring).

58 Michael Heller & James Saltzman, *Mine! How the Hidden Rules of Ownership Control Our Lives* 7 (2021).

59 Id. at 15.

60 See Jeffrey Bellin, *Fourth Amendment Textualism*, 118 Mich. L. Rev. 233, 254–60 (2020) (making this point).

61 565 U.S. at 404 (emphasis added).

62 See Judith Resnick & Julie Chi-hye Suk, *Adding Insult to Injury: Questioning the Role of Dignity in Conceptions of Sovereignty*, 55 Stanford L. Rev. 1921, 1935 (2003) (finding dignity mentioned in the Supreme Court's Eighth Amendment and Fourth Amendment cases, Fourteenth and Fifteenth Amendment discrimination cases, and Ninth and Fourteenth Amendment right to procreative choice cases).

63 *Katz*, 389 U.S. at 361.

64 Anthony Amsterdam, *Perspectives on the Fourth Amendment*, 58 Minn. L. Rev. 349, 384, 407 (1974).

65 See Christopher Slobogin, *Making the Most of* United States v. Jones *in a Surveillance Society: A Statutory Implementation of Mosaic Theory*, 8 Duke J. Const'al L. & Pub. Pol'y 1, 17–18 (2012); Bellin, *Fourth Amendment Textualism*, supra note 60, at 254–60 (although also emphasizing that a search must be of a person, house, paper, or effect to implicate the Fourth Amendment); Daniel J. Solove, *Fourth Amendment Pragmatism*, 51 B.C. L. Rev. 1511, 1524 (2010).

66 *Johnson v. United States*, 333 U.S. 10, 14 (1948).

67 Richard Van Duizend, L. Paul Sutton & Charlotte A. Carter, *The Search Warrant Process: Preconceptions, Perceptions and Practices* 148–149 (National Center for State Courts, 1985).

68 William J. Stuntz, *Warrants and Fourth Amendment Remedies*, 77 Va. L. Rev. 881, 910–918 (1991).

69 Van Duizend et al., *The Search Warrant Process*, supra note 67, at 85–87 (noting the practice as far back as the early 1980s). See Fed.R.Crim.P. 41(c)(2).

70 *Missouri v. McNeely*, 569 U.S. 141, 154–55 (2013) (making this observation in a case in which a warrantless draw of the defendant's blood occurred 25 minutes after his arrest).

71 *Illinois v. Gates*, 462 U.S. 213, 238–239 (1983).

72 *Brinegar v. United States*, 388 U.S. 160, 171 (1949).

73 Id. at 175.

74 For an overview of these exceptions, see chapter 4 of Christopher Slobogin, *Advanced Introduction to U.S. Criminal Procedure* 54–86 (2020). More detail about the exceptions is provided in this book when relevant to virtual searches.

3. Proportionality Analysis

1 Emily Riley, *Privacy Experts: Sensor Devices Threaten "New Age of Excessive Police Surveillance,"* The Crime Report, Feb. 3, 2021, at https://thecrimereport.org.

2 Alfred McCoy, *Surveillance Blowback: The Making of the US Surveillance State, 1898–2020,* Truthout, July 15, 2013, at http://truth-out.rg.

3 See, e.g., Nat'l Ass'n Crim. Defense Lawyers, *Garbage In, Garbage Out: How Data-Driven Police Technologies Entrench Historic Racism and "Tech-Wash" in the Criminal Legal System* 63 (2021) (arguing that "surveillance technologies . . . should never be used," but recommending several limitations if they are used).

4 Orin Kerr, *An Equilibrium-Adjustment Theory of the Fourth Amendment,* 125 Harvard L. Rev. 476, 480 (2011) ("When changing technology or social practice makes evidence substantially harder for the government to obtain, the Supreme Court generally adopts lower Fourth Amendment protections for these new circumstances to help restore the status quo ante level of government. On the other hand, when changing technology or social practice makes evidence substantially easier for the government to obtain, the Supreme Court often embraces higher protections to help restore the prior level of privacy protection.").

5 *Carpenter,* 138 S.Ct. at 2218.

6 Ric Simmons, *Smart Surveillance: How to Interpret the Fourth Amendment in the Twenty-First Century* 161 (2019).

7 Shima Baradaran Baughman, *Crime and the Mythology of the Police,* 99 Wash. U. L. Rev. 65, 116 (2021).

8 Id. at 49 n. 236.

9 387 U.S. 523 (1967).

10 392 U.S. 1 (1968).

11 Id. at 30.

12 Id. at 31 (Harlan, J., concurring). While this phrase came from a concurring opinion, it describes the majority's view, which required "specific reasonable inferences which [the officer] is entitled to draw from the facts in light of his experience"). Id. at 27.

13 *Camara,* 387 U.S. at 537–38.

14 Christopher Slobogin, *Privacy at Risk: The New Government Surveillance and the Fourth Amendment,* ch. 2 (2007).

15 Id. at 30.

16 See Christopher Slobogin, *Advanced Introduction to U.S. Criminal Procedure* § 4.5 (2020).

17 *New Jersey v. T.L.O.,* 469 U.S. 325, 340 (1985).

18 *United States v. Knotts,* 460 U.S. 276, 285 (1983).

19 Id. at 287 (Stevens, J., joined by Brennan, J. and Marshall, J., concurring).

20 *United States v. Miller*, 425 U.S. 435, 447, 455 (1976) (Brennan, J., dissenting), (Marshall, J., dissenting).

21 Id. at 450 (Brennan, J., dissenting) (emphasis added).

22 *United States v. Jones*, 565 U.S. 400, 430–31 (2012) (Alito, J., concurring) ("[R]elatively short-term monitoring of a person's movements on public streets accords with expectations of privacy that our society has recognized as reasonable. But the use of longer term GPS monitoring in investigations of most offenses impinges on expectations of privacy") (citations omitted).

23 Id. at 416 (Sotomayor, J., concurring) ("I would ask whether people reasonably expect that their movements will be recorded and aggregated in a manner that enables the government to ascertain, more or less at will, their political and religious beliefs, sexual habits, and so on.").

24 Id. at 430 n. 11 (Alito, J., concurring).

25 575 U.S. 373 (2014).

26 Id. at 393.

27 Slobogin, *Privacy at Risk*, supra note 14, at 44–45.

28 Id. at 39.

29 See, e.g., *Illinois v. Gates*, 462 U.S. 213, 239 (1983).

30 American Bar Association, *Standards for Criminal Justice: Electronic Surveillance: Technologically-Assisted Physical Surveillance* (3d ed. 1999) at www.americanbar.org.

31 American Bar Association, *Standards for Criminal Justice: Law Enforcement Access to Third Party Records*, stds. 25–4.1, 25–5.2 & 25–5.3 (3d ed. 2013), at www.americanbar.org.

32 American Law Institute, *Principles of Policing*, § 3.02(b)(1).

33 Compare 18 U.S.C. § 2518(3) (real-time interception of content of communications); 18 U.S. § 2703(a), (b)(1)(B) (stored communications); 18 U.S.C. § 2703(d) (subscriber information); 18 U.S.C. § 3123(a)(1) (real-time interception of envelope information).

34 See David J. Roberts & Meghann Casanova, *Automated License Plate Recognition Systems: Policy and Operational Guidance for Law Enforcement*, U.S. Department of Justice, National Institute of Justice (2012).

35 Jones, 565 U.S. at 429 (Alito, J., concurring).

36 Orin Kerr, *The Fourth Amendment and New Technologies: Constitutional Myths and the Case for Caution*, 102 Mich. L. Rev 801 (2004).

37 Id. at 861.

38 Id. at 871–73.

39 Akhil Amar, *Fourth Amendment First Principles*, 107 Harv. L. Rev. 757, 599 (1995) ("Judges do not like excluding bloody knives, so they distort doctrine, claiming the Fourth Amendment was not really violated.")

40 John Rappaport, *Second-Order Regulation of Law Enforcement*, 103 Cal. L. Rev. 205, 237–43 (2015).

41 Daniel J. Solove, *Fourth Amendment Codification and Professor Kerr's Misguided Call for Judicial Deference*, 74 Fordham L. Rev. 747, 771–772 (2005).

42 Id. at 770–771.

43 Id. at 763–765.

44 Peter P. Swire, Katz *Is Dead, Long Live* Katz, 102 Mich. L. Rev. 904, 914 (2004).

45 Erin Murphy, *The Politics of Privacy in the Criminal Justice System: Information Disclosure, the Fourth Amendment, and Statutory Law Enforcement Exemptions*, 111 Mich. L. Rev. 485, 536 (2013).

46 Numerous scholars have described this dynamic in other areas of law. See, e.g., Erik Luna, *Constitutional Roadmaps*, 90 J. Crim. L. & Criminol. 1125, 1127 (2000) (discussing how, and advocating for, decisions in which the Supreme Court "offers a 'road map' for lawmakers to following in creating a constitutional statute").

47 Solove, *Fourth Amendment Codification*, supra note 41, at 775.

48 Erin Murphy & Peter P. Swire, *How to Address Standardless Discretion After* Jones, http://ssrn.com.

49 Id.

50 Alan Westin, *Privacy and Freedom* 7, 31 (1967).

51 Daniel J. Solove, *Conceptualizing Privacy*, 90 Calif. L. Rev. 1087, 1092 (2002).

52 David Alan Sklansky, *Too Much Information: How Not to Think About Privacy and the Fourth Amendment*, 102 Cal. L. Rev. 1069, 1113 (2014).

53 In addition to the problems in the text, one might point to the fact that positive law differs from state to state and thus will result in inconsistent Fourth Amendment protection. However, it is not clear that this consequence is a bad one, from either a constitutional or policy perspective. See Michael Mannheimer, *The Fourth Amendment: Original Understandings and Modern Policing* (forthcoming, U. Mich. Press, 2022) (arguing, based on colonial and Civil War history, that the Fourth and Fourteenth Amendments were meant to give the primary power of defining the law of searches to the states).

54 Richard Re, *The Positive Law Floor*, 129 Harv. L. Rev. Forum 313, 314 (2016).

55 Id. at 322.

56 Id. at 332.

57 The first survey was reported in Christopher Slobogin & Joseph Schumacher, *Reasonable Expectations of Privacy and Autonomy in Fourth Amendment Cases: An Empirical Look at Understandings Recognized and Permitted by Society*, 42 Duke L.J. 727 (1993) (hereafter Duke); see also, Christopher Slobogin, *Public Privacy: Camera Surveillance of Public Places and the Right to Anonymity*, 72 Miss. L.J. 213 (2002) (hereafter Mississippi); Christopher Slobogin, *Government Data Mining and the Fourth Amendment*, 75 U. Chi. L. Rev. 317 (2008) (hereafter Chicago).

58 Duke, supra note 57, at 737–738 (Table 1).

59 Chicago, supra note 57, at 335.

60 Duke, supra note 57, at 737–738 (Table 1).

61 Id.

62 See id. (ranking patdown 54.7 on a 100-point scale and 19th out of 50 scenarios, and perusal of bank records 71.6 and 38th); Chicago, supra note 57, at 335 (ranking patdown 71.5 and 16th out of 25 scenarios, and bank records 80.3, 24th out of 25 scenarios).

63 Jeremy A. Blumenthal et al., *The Multiple Dimensions of Privacy: Testing Law Expectations of Privacy*, 11 U. Pa. J. Const. L. 331, 345 (2009) ("Our subjects' intrusiveness ratings are quite consistent with [Slobogin's and Schumacher's] results; each of our samples correlated highly with their overall data.").

64 Henry Fradella et al., *Quantifying Katz: Empirically Measuring "Reasonable Expectations of Privacy" in the Fourth Amendment*, 38 Am. J. Crim. L. 289, 294 (2011).

65 Christine S. Scott-Hayward, Henry F. Fradella & Ryan G. Fischer, *Does Privacy Require Secrecy? Societal Expectations in the Digital Age*, 43 Am. J. Crim. L. 19, 49–58 (2015).

66 Bernard Chao et al., *Why Courts Fail to Protect Privacy: Race, Age, Bias and Technology*, 106 Calif. L. Rev. 263 (2018).

67 Matthew Kugler & Lior Strahilevitz, *Actual Expectations of Privacy, Fourth Amendment Doctrine and the Mosaic Theory*, 2015 S.Ct. Rev. 4 (2016).

68 Marc McAllister, *The Fourth Amendment and New Technologies: The Misapplication of Analogical Reasoning*, 36 S.Ill. U.L.J. 475 (2012); Emma Marshall et al., *Police Surveillance of Cellphone Location Data: The Supreme Court v. Public Opinion*, 37 Beh. Sci. & L. 751 (2019).

69 See, e.g., Chao et al., *Why Courts Fail to Protect Privacy*, supra note 66, at 295 (using my intrusiveness scale but also asking the expectation of privacy question).

70 I reported these results in Christopher Slobogin, *Proportionality, Privacy and Public Opinion: A Reply to Kerr and Swire*, 94 Minn. L. Rev. 1558. 1595 (2010), where I noted there were "well over 200" such opinions; I've now updated that count through the 2020–2021 Term.

71 Chao, *Why Courts Fail to Protect Privacy*, supra note 66, at 300, tbl. 2 (showing survey findings equating a pat-down to "police obtaining data from a website operator that reflects the name, email address, telephone number, and physical address you entered when you opened an account on the website").

72 Id. (showing survey findings that tracking on *Jones* facts was more intrusive than searching a bedroom); Kugler & Strahilevitz, *Actual Expectations of Privacy*, supra note 67, at 246–47 ("People were more inclined to say that a person's reasonable expectation of privacy is violated by month-long tracking than by week-long, more by weeklong than day-long, and more by day-long than instantaneous."); Scott-Hayward et al., *Does Privacy Require Secrecy*, supra note 65, at 54 (results showing "very modest support for the Mosaic Theory").

Unfortunately, the latter two surveys did not ask about relative intrusiveness, only threshold questions about whether expectations of privacy were infringed or whether "probable cause" should be required; these are questions the courts, not survey participants, should be asking.

73 Chao, *Why Courts Fail to Protect Privacy,* supra note 66, at 300, tbl. 2; Fradella et al., *Quantifying* Katz, supra note 64, at 366.

74 Chao, *Why Courts Fail to Protect Privacy,* supra note 66, at 300, tbl. 2; Fradella et al., *Quantifying* Katz, supra note 64, at 365.

75 5 U.S. 137 (1803).

76 This phrase first appeared in *West Virginia State Bd. Educ. v. Barnette,* 319 U.S. 624, 638 (1943) ("One's right to life, liberty, and property, to free speech, a free press, freedom of worship and assembly, and other fundamental rights may not be submitted to vote; they depend on the outcome of no elections.").

77 *Trop v. Dulles,* 356 U.S. 86, 101 (1958).

78 Robert C. Post, *Three Concepts of Privacy,* 89 Geo. L.J. 2086, 2092 (2001).

79 Id. at 2094.

80 David L. Faigman, *Constitutional Fictions: A Unified Theory of Constitutional Facts* 18 (2008).

81 See, e.g., *Stanford v. Kentucky,* 492 U.S. 361, 379 (1989) (Scalia, J.) ("[t]o say, as the dissent says, that 'it is for us ultimately to judge whether the Eighth Amendment permits imposition of the death penalty,' . . . to say and mean that, is to replace judges of the law with a committee of philosopher-kings").

82 138 S.Ct. at 2218.

83 *Valador, Inc. v. HTC Corporation,* 242 F.Supp.3d 448, 455 (2017) ("Consumer surveys are generally admissible in trademark infringement cases"); *State v. Williams,* 598 N.E.2d 1250 (Ohio, 1991) ("opinion polls and surveys may be relevant and, thus, admissible on the question whether a work is obscene so long as the poll or survey is properly conducted"); *Applera Corp. v. MJ Research Inc.,* 389 F.Supp.2d 344, 350–351 (D. Conn. 2005) (using survey data from customers to establish induced patent infringement).

84 American Bar Association Standards for Criminal Justice, *Law Enforcement Access to Third Party Records* § 25–4.1 (2013). A fourth factor is the extent to which "existing law, including the law of privilege, restricts or allows access to and dissemination of such information or of comparable information."

85 Paul Ohm, *The Many Revolutions of* Carpenter, 32 Harv. J. L. & Tech. 357, 369–83 (2019).

86 Matthew Tokson, *Inescapable Surveillance,* 106 Cornell L. Rev. 409, 425–439 (2021). While *Carpenter* can also be said to adopt the inescapability factor, given its statement that "carrying [a cell phone] is indispensable to participation in modern society," 138 S.Ct. at 2220, the principal reason for this language was to undercut the government's assertion that CSLI is "voluntarily" disclosed to the common carrier. See id. ("in no meaningful sense does the user voluntarily

'assume[ ] the risk' of turning over a comprehensive dossier of his physical movements."). That point holds true whether or not use of a cell phone is "inescapable."

87 338 U.S. 632 (1950)

88 Id. at 652.

89 50 U.S.C. 50 § 1861(d)(1).

90 18 U.S.C. § 2703(c)(d).

91 See, e.g., Right to Financial Privacy Act, 12 U.S.C. § 3409; 18 U.S.C. § 2703(b)(1) (B).

92 *Hale v. Henkel*, 201 U.S. 43, 75–76 (1906).

93 530 U.S. 27 (2000).

94 Id. at 42.

95 392 U.S. at 17.

96 Id. at 27.

97 18 U.S.C. § 2703(d).

98 See Christopher Slobogin, *Cause to Believe What?: The Importance of Defining a Search's Object, or, How the ABA Would Analyze the NSA Phone Metadata Surveillance Program*, 66 Okla. L. Rev. 725, 727 (2014) ("probable cause to believe that a search might lead to evidence of wrongdoing triggers a very different inquiry than probable cause to believe that a search will produce evidence of criminal activity").

99 One former magistrate believes that "there is really not that much difference between a 2703(d) specific and articulable facts standard and Rule 41 probable cause . . . Provider legal response teams have told me they see little discernible difference between the pre-*Carpenter* '(d)' order applications for CSLI and the post-*Carpenter* Rule 41 applications for the same data." Email to author from Stephen Smith, April 4, 2021.

100 *Safford Unified School District No. 1 v. Redding*, 557 U.S. 365, 371 (2009).

101 *Illinois v. Gates*, 462 U.S. 213, 239, 236 (1983).

102 William J. Stuntz, *Warrants and Fourth Amendment Remedies*, 77 Va. L. Rev. 881 (1991).

103 Id. at 911–913.

104 The "mere evidence" nomenclature comes from *Gouled v. United States*, 255 U.S. 298, 309 (1921).

105 See *Boyd v. United States*, 116 U.S. 616 (1886) (holding that the Fourth and Fifth Amendments, acting together, prohibited seizure of private papers).

106 387 U.S. 294 (1967).

107 Id. at 302.

108 See, e.g., *Messerschmidt v. Millender*, 565 U.S. 535 (2012) (upholding search of a third party's home for gang insignia in a domestic assault case).

109 I develop these points further in Christopher Slobogin, *Cause to Believe What?*, supra note 98.

110 470 U.S. 753 (1985).

111 Id. at 763 n. 6 ("Because the State has afforded respondent the benefit of a full adversary presentation and appellate review, we do not reach the question whether the State may compel a suspect to undergo a surgical search of this magnitude for evidence absent such special procedural protections.").

112 388 U.S. 41 (1967).

113 Id. at 60.

114 18 U.S.C. § 2518(5).

115 Duke, supra note 57, at 738, tbl. 1 (reporting survey results finding that "monitoring a phone for 30 days" and "body cavity search at the border" were the 49th and 50th most intrusive scenarios out of 50 scenarios); Blumenthal et al., *The Multiple Dimensions of Privacy*, supra note 63, at 355, tbl. 1 (reporting survey finding the same scenarios 44th and 45th out of the same 50 scenarios).

116 138 S.Ct. at 2247 (Alito, J., dissenting).

117 565 U.S. at 431 (Alito, J., concurring).

118 See Simmons, *Smart Surveillance*, supra note 6, at 31 ("the more severe the crime that is being investigated, the greater the societal benefit of the surveillance"); Jeffrey Bellin, *Crime Severity Distinctions and the Fourth Amendment: Reassessing Reasonableness in a Changing World*, 97 Iowa L. Rev. 1 (2011); Orin Kerr, *Do We Need a New Fourth Amendment?*, 107 Mich. L. Rev. 951, 962–963 (2009).

119 437 U.S. 385 (1978).

120 Id. at 393 (citing *Chimel v. California*, 395 U.S. 752, 766 (1969)).

121 Id.

122 See Yale Kamisar, *Comparative Reprehensibility and the Fourth Amendment Exclusionary Rule*, 86 Mich. L. Rev. 1, 20–29 (1987).

123 *In re Winship*, 397 U.S. 358 (1970).

124 466 U.S. 740 (1984).

125 Id. at 753.

126 141 S.Ct. 2011 (2021).

127 Id. at 2020.

128 See, e.g., 18 U.S.C. § 2516(1) (2) (limiting federal surveillance to "any Federal felony" and state surveillance to designated felonies and "other crime dangerous to life, limb, or property" punishable by more than one year); 50 U.S.C. § 1861(a)(1) (authorizing access to business records to investigate "international terrorism or clandestine intelligence activities").

129 392 U.S. at 27.

130 See, e.g., *Brigham v. Stuart*, 547 U.S. 398, 406 (2006) (permitting warrantless entry into a home when there is an "objectively reasonable basis" to believe an assault is imminent); *Maryland v. Buie*, 494 U.S. 325, 336–37 (1990) (permitting a protective sweep of premises upon reasonable suspicion that a confederate is on the premises).

131 *Addington v. Texas*, 441 U.S. 418, 433 (1979); *United States v. Salerno*, 481 U.S. 739, 751 (1987).

132 See President Barack Obama, Speech at the United States Department of Justice (Jan. 17, 2014), at www.nytimes.com (stating that "[e]ffective immediately" NSA officials would pursue calls only two steps removed from the seed identifier and indicating that the NSA would have to confirm the seed identifier with the FISC).

133 201 U.S. 43 (1906).

134 Id. at 70.

135 Id.

136 *Parks v. F.D.I.C.*, 65 F.3d 207, 218 (1995) (Selya, J., dissenting).

137 ABA Standards, supra note 84, at § 25–4.2(b).

138 As evidenced by *Zurcher v. Stanford Daily*, 436 U.S. 547 (1978) (holding that a warrant is sufficient authorization to search a newspaper's office for photographic evidence of crime committed by a third party).

139 475 U.S. 868 (1986).

140 Id. at 875.

141 I dive into detail on these matters in Slobogin, *Privacy at Risk*, supra note 14, at 98–106.

142 See e.g., 18 U.S.C. § 2709 (authorizing access to telephone toll and transactions records "provided that such an investigation of a United States person is not conducted solely upon the basis of activities protected by the first amendment to the Constitution of the United States."); 50 U.S.C. § 1861(a)(1) (same re metadata collection).

143 See Blumenthal, *The Multiple Dimensions of Privacy*, supra note 63, at 358 (reporting that survey participants found search of a diary to be the most intrusive out of 47 scenarios).

144 See generally The Slaughterhouse Cases, 83 U.S. 36, 81 (1872) ("The existence of laws in the States where the newly emancipated negroes resided, which discriminated with gross injustice and hardship against them as a class, was the evil to be remedied by this [equal protection] clause, and by it such laws are forbidden.").

145 Movement for Black Lives, The Breathe Act, https://breatheact.org.

146 See *Washington v. Davis*, 426 U.S. 229, 239 (1976) ("[O]ur cases have not embraced the proposition that a law or other official act, without regard to whether it reflects a racially discriminatory purpose, is unconstitutional solely because it has a racially disproportionate impact.").

147 William M. Carter, Jr., Whren's *Flawed Assumptions about Race, History and Unconscious Bias*, 66 Case Western L. Rev. 947, 954 (2016) (stating that "the promise of serious equal protection review of racially motivated pretextual searches and seizures has . . . proved hollow").

148 Sarah Elbeshbishi & Mabinty Quarshie, *Fewer Than One in Five Support "Defund the Police Movement," USA Today Poll Shows*, USA Today (Mar 8, 2021), at www.usatoday.com (survey finding that only 28% of Blacks were in favor of defunding the police); Ibrahim Hursi, *Black Residents of Minneapolis Say They Need More Cops—Not Fewer*, The Nation (Sept. 30, 2021), www. thenation.com.

4. Suspect-Driven Virtual Searches

1 *United States v. Jones*, 565 U.S. 400, 402 (2012); See Brief for the United States, *4.

2 Defendant's Motion in Limine to Exclude the Expert Testimony and Cellular Analysis Report of FBI Special Agent Scott Eicher, 2013 WL 1150165 at 2.

3 Brief for the United States, *United States v. Jones*, *34–35.

4 Brief for Respondent, *6.

5 Brief for the United States, *United States v. Jones*, *4.

6 William H. Rehnquist, *Is an Expanded Right of Privacy Consistent with Fair and Effective Law Enforcement? Or: Privacy, You've Come a Long Way, Baby*, 23 Kan. L. Rev. 1, 9 (1974).

7 Christopher Slobogin: *Camera Surveillance of Public Places and the Right to Anonymity*, 72 Miss. L.J. 213, 277, tbl. 1 (2002).

8 *Florida v. Riley*, 488 U.S. 445 (1989) (helicopter hover not a search); *Michigan v. Chesternut*, 486 U.S. 567 (1988) (police chase not a seizure); *California v. Greenwood*, 486 U.S. 35 (1988) (going through garbage not a search).

9 Slobogin, *Camera Surveillance*, supra note 7, at 277.

10 See *United States v. Martinez-Fuerte*, 428 U.S. 543, 556, 558 (1976) (holding that "checkpoint stops are 'seizures' within the meaning of the Fourth Amendment," but going on to hold that a brief initial stop at a checkpoint set up to detect illegal immigrants miles from the border need not be based on reasonable suspicion); *Edmond v. City of Indianapolis*, 531 U.S. 32, 47 (2000) (holding that stops at a checkpoints set up for the purpose of "crime control" (i.e., narcotics interdiction) "can only be justified by some quantum of individualized suspicion").

11 *People v. Tafoya* (Colo. 2021) (three-month camera surveillance of backyard a search); *United States v. Cuevas-Sanchez*, 841 F.2d 248, 251 (5th Cir. 1987); *United States v. Houston*, 965 F.Supp.2d. 855, 871 (2013). Most, however, are not. See *United States v. Tuggle*, F.3d (7th Cir. 2021) (summarizing caselaw).

12 442 U.S. 735 (1979).

13 *Carpenter*, 138 S.Ct. at 2219.

14 Christopher Slobogin, *Government Data Mining and the Fourth Amendment*, 75 U. Chicago L. Rev. 317, 335 (Table) (2008).

15 See, e.g., Matthew Kugler & Lior Strahilevitz, *Actual Expectations of Privacy, Fourth Amendment Doctrine and Mosaic Theory*, 2015 Sup. Ct. Rev. 205, 246

(finding a majority of those surveyed believed tracking violated "people's reasonable expectations of privacy").

16 Slobogin, *Camera Surveillance*, supra note 7, at 277 (finding that tracking for three days—a mean intrusiveness rating of 63—was viewed as more intrusive than short-term tracking—a mean of 50). Kugler and Strahilevitz, *Actual Expectations of Privacy*, supra note 15, found that only about 16% of subjects differentiated between tracking for different lengths of time. Id., at 247. However, they asked their participants an either/or question (Does tracking violate expectations of privacy?) rather than a relative one, as I did.

17 *United States v. Maynard*, 615 F.3d 544, 562 (D.C. Cir. 2010). See also *State v. Zahn*, 812 N.W.2d 490, 497–98 (S.D. 2012) (adopting the mosaic theory and holding that 26 days of warrantless GPS vehicle tracking violated reasonable expectations of privacy).

18 For a summary, see *United States v. Howard*, 426 F.Supp.3d 1247, 1256 (M.D. Ala. 2019).

19 *United States v. Graham*, 846 F.Supp.2d 384, 402 (D. Md. 2012).

20 18 U.S.C. § 2518.

21 *United States v. Williams*, 737 F.2d 594, 601 (7th Cir. 1984). The court continued: "The authorizing judge must be sufficiently informed about the results of the prior interceptions to answer intelligently the question whether probable cause exists to believe relevant conversations will be intercepted in the future. Accordingly, [Title III] requires that the extension application contain a statement of results previously obtained, or an explanation of the failure to obtain results"; see also *United States v. Glover*, 681 F.3d 411, 420 (D.C. Cir. 2012) (before granting an extension order, court must find surveillance continues to be necessary).

22 Fed. R. Crim. P. 41(e)(2)(C).

23 18 U.S.C. 3123(c).

24 500 U.S. 44 (1991).

25 Id. at 57.

26 Id. at 55–56.

27 Id. at 56.

28 The county policy in question in Riverside required review within 48 hours, unless a weekend or holiday interceded. It was the weekend/holiday exception that the Court held was unconstitutional.

29 *Miller*, 425 U.S. 435, 450 (Brennan, J., dissenting).

30 138 S.Ct. at 2212.

31 Id. at 2210.

32 Bernard Chao et al., *Why Courts Fail to Protect Privacy: Race, Age, Bias and Technology*, 106 Calif. L. Rev. 263, 300, tbl. 2 (2018); Slobogin & Schumacher, *Reasonable Expectations of Privacy and Autonomy in Fourth Amendment Cases: An Empirical Look at "Understandings Recognized and Permitted by Society,"* 42

Duke L.J. 727, 738, tbl. 1 (1991); Rachel Adler, *What Metadata Reveals About You*, The Century Foundation, July 21, 2016, at https://tcf.org.

33 Id. at 2232 (Kennedy, J., dissenting) (citations omitted).

34 Id. at 2247 (Alito, J., dissenting).

35 Paul Ohm, *Probably Probable Cause: The Diminishing Importance of Justification Standards*, 94 Minn. L. Rev. 1514, 1515 (2010) ("In increasingly common situations, whenever the police have any suspicion at all about a piece of evidence, they almost always have probable cause and can meet the highest level of justification."); see also comments of former federal magistrate Stephen Smith, note 99 of chapter 3.

36 Slobogin, *Government Data Mining*, supra note 14, at 335, Table (corporate records—40.6—were ranked between criminal records—36.2—and real estate records—45.5—and well below utility records—57.5—high school records—58.3—and phone records—74.1).

37 *Hale v. Henkel*, 201 U.S. 43, 74 (1906) (overruled in part by *Murphy v. Waterfront Com'n of New York Harbor*, 378 U.S. 52 (1964)).

38 *SEC v. Vacuum Can Co.*, 157 F.2d 530, 532 (7th Cir. 1946).

39 338 U.S. 632, 652 (1950).

40 See Christopher Slobogin, *Subpoenas and Privacy*, 54 DePaul L. Rev. 805, 817–822 (2005) (replicated and updated in chapter 6 in *Privacy at Risk*).

41 138 S.Ct. at 2222.

42 Id. at 2221.

43 Id. at 2222.

44 See Slobogin, *Subpoenas and Privacy*, supra note 40, at 841 (parsing Supreme Court case law regarding the Fifth Amendment's application to corporations, partnerships, labor unions, and sole proprietorships).

45 See, e.g., Zoey Chung, *FBI Tried to Break into 6,900 Phones—and Failed*, CNN, Oct. 23, 2017,

46 James B. Comey, *Going Dark: Are Technology, Privacy, and Public Safety on a Collision Course?*, Oct. 16, 2014, www.fbi.gov.

47 *Fisher v. United States*, 425 U.S. 391, 408 (1976) (the Fifth Amendment "applies only when the accused is compelled to make a Testimonial Communication that is incriminating").

48 *United States v. Apple Macpro Computer et al.*, 851 F.3d 238, 247 (3d Cir. 2017).

49 Eric Lichtblau, *Judge Tells Apple to Help Unlock iPhone Used by San Bernadino Gunman*, N.Y. Times, Feb. 16, 2016.

50 Eric Lichtblau, *In Apple Debate on Digital Privacy and iPhone, Questions Still Remain*, N.Y. Times, Mar. 28, 2016.

51 28 U.S.C. § 1651.

52 *United States v. N.Y. Tel. Co.*, 434 U.S. 159, 172 (1977).

53 Joe Palazzolo, *Apple Tells Judge It Can't Unlock Phones*, Wall. St. J. Oct. 20, 2015 (quoting filing submitted by Apple to a federal magistrate stating that "[a]mong

the security features in iOS 8 is a feature that prevents anyone without the device's passcode from accessing the device's encrypted data. This includes Apple.").

54 Anthony Ha, *Apple's App Tracking Transparency Feature Has Arrived*, TechCrunch, April 26, 2021, https://techcrunch.com.

55 For a description of this and other approaches to encryption and decryption, see Geoffrey S. Corn & Dru Brenner-Beck, *"Going Dark": Encryption, Privacy, Liberty, and Security in the "Golden Age of Surveillance,"* in *The Cambridge Handbook of Surveillance Law* 330, 361 (2015).

56 Id. at 363–368.

57 Cyrus Vance, *5 Ways Tech Companies Distort the Encryption Debate*, Wash. Post, Dec. 15, 2015.

58 See Orin Kerr & Bruce Schneier, *Encryption Work-arounds*, 107 Geo. L. J. 989 (2018).

59 Nicholas Weaver, *We Think Encryption Allows Terrorists to Hide. It Doesn't*, Wash. Post., Dec. 14, 2015.

60 Id.

61 It must also be recognized, however, that any American legislative effort will at most affect companies over which the United States has control; there are many other means of communicating that are completely immune from domestic laws. See Corn & Brenner-Beck, *"Going Dark"*, supra note 55, at 360 (mentioning, inter alia, the "Snowden-approved" Signal messaging app, Telegram, a Russian-designed app, the "dark web," and in-game chat messaging).

62 See Slobogin, *Government Data Mining*, supra note 14, at 335 (car search—74.6; search of phone records—74.1).

63 460 U.S. 276 (1983).

64 565 U.S. at 416 (Sotomayor, J., concurring).

65 See Brian A. Jackson et al. (RAND Corporation), *Police Department Investments in Information Technology Systems* 1 (2014), at www.rand.org; Mariana Oliver & Matthew Kugler, *Surveying Surveillance: A National Survey of Police Department Surveillance Technologies*, 54 Ariz. St. L.J. (2022).

66 Amitai Etizoni, *Privacy in a Cyber Age: Policy and Practice* 11–12 (2015).

67 Sarah Brayne, *Predict and Surveil: Data, Discretion and the Future of Policing* 157, Appendix D (2021).

68 LexisNexis Risk Solutions: Crime and Criminal Investigations, https://risk.lexisnexis.com.

69 Id.

70 See, e.g., DocuSearch, at www.docusearch.com.

71 Alan Feuer, *Council Forces N.Y.P.D. to Disclose Use of Drones and Other Spy Tech*, N.Y. Times, June 6, 2018; Etzioni, *Privacy in a Cyber Age*, supra note 66, at 43.

72 Fusus, Real-Time Crime Center in the Cloud, www.fusus.com.

73 Id.

5. Profile-Driven Virtual Searches (Predictive Policing)

1 Andrew Ferguson, *The Rise of Big Data Policing: Surveillance, Race, and the Future of Law Enforcement* 64 (2017).

2 See, e.g., Shotspotter website, at www.shotspotter.com, Predpol website, at www.predpol.com.

3 See Ferguson, *The Rise of Big Data Policing*, supra note 1, at 68–69.

4 Nissa Rhee, *Can Police Big Data Stop Chicago's Spike in Crime*, Chicago Sun Times, June 2, 2016.

5 Justin Jouvenal, *The New Way Police Are Surveilling You: Calculating Your Threat "Score,"* Wash. Post, Jan. 10, 2016.

6 Michael Kwet, *ShadowDragon: Inside the Social Media Surveillance Software That Can Watch Your Every Move*, The Intercept, Sept. 21, 2021, available at https://theintercept.com.

7 See Ferguson, *The Rise of Big Data Policing*, supra note 1, at 44.

8 See Cynthia Lum & Christopher S. Koper, *Evidence-Based Policing: Translating Research into Practice* 76 (2017) (stating, based on the research, that "[t]argeting high crime places is one of the most effective approaches that the police can use to prevent crime and increase their legitimacy," although also noting that this effectiveness depends on numerous implementation variables).

9 Jessica Saunders, Priscilla Hunt & John S. Hollywood, *Predictions Put into Practice: A Quasi-Experimental Study of Chicago's Predictive Policing Project*, 12 J. Exper. Criminol. 347 (2016).

10 Anthony A. Braga & David L. Weisburd, *Policing Problem Places: Crime Hot Spots and Effective Prevention* 225 (2010).

11 David Weisburd & Malay Majmundar eds., *Proactive Policing: Effects on Crime and Communities* 282 (2018).

12 392 U.S. 1 (1968).

13 Id. at 30.

14 See Ben Grunwald & Jeffrey Fagan, *The End of Intuition-Based High Crime Areas*, 107 Calif. L. Rev. 345, 353 (2019) ("once courts recognized 'furtive movement' as a cognizable factor in the reasonable suspicion analysis, police began to see furtive movements everywhere").

15 Jeremey Gorner, *Chicago Police Use 'Heat List' as Strategy to Prevent Violence*, Chicago Tribune (Aug. 21, 2013), http://articles.chicagotribune.com [https://perma.cc/GKJ7-29LQ].

16 Hunchlab website, https://teamupturn.gitbooks.io; see also Geolitica/PredPol website, www.predpol.com ("PredPol uses ONLY 3 data points—crime type, crime location, and crime date/time—to create its predictions. No personally identifiable information is ever used. No demographic, ethnic or socio-economic information is ever used.")

17 C.M.A. McCauliff, *Burdens of Proof: Degrees of Belief, Quanta of Evidence, or Constitutional Guarantees?*, 35 Vand. L. Rev. 1293, 1327–28 (1982).

18 *Chavez v. Ill. St. Police*, 251 F.3d 612, 645 (7ᵗʰ Cir. 2001).

19 *Navarette v. California*, 572 U.S. 393, 410 (2014) (Scalia, J., dissenting).

20 Editorial, *Who Will Kill or Be Killed in Violence-Plagued Chicago? The Algorithm Knows*, Chi. Trib., May 10, 2016.

21 See Jeff Asher & Rob Arthur, *Inside the Algorithm That Tries to Predict Gun Violence in Chicago*, N.Y. Times, June 13, 2017.

22 Stephanie Kollman, *An Enormous List of Names Does Nothing to Combat Chicago Crime*, Chicago Sun-Times, May 16, 2017.

23 Sharad Goel et al., *Combatting Police Discrimination in the Age of Big Data*, 20 New Crim. L. Rev. 181, 212 (2017).

24 Sharad Goel, Justin A. Rao & Ravi Shroff, *Precinct or Prejudice?: Understanding Racial Disparities in New York City's Stop and Frisk Policy*, 10 Annals App. Stat. 365, 375 (2016). More specifically, the team found that, comparing a randomly selected weapon-carrier with a randomly selected person who did not have a weapon, the weapon-carrier would have a higher score on the algorithm 83% of the time, a result much higher than chance, which would produce a 50% rate.

25 Id. at 384.

26 Id. at 386.

27 Data on file with author.

28 Goel et al., *Combatting Police Discrimination in the Age of Big Data*, supra note 24, at 386.

29 Id.

30 959 F.Supp.2d 540 (S.D. N.Y. 2013).

31 Id. at 559 ("weapons were seized in 1.0% of the stops of blacks, 1.7% of the stops of Hispanics, and 1.4% of the stops of whites").

32 See Goel et al., *Combatting Police Discrimination in the Age of Big Data*, supra note 24, at 386 ("We note that if such stop rules were ultimately adopted, the model would likely require periodic updating since changes in officers' behavior could affect model performance.").

33 *Illinois v. Wardlow*, 528 U.S. 119, 124–25 (2000).

34 John Stuart Mill, *On Liberty*, in *The Philosophy of John Stuart Mill* 197 ("the preventive function of government . . . is far more liable to be abused, to the prejudice of liberty, than the punitory function, for there is hardly any part of the legitimate freedom of action of a human being which would not admit of being represented, and fairly too, as increasing the facilities for some form or other of delinquency. [However, if] a public authority, or even a private person, sees any one evidently preparing to commit a crime, they are not bound to look on inactive. . . .").

35 See Christopher Slobogin, *Prevention as the Primary Goal of Sentencing: The Modern Case for Indeterminate Dispositions in Criminal Cases*, 48 San Diego L. Rev. 1127, 1132–34 (2011).

36 *United States v. Hensley*, 469 U.S. 221, 227 (1985) (making this statement while holding that police may also stop and question an individual on reasonable suspicion the person has already committed a serious crime).

37 Neil Bedi & Katherine McGrory, *Pasco's Sheriff Uses Grades and Abuse History to Label School Children Potential Criminals*, Tampa Bay Tribune (Nov. 19, 2020), available at https://projects.tampabay.com.

38 Id.

39 Cf. *Minnesota v. Dickerson*, 508 U.S. 366 (1993).

40 392 U.S. at 27.

41 See Orin Kerr, *Why Courts Should Not Quantify Probable Cause*, in *The Political Heart of Criminal Procedure: Essays on Themes of William J. Stuntz* 131, 135–37 (Michael Klarman, David Skeel & Carol Steiker eds., 2012).

42 See Kiel Brennan-Marquez, *"Plausible Cause": Explanatory Power in an Age of Machines*, 70 Vand. L. Rev. 1249, 1252 (2017).

43 Christopher Slobogin, *A World Without a Fourth Amendment*, 39 UCLA L. Rev. 1, 82–84 (1991).

44 Terry, 392 U.S. at 5.

45 Barbara Underwood, *Law and the Crystal Ball: Predicting Behavior with Statistical Inference and Individualized Judgment*, 88 Yale L.J. 1408, 1427 (1979) ("Although the clinician need not identify in advance the characteristics he will regard as salient, he must nevertheless evaluate the applicant on the basis of a finite number of salient characteristics, and thus, like the statistical decision-maker, he treats the applicant as a member of a class defined by those characteristics.").

46 Frederick Schauer, *Profiles, Probabilities, and Stereotypes* 107 (2003).

47 Richard M. Re, *Fourth Amendment Fairness*, 116 Mich. L. Rev. 1409, 1433 (2018).

48 Christopher Slobogin, *Minding Justice: Laws that Deprive People with Mental Disability of Life and Liberty* 115–122 (2006).

49 Jane Bambauer, *Hassle*, 113 Mich. L. Rev. 461, 462–465 (2015) ("Hit rates measure suspicion. . . . Hassle rates, by contrast, measure the probability that an innocent person within the relevant population will be stopped or searched under the program.").

50 If instead the police want to arrest an individual for a *past* crime based on a profile, blameworthy conduct has already occurred and the only issue is whether the requisite suspicion (for an arrest, probable cause) exists.

51 Tom Tyler, *Can the Police Enhance Their Legitimacy through Their Conduct: Using Empirical Research to Inform Law*, 2017 U. Ill. L. Rev. 1971, 1973, 1998 tb. 6 (2017).

52 See George Yancy, Op-Ed., *Walking While Black in the "White Gaze,"* N.Y. Times (Sept. 1, 2013), http://opinionator.blogs.nytimes.com; David A. Harris, *"Driving While Black" and All Other Traffic Offenses: The Supreme Court and Pretextual Traffic Stops*, 87 J. Crim. L. & Criminol. 544 (1997).

53 See https://crimprof.law.ou.edu; *Louisville Metro PD Falsely Alert K-9 to Conduct an Illegal[] Search*, YouTube (Feb. 11, 2019), www.youtube.com (March 23, 2012).

54 See Michael K. Brown, *Working the Street* 170–179 (1981) (describing the "incongruity," "prior information," and "appearance" bases for police detention).

55 See, e.g., studies in San Diego, Houston, Newark, Kansas City, and Minneapolis reported in Lawrence W. Sherman, *Police and Crime Control*, in *Modern Policing* (Michael Tonry & Norval Morris, eds.), 197 (1992).

56 See, e.g., *Floyd v. City of New York*, 959 F.Supp.2d 540, 578–579, 588–589, 606 (S.D.N.Y. 2013) (recounting data in New York and its impact).

57 Sendhil Mullainathan, *Biased Algorithms Are Easier to Fix Than Biased People*, N.Y. Times (Dec. 6 2019), https:///www.nytimes.com. I develop these points in more detail in Christopher Slobogin, *Just Algorithms: Using Science to Reduce Incarceration and Inform a Jurisprudence of Risk* 90–97 (2021).

58 Robert E. Worden et al, *The Impacts of Implicit Bias Training in the NYPD* (2020) (finding no meaningful change in behavior in NYPD police after receiving training about implicit bias); Michael Hobbes, *"Implicit Bias" Trainings Don't Actually Change Police Behavior*, Huffington Post (June 12, 2020), www.huffpost.com/ [https://perma.cc/32NJ-YVHY] (citing similar study).

59 Bryan Llenas, Fox News Latino (Feb. 25, 2014), http://latino.foxnews.com (quoting Hanni Fakhoury, staff attorney at the Electronic Frontier Foundation, as saying: "The algorithm is telling you exactly what you programmed it to tell you. 'Young black kids in the south side of Chicago are more likely to commit crimes,' and the algorithm lets the police launder this belief. It's not racism, they can say.").

60 See Megan Stevenson & Sandra G. Mayson, *The Scale of Misdemeanor Justice*, 98 B.U. L. Rev. 731, 769–770 (2018) ("We find that black people are arrested at more than twice the rate of white people for nine of twelve likely-misdemeanor offenses: vagrancy, prostitution, gambling, drug possession, simple assault, theft, disorderly conduct, vandalism, and 'other offenses'"); Ojmarrh Mitchell & Michael S. Caudy, *Examining Racial Disparities in Drug Arrests*, Just. Q., Jan. 2013, at 22 ("[R]acial disparity in drug arrests between black and whites cannot be explained by race differences in the extent of drug offending, nor the nature of drug offending.").

61 See Jeff Brantingham, *The Logic of Data Bias and Its Impact on Place-Based Predictive Policing*, 15 Ohio St. J. Crim. L. 473 (2018) (suggesting these and other possibilities).

62 Cf. Sandra G. Mayson, *Bias In, Bias Out*, 128 Yale L. J. 2218, 2264 (2019) (noting that, in New Orleans, where she was a public defender for a number of years, a black person with three arrests was not much of a concern—but a white with three arrests was "really bad news").

63 See Rashida Richardson, Jason Schultz & Kate Crawford, *Dirty Data, Bad Predictions: How Civil Rights Violations Impact Police Data, Predictive Policing Systems, and Justice*, 94 NYU L. Rev. Online 192 (2019).

64 Andrew Ferguson, *Policing Predictive Policing*, 94 Wash. U. L. Rev. 1109, 1127 (2017).

65 Ben Grunwald, *Measuring Racial Bias in Criminal Records* (forthcoming).

66 Kimberly Jenkins Robinson, *The Constitutional Future of Race-Neutral Efforts to Achieve Diversity and Avoid Racial Isolation in Elementary and Secondary Schools*, 50 B.C. L. Rev. 277, 315 (2009) ("The Court's current approach to equal protection, which has been labeled an antidiscrimination, anticlassification, or color-blind approach, emphasizes the impropriety of government use of racial classifications.").

67 See Aziz Z. Huq, *Constitutional Rights in the Machine Learning State*, 105 Cornell L. Rev. 1875, 1920 (2020) ("[A]n official's mere awareness of race raises no constitutional problem. By analogy, it may also be that mere inclusion of race as a feature of training data should not be per se problematic.").

68 Goel, *Combatting Police Discrimination in the Age of Big Data*, supra note 24, at 386.

69 Bernard E. Harcourt, *Against Prediction: Profiling, Policing and Punishing in an Actuarial Age* 147 (2007).

70 Bernard E. Harcourt & Tracey L. Meares, *Randomization and the Fourth Amendment*, 78 U. Chi. L. Rev. 809, 866–868 (2011).

71 Maurice Chammah, *Policing the Future*, The Marshall Project, www.the marshallproject.org.

72 See Mayson, supra note 62, at 2285–86 (2019) (noting that risk algorithms can be used as a "diagnostic tool" that can "identify[] sites and causes of racial disparity in criminal justice" and "help[] to illuminate the causal pathways of crime and arrest risk").

73 Sonia K. Katyal, *Private Accountability in the Age of Artificial Intelligence*, 66 UCLA L. Rev. 54 (2019) (exploring ways of improving algorithmic accountability).

74 Andrew Selbst & Simon Barocas, *The Intuitive Appeal of Explainable Machines*, 87 Ford. L. Rev. 1085, 1091 (2018).

75 371 Wis.2d 235 (2016).

76 Id. at 260.

77 430 U.S. 349 (1977).

78 *Loomis*, 371 Wis.2d at 257 (quoting *State v. Travis*, 347 Wis.2d 142, 153 (2013)).

79 353 U.S. 53 (1957).

80 Id. at 63.

81 Andrea Roth, *Machine Testimony*, 126 Yale L.J. 1972, 2042 (2017).

82 See Richard Van Duizend, L. Paul Sutton & Charlotte A. Carter, *The Search Warrant Process: Preconceptions, Perceptions and Practices* 24 (National Center

for State Courts, 1985) ("Law enforcement officers and prosecutors prefer to forgo the possibility of a conviction rather than to jeopardize the safety of informants by divulging their identity.").

83 See Z. A. G. Perez, *Piercing the Veil of Informant Confidentiality: The Role of In Camera Hearings in the* Roviaro *Determination*, 46 Am. Crim. Law Rev. 179, 202–13 (2009) (describing Federal Circuit of Appeals approaches to *Roviaro*).

84 *United States v. Millán-Isaac*, 749 F.3d 57, 70 (1st Cir. 2014); *Smith v. Woods*, 505 F. App'x 560, 568 (6th Cir. 2012); *United States v. Hayes*, 171 F.3d 389, 394 (6th Cir. 1999).

85 528 U.S. at 124.

86 Jay Stanley, *The Dawn of Robotic Surveillance*, ACLU (June 2019), www.aclu. org.

87 Department of Homeland Security, www.dhs.gov.

88 Joseph Kennedy, Isac Unah & Kasi Wahlers, *Sharks and Minnows in the War on Drugs: A Study of Quantity, Race, and Drug Type in Drug Arrests*, 52 U.C. Davis L. Rev. 729, 732 (2018).

89 Compare Ram Subramanian et al., Vera Inst. of Justice, *Incarceration's Front Door: The Misuse of Jails in America* 22 (Patricia Connelly ed., 2015), at www. vera.org (95% jailing rate in U.S.) with Christine Morgenstern, *Alternatives to Pre-trial Detention* (Gerben Bruinsma & David Weisburd eds., 2014), at https:// research-paper.essayempire.com (3–5% jailing rate in Germany).

90 For a discussion of this approach, see Jordan Blair Woods, *Decriminalization, Police Authority and Traffic Stops*, 62 UCLA L. Rev. 672, 754–59 (2015).

91 The latest study, of many, to so find is reported in Emma Pierson et al., *A Large-Scale Analysis of Racial Disparities in Police Stops Across the United States*, 4 Nat. Human Behav. 729, 732 (2020).

92 See Christopher Slobogin, *Why Liberals Should Chuck the Exclusionary Rule*, 1999 Ill. L. Rev. 363, 404–423 (making the case for reforming Fourth Amendment damages actions).

93 Elizabeth E. Joh, *Discretionless Policing: Technology and the Fourth Amendment*, 95 Calif. L. Rev. 199 (2007).

94 See generally, Mary Fan, *Body Cameras, Big Data, and Police Accountability*, 43 L. & Soc. Inquiry 1236 (2018).

95 Ferguson, *Policing Predictive Policing*, supra note 64, at 1170–1171.

96 See Stephen Henderson, *Fourth Amendment Time Machines (and What They May Say About Police Body Cameras)*, 18 Penn. J. Const'al L. 933, 933 (2016).

6. Event-Driven Virtual Searches

1 Misuki Hisaka, *Police Obtain Warrants to Find Out Which Google Users Were Present at Crime Scenes*, The Inquistr, Mar. 18, 2018, at www.inquisitr.com.

2 Id.

3 Jennifer Valentino-DeVries, *Google's SensorVault Is a Boon for Law Enforcement: This Is How It Works*, N.Y. Times (Apr. 13, 2019), www.nytimes.com.

4 Brief of Amicus Curiae Google LLC in Support of Neither Party Concerning Defendant's Motion to Suppress Evidence from a "Geofence" General Warrant at 3, *United States v. Chatrie*, No. 3:19-cr-00130 (E.D. Va. Dec. 23, 2019).

5 Zach Whittaker, *Google Says Geofence Warrants Make Up One-Quarter of all U.S. Demands*, TechCrunch, https://techcrunch.com.

6 540 U.S. 419 (2004).

7 Id. at 427 (citing *Brown v. Texas*, 443 U.S. 47, 51 (1979)).

8 Declaration of Sarah Rodriguez at 2, *United States v. Chatrie*, No. 3:19-cr-00130 (E.D. Va. Mar. 11, 2019).

9 *Commonwealth v. Perry*, 2021 WL 2019293 (2021); *Matter of Search Warrant Application for Geofence Location Data Stored at Google Concerning an Arson Investigation*, No. 20 M 525, 2020 WL 6343084, at *2 (N.D. Ill. Oct. 29, 2020).

10 *Matter of Search of Info. Stored at Premises Controlled by Google*, 481 F. Supp. 3d 730, 733 (N.D. Ill. Aug. 24, 2020).

11 Id.

12 *Sealed Memorandum and Order*, No. 20 M 297, N.D. Ill. (Jul. 8, 2020), at www.eff.org.

13 See Charlie Warzel and Stuart A. Thompson, *They Stormed the Capitol. Their Apps Tracked Them*, N.Y. Times (Feb. 5, 2021), www.nytimes.com (describing how *Times* reporters were "able to connect dozens of devices to their owners, tying anonymous locations back to names, home addresses, social networks and phone numbers of people in attendance").

14 See Sidney Fussell, *Creepy 'Geofence' Finds Anyone Who Went Near a Crime Scene*, Wired (Sept. 4, 2020), www.wired.com.

15 Matthew Feeney, *Baltimore Surveillance Program Should Cause Concerns*, The Hill (Aug. 25, 2016) https://thehill.com.

16 Nathan Sherard, *Officials in Baltimore and St. Louis Put the Brakes on Persistent Surveillance Systems Spy Planes*, Electronic Frontier Foundation (March 28, 2021), at www.eff.org.

17 2 F.4th 330 (4th Cir. 2021).

18 Id. at 344–345.

19 Id. at 366 (Wilkinson, J., dissenting).

20 *DNA Sample Collection from Arrestees*, Nat'l Inst. Just. (Dec.6, 2012), https://nij.ojp.gov[https://perma.cc.4SQT-2F4F].

21 For a description of the process, see Erin Murphy, *Relative Doubt: Familial Searches of DNA Databases*, 109 Mich. L. Rev. 291, 297–300 (2010).

22 Yaniv Erlich, Tal Shor, Itsik Pe'er & Shai Carmi, *Identity Inference of Genomic Data Using Long-Range Familial Searches*, 362 Sci. 690, 690 (2018) ("[A] genetic database needs to cover only 2% of the target population to provide a third-cousin match to nearly any person.").

23 Paige St. John, *The Untold Story of How the Golden State Killer Was Found*, L.A. Times, Dec. 8, 2020, at www.latimes.com.

24 Id.

25 Jon Schuppe, *Police Were Cracking Cold Cases with a DNA Website. Then the Fine Print Changed.*, NBC NEWS (Oct. 25, 2019, 9:53 AM), www.nbcnews.com [https://perma.cc/PFE6-YHR3].

26 See Peter Aldhous, *A Court Tried to Force Ancestry.com to Open Up Its DNA Database to Police. The Company Said No.*, BuzzFeed News (Feb. 3, 2020), www.buzzfeednews.com [https://perma.cc/V8PJ-GLKR] ("Ancestry and its main competitor, 23andMe . . . have publicly vowed to defend their customers' genetic privacy, and say they will fight efforts to open up their databases to searches by police.").

27 *You Can Help*, FamilyTreeDNA, www.familytreedna.com [https://perma.cc/4X5S-6DQL]; *Ed Smart, Father of Elizabeth Smart Teams Up with FamilyTreeDNA*, PR Newswire (Mar. 26, 2019), https://prn.to [https://perma.cc/2QNG-7P5U].

28 Sara Debus-Sherrill & Michael B. Field, ICF, *Understanding Familial DNA Searching: Policies, Procedures, and Potential Impact* 11–12 (2017), www.ncjrs.gov [https://perma.cc/6T95-BU2A].

29 See Murphy, *Relative Doubt*, supra note 21, at 330–340.

30 *Carpenter v. United States*, 138 S.Ct. 2206, 2220 (2018).

31 *Maryland v. King*, 569 U.S. 435 (2013).

32 *Carpenter*, 138 S.Ct. at 2262 (Gorsuch, J., dissenting) (citing Kerr, *The Case for the Third-Party Doctrine*, 107 Mich. L. Rev. 561, 563, n. 5, 564 (2009)).

33 James W. Hazel & Christopher Slobogin, *"A World of Difference"? Law Enforcement, Genetic Data, and the Fourth Amendment*, 70 Duke L.J. 705, 745, tbl. 1 (2021).

34 Id. at 759–760.

35 Cf. *Maryland v. King*, 569 U.S. at 464 (emphasizing that the DNA collected from arrestees in the program in question was analyzed "for the sole purpose of generating a unique identifying number against which future samples may be matched").

36 Elizabeth E. Joh, *DNA Theft: Recognizing the Crime of Nonconsensual Genetic Collection and Testing*, 91 B.U. L. Rev. 665, 699 & n.197 (2011).

37 Hazel & Slobogin, *"A World of Difference,"* supra note 33, at 745, tbl. 1.

38 Erin Murphy & Jun H. Tong, *The Racial Composition of Forensic DNA Databases*, 108 Calif. L. Rev. 1847 (2020).

39 Ryan Mac et al., *Clearview AI Offered Thousands of Cops Free Trial*, BuzzFeed New (Apr. 6, 2021), www.buzzfeednews.com.

40 Id.

41 Tom Simonite, *Photo Algorithms Identify White Men Fine—Black Women, Not So Much*, Wired (Feb. 6, 2018) (reporting studies from MIT and Georgetown);

Henry Kenyon, *ACLU Rips Clearview AI Claims of Facial Recognition Accuracy*, 2020 CQDPRPT 0115 (reporting ACLU study finding that FRT misidentified numerous members of Congress, particularly those of color).

42 Sean O'Brien, *Time to Face Up to Big Brother*, New Haven Independent (Mar. 9, 2020), at www.newhavenindependent.org. As a result, the ACLU filed a suit claiming that Clearview was violating Illinois's Biometric Information Privacy Act, 740 Ill. Comp. St. 14/1 et. seq. (2008), which requires companies to obtain a person's consent before they can obtain his or her biometric information. See www.aclu.org.

43 See Federal Bureau of Investigation, *Next Generation Identification (NGI)*, www.fbi.gov, at Electronic Privacy Information Center.

44 See, e.g., Woodrow Hartzog & Evan Selinger, *Surveillance as Loss of Obscurity*, 72 Wash. & Lee L. Rev. 1353 (2015).

45 Slobogin, *Privacy at Risk* 98–106 (2017) (making the arguments, although also admitting that the Court's ungenerous interpretation of those rights makes them tenuous).

46 Id. at 112, tbl.

47 N.Y.C. Police Department, Procedure No. 212–129 (Mar. 12, 2020).

48 462 U.S. 213 (1983).

49 Id. at 241.

50 Ryan Saavedra, *"Groundbreaking" Clearview AI Technology Used to Take Down Alleged Child Sex Predators*, The Daily Wire (Jan. 21, 2020), at www.dailywire.com.

51 Government Accountability Office, *Facial Recognition Technology: Federal Law Enforcement Agencies Should Assess Privacy and Other Risks* (June 29, 2021), at www.gao.gov.

52 Lindsey Barrett, *Ban Facial Recognition Technology for Children—and for Everyone Else*, 26 B.U. J. Sci. & Tech. L. 223 (2020).

53 Gregory Barber, *San Francisco Bans Agency Use of Facial Recognition Tech*, Wired (May 14, 2019).

54 See *China Has Turned Xinjiang into a Police State Like No Other*, The Economist (May 31, 2018), www.economist.com; *China's Algorithms of Repression, Human Rights Watch* (May 1, 2019), www.hrw.org.

55 *Street-Level Surveillance: Automated License Plate Readers*, Electronic Frontier Foundation, www.eff.org [https://perma.cc/3ZJH-WD2K].

56 See Marcia Hofmann, *Arguing for Suppression of "Hash" Evidence*, Champion, May 2009, at 20; *United States v. Reddick*, 900 F.3d 636, 649–640 (5th Cir. 2018).

57 Brian Charles, *NYPD's Big Artificial-Intelligence Reveal*, Governing (Mar. 19, 2020), at www.governing.com.

58 Sindh Today, *Canadian Changes Name to Dodge U.S. No-Fly List*, Sept. 13, 2008, at www.sindhtoday.net (stating that 32,000 Americans have applied to have their names removed from the list).

59 *Research in Brief: Assessing the Effectiveness of Automated License Plate Readers*, The Police Chief, 14–15, March, 2018.

60 462 U.S. 696 (1983).

61 Robert C. Bird, *An Examination of the Training and Reliability of the Narcotics Detection Dog*, 85 KY. L.J. 405 (1996).

62 568 U.S. 237 (2013).

63 Id. at 248.

64 Id. at 246–247.

65 If testing is carried out appropriately, arguments that reasonable suspicion should be required before a dog can be used (based on Bayesian analysis) are inapposite. See Richard E. Myers, *Detector Dogs and Probable Cause*, 14 Geo. Mason L. Rev. 1, 12–18 (2006).

66 See *United States v. Sundby*, 186 F.3d 873, 876 (8th Cir. 1999) (citing cases).

67 See Charles, *NYPD's Big Artificial-Intelligence Reveal*, supra note 57.

68 Id.

7. Program-Driven Virtual Searches

1 See Glenn Greenwald, *No Place to Hide: Edward Snowden, the NSA, and the U.S. Surveillance State* 97 (2014) (noting an NSA slide describing the program as "Collect It All").

2 See Consolidated Appropriations Resolution, 2003, Pub. L. No. 108–7, 117 Stat. 11, 534 (stating that "no funds appropriated or otherwise made available to the Department of Defense may be obligated or expended on research and development on the Total Information Awareness program, unless [statutory exceptions apply]").

3 Rachel Levinson-Waldman, *NSA Surveillance in the War on Terror*, in *The Cambridge Handbook of Surveillance Law*, 7, 8, 30 (2017); Dalia Naamani-Goldman, *Anti-terrorism Program Mines IRS' Records; Privacy Advocates Are Concerned That Tax Data and Other Information May Be Used Improperly*, L.A. Times C1 (Jan 15, 2007).

4 See The Constitution Project, *Recommendations for Fusion Centers: Preserving Privacy & Civil Liberties While Protecting Against Crime & Terrorism* 4 (2012), www.constitutionproject.org [https://perma.cc/2D3K-HXXH] (describing the establishment of 77 fusion centers nationwide and the types of information these centers collect).

5 Harold Krent, *Of Diaries and Databanks: Use Restrictions under the Fourth Amendment*, 74 Tex. L. Rev. 49, 51 (1995) (as a result of "rapidly developing technology, . . . what the government does with information may now threaten privacy more than the collection itself"; thus, the absence of use restrictions on collected information could constitute an unreasonable "seizure").

6 Julie Cohen, *What Privacy Is For*, 126 Harv. L. Rev. 1904, 1912 (2013).

7 Curt Gentry, *J. Edgar Hoover: The Man and the Secrets* 51 (1991).

8 See, e.g., Rachel Levinson-Waldman, *Hiding in Plain Sight: A Fourth Amendment for Analyzing Public Government Surveillance*, 66 Emory L.J. 527, 553 (2017) (detailing government efforts to obtain and retain data on political opponents, protesters, and religious groups); Amy Pavuk, *Law-Enforcer Misuse of Driver Database Soars*, Orlando Sentinel (Jan. 22, 2013), [https://perma.cc/B8XP-4PJ4] (detailing abuse of driver databases); James Hamilton & Steve Blum, *Top Ten List of Police Database Abuses*, Rense.com (June 12, 2002), [https://perma.cc/E4HB-ASQP] (detailing sale of police data to organized-crime syndicates, probing of political opponents, and stalking of acquaintances); *Camaj v. Dep't of Homeland Sec.*, 542 F. App'x 933, 933 (Fed. Cir. 2013) (per curiam) (immigration officer admitted to 314 unauthorized queries).

9 Michael Schmidt, David E. Sanger & Nicole Perlroth, *Chinese Hackers Pursue Key Data on U.S. Workers*, N.Y. Times (July 9, 2014), [https://perma.cc/27NE-FVE9]; David E. Sanger, *Russian Hackers Broke into Federal Agencies, Officials Suspect*, N.Y. Times, Dec. 13, 2020, www.nytimes.com.

10 See generally Wayne A. Logan & Andrew Guthrie Ferguson, *Policing Criminal Justice Data*, 101 Minn. L. Rev. 541 (2016); Robert Patrick & Jennifer S. Mann, *Jailed by Mistake*, St. Louis Post-Dispatch (Oct. 26, 2013), [https://perma.cc/N3RR-P7KR]. Similarly, watchlist errors can have negative effects on a person's ability to work, as well as to travel and even to vote. Margaret Hu, *Big Data Blacklisting*, 67 Fla. L. Rev. 1735, 1777–1792 (2016) (documenting impact of no-work, no-vote, no-citizenship, no-fly, and terrorist watchlists).

11 Danielle Keats Citron & Frank Pasquale, *Network Accountability for the Domestic Intelligence Apparatus*, 62 Hastings L.J. 1441, 1463–1466 (2011) (describing privacy, mission creep, and transparency concerns); Clive Norris, *From Personal to Digital: CCTV, the Panopticon and the Technological Mediation of Suspicion and Social Control*, in *Surveillance and the Social Sorting: Privacy Risk and Automatic Discrimination* 28 (David Lyon ed., 2003).

12 Ryan Lizza, *State of Deception*, New Yorker (Dec. 16, 2013), www.newyorker.com.

13 Office of the Dir. Of Nat'l Intelligence, *FISC Approves Government's Request to Modify Telephony Metadata Program*, IC on the Record (Feb. 6, 2014, https://icontherecord.temblr.com).

14 Sarah Brayne, *Predict and Surveil: Data, Discretion and the Future of Policing* 24 (2021).

15 Cade Metz, Erin Griffith & Kate Conger, *What Is Palantir?: The Tech Industry's Next Big I.P.O.*, N.Y. Times (Aug. 26, 2020), www.nytimes.com.

16 Brayne, *Predict and Surveil*, supra note 14, at 107–117.

17 *Leaders of a Beautiful Struggle v. Baltimore Police Department*, 4 F.4th 330, 359 (4th Cir. 2021) (Wilkinson, J., dissenting).

18 4 F.4th 330 (4th Cir. 2021).

19 Id. at 345.

20 Id. at 341.

21 Id. at 342.

22 Id. at 343.

23 Id. at 348 (citing *Messerschmidt v. Millender*, 565 U.S. 560, 560 (2012) (Sotomayor, J., dissenting).

24 Id. at 353 (Wilkinson, J., dissenting).

25 Id. at 367–368.

26 Id. at 367 (citing Luke Broadwater, *Surveillance Airplane Gains a New Sales Pitch,* Balt. Sun, Feb. 25, 2018, at A1).

27 Id. at 366.

28 *United States v. Jones*, 565 U.S. 400, 429–430 (Alito, J., concurring).

29 American Law Institute, *Principles of the Law: Policing*, March 18, 2019.

30 Id. § 5.01(b).

31 Id. § 5.03.

32 Id. § 5.02.

33 Id. § 5.03.

34 Id., comment to § 5.01.

35 *Ry. Express Agency, Inc. v. New York*, 336 U.S. 106, 112–113 (1949) (Jackson, J. concurring).

36 ALI, *Principles of Policing*, supra note 29, § 6.01.

37 Id., § 6.02.

38 Id., § 6.03.

39 Id., §§ 6.04; 6.05.

40 Id., § 6.06.

41 See, e.g., *American Bar Association Standards for Law Enforcement Access to Third Party Records*, std. 25.6.1; *Technologically Assisted Physical Surveillance*, std. 2–9.1(f), at www.americanbar.org; The Constitution Project, *Guidelines for Video Surveillance*, §§ 325–327; Barry Friedman, *Unwarranted: Policing Without Permission* 211–282 (2017); David Gray, *The Fourth Amendment in an Age of Surveillance* 267–275 (2017).

42 Much of this analysis is taken from Christopher Slobogin, *Policing as Administration*, 165 U. Pa. L. Rev. 91 (2016).

43 David Gray, *Collective Civil Rights and the Fourth Amendment After* Carpenter, 79 Md. L. Rev. 66, 82 (2019) ("[T]he Fourth Amendment is not a defense of individual property rights. It is, instead, a restraint on government power—a restraint designed to preserve the independence and integrity of the people as a whole. It is a bulwark against tyranny.").

44 Neil M. Richards, *Intellectual Privacy*, 87 Tex. L. Rev. 387, 431–441 (2008) (arguing that First Amendment values enhance individual interests vis-à-vis government surveillance and access to personal records).

45 460 U.S. 276 (1983).

46 Id. at 283.

47 429 U.S. 589 (1977).

48 Id. at 605.

49 *T.L.O. v. New Jersey*, 470 U.S. 276, 351 (Blackmun, J., concurring).

50 452 U.S. 594 (1981).

51 Id. at 603–604.

52 *United States v. Martinez-Fuerte*, 428 U.S. 543, 554, 566 (1976).

53 *Delaware v. Prouse*, 440 U.S. 648, 664 (Blackmun, J., concurring).

54 Christopher Slobogin, *Panvasive Surveillance, Political Process Theory and the Nondelegation Doctrine*, 102 Geo. L. Rev. 1721, 1727–1733 (2014).

55 555 U.S. 135 (2009).

56 Id. at 146–147.

57 429 U.S. at 605.

58 *NASA v. Nelson*, 562 U.S 134, 138 (2011).

59 569 U.S. 435 (2014).

60 5 U.S.C. § 552a(e)(1) (2012).

61 16 C.F.R. § 314.4(b)(2), (c) (2017) (financial institutions), 45 C.F.R. § 164.310(d)(2)(ii) (2017) (medical establishments), 18 U.S.C. § 2710(e) (video businesses), N.Y. Gen. Bus. Law § 399-H (McKinney 2017) (business organizations), 16 C.F.R. § 682(a) (2017) (consumer data).

62 5 U.S.C. § 552a(k)(2).

63 See Colleen Long, *NYPD, Microsoft Create Crime-Fighting "Domain Awareness" Tech System*, Huffington Post, Feb. 25, 2013. See also *Privacy Security Guidelines* (*Guidelines*), New York City (Feb. 2009) (describing the program), www.nyc.gov/html/nypd/downloads/pdf/crime_prevention/public_security_privacy_guidelines.pdf.

64 On the increase in drone surveillance and attempts to regulate it, see Marc Jonathan Blitz, James Grimsley, Stephen A. Henderson & Joseph Thai, *Regulating Drones under the First and Fourth Amendments*, 57 Wm. & Mary L. Rev. 49 (2015).

65 See The Constitution Project, *Recommendations for Fusion Centers*, supra note 4, at 7.

66 N.Y.C. Charter, Ch. 45, §§ 1041 et seq.

67 5 U.S.C. § 551(4) (2011) (defining "rule" in this manner).

68 See, e.g., *Long Island Care at Home, Inc. v. Coke*, 551 U.S. 158, 172–73 (2007).

69 Kenneth Culp Davis & Richard J. Pierce, Jr., *Administrative Law Treatise* 1 (3d ed. 1994) (emphasis added).

70 See *Chamber of Commerce v. U.S. Dep't of Labor*, 174 F.3d 206, 211–13 (D.C. Cir. 1999) (ergonomics); *Hoctor v. U.S. Dep't of Agric.*, 82 F.3d 165, 1771–72 (7th Cir. 1996) (fence height); *Davidson v. Glickman*, 169 F.3d 996, 999 (5th Cir. 1999) (farm acreage).

71 Eugene Mcquillin, *The Law of Municipal Corporations* 2.8.10 (3d ed. 1999).

72 436 U.S. 307 (1978).

73 Id. at 323.

74 397 U.S. 72 (1970).

75 Id. at 77.

76 5 U.S.C. § 553(b)(3) (1966).

77 See, e.g., *AFL-CIO v. Donovan*, 757 F.2d 330 (D.C. Cir. 1985).

78 See, e.g., Torin Monahan & Neal A. Palmer, *The Emerging Politics of DHS Fusion Centers*, 40 Sec. Dialogue 617, 630 (2009).

79 *Leaders of a Beautiful Struggle v. Baltimore Police Dep't*, 4 F.4th 330, 368 (4th Cir. 2021) (Wilkinson, J., dissenting).

80 See ACLU, *Community Control Over Police Surveillance*, www.aclu.org.

81 The Oakland experience is described in John Fasman, *We See It All: Liberty and Justice in an Age of Perpetual Surveillance* 207–221 (2021).

82 See Jennifer Valentino-Devries, *Stingray Phone Tracker Fuels Constitutional Class*, Wall St. J. (Sept 22, 2011), www.wsj.com (discussing *United States v. Rigmaiden*, 844 F.Supp. 2d 982 (D. Ariz. 2012).

83 5 U.S.C. § 552(b)(7)(E) (2009).

84 David Alan Sklansky, *Democracy and the Police* 157–58 (2008) (defending the idea that policing practices and fundamental aspects of democracy are irretrievably linked).

85 This ruse is most commonly used when agencies want to hide information obtained through national security programs. See Joe Kloc, *DEA Investigated for Using NSA Data for Drug Busts*, Daily Dot (Aug. 7, 2013), www.dailydot.com.

86 See, e.g., *Maryland v. Andrews*, 134 A.3d 324, 327–29 (Md. Ct. Spec. App. 2016).

87 The APA requires that the rules incorporate "a concise general statement of [their] basis and purpose," *Tri-State Generation and Transmission Ass'n., Inc. v. Environmental Quality Council*, 590 P.2d 1324, 1330 (Wyo. 1979), but the agency need not discuss "every item or factor or opinion in the submissions made to it." Bernard Schwartz, *Administrative Law* 200–01 (1991).

88 5 U.S.C. § 706(2)(A) (1966) (authorizing reviewing courts to "set aside agency action, findings, and conclusions found to be . . . arbitrary, capricious, and abuse of discretion, or otherwise not in accordance with law").

89 *SEC v. Chenery Corp.*, 332 U.S. 194, 196 (1947).

90 *Motor Vehicle Mfrs. Ass'n of U.S., Inc. v. State Farm Mut. Auto. Ins. Co.*, 463 U.S. 29, 41–42 (1983) (indicating that agency rationales that do not meet this test risk judicial invalidation on "arbitrary and capricious" grounds).

91 Kevin Stack, *Interpreting Regulations*, 111 Mich. L. Rev. 355, 379 (2012).

92 Id. at 379 ("Hard-look review further distinguishes regulations from legislation; it has long been understood as requiring a higher standard of rationality than the minimum rational basis standard of constitutional review.").

93 Chris Francescani, *NYPD Expands Surveillance Net to Fight Crime as Well as Terrorism*, Reuters (June 31, 2013), www.reuters.com (recounting how the

system brings together data from multiple technological sources and makes it available to the individual police officer).

94 See Department of Homeland Security, *Fusion Center Success Stories*, www.dhs.gov. But see Danielle Keats Citron & Frank Pasquale, *Network Accountability*, 64 Hastings L.J. 1141, 1444 (2001) ("Years after they were initiated, advocates of fusion centers have failed to give more than a cursory account of the benefits they provide.").

95 National Institute of Justice, *How to Identify Hot Spots*, http://nij.gov (describing the use of Geographic Information Systems "to more accurately pinpoint hot spots to confirm trouble areas, identify the specific nature of the activity occurring within the hot spot and then develop strategies to respond").

96 Joseph T. Small, Jr. & Robert A. Burgoyne, *Criminal Prosecutions Initiated by Administrative Agencies: The FDA, the* Accardi *Doctrine, and the Requirement of Consistent Agency Treatment*, 78 J. Crim. L. & Criminology 87, 103–04 (1987).

97 See, e.g., *Green County Mobilephone, Inc. v. FCC*, 765 F.2d 235, 237 (D.C. Cir. 1985) ("We reverse the Commission not because the strict rule it applied is inherently invalid, but rather because the Commission has invoked the rule inconsistently. We find that the Commissioner has not treated similar cases similarly."); *Distrigas of Mass. Corp. v. Fed. Power Comm'n*, 517 F.2d 761, 765 (1st Cir. 1975) ("[An administrative agency] has a duty to define and apply its policies in a minimally responsible and evenhanded way."); *Crestline Memorial Hosp. Ass'n, Inc. v. NLRB*, 668 F.2d 243, 245 (6th Cir. 1982) (stating that the NLRB cannot "treat similar situations in dissimilar ways"); *Contractors Transport Corp. v. United States*, 537 F.2d 1160, 1162 (4th Cir. 1976) ("Patently inconsistent application of agency standards to similar situations lacks rationality" and is prohibited under the APA's arbitrary and capricious standard.).

98 Nirej S. Sekhon, *Redistributive Policing*, 101 J. Crim. L. & Criminology 1171, 1211 (2011) ("In proactive policing, police departments have considerable discretion to ration arrests as they see fit. These departmental choices generate winners and losers, with significant distributive consequences.").

99 Schwartz, *Administrative Law*, supra note 87, at 171 ("The statute is the source of agency authority as well as of its limits. If an agency act is within the statutory limits (or vires), its action is valid; if it is outside them (or ultra vires), it is invalid.").

100 Cal. Civ. Code § 1798.90.51.

101 *Privacy Security Guidelines* (*Guidelines*) New York City 1 (Feb. 2009) (describing the statute), www.nyc.gov.

102 See The Constitution Project, *Recommendations for Fusion Centers*, supra note 4, at 6 (stating that fusion centers "derive their authority from general statutes creating state police agencies or memoranda of understanding among partner agencies."); see also Danielle Citron & Frank Pasquale, *Network Accountability*,

supra note 11, at 1453–55 (discussing "confusing lines of authority" with respect to fusion centers).

103 *2014 National Network of Fusion Centers Final Report*, Dept' Homeland Security 10 (2015), www.archives.gov.

104 Government Accountability Office, *Facial Recognition Technology: Federal Law Enforcement Agencies Should Assess Privacy and Other Risks* (June 29, 2021), at www.gao.gov.

105 Schwartz, *Administrative Law*, supra note 87, at 171.

106 See *Whiteman v. Am. Trucking Ass'ns, Inc.*, 531 U.S. 457, 472 (2001) (quoting *J. W. Hampton, Jr. & Co. v. United States*, 276 U.S. 394, 409 (1928).

107 Jim Rossi, *Institutional Design and the Lingering Legacy of Antifederalist Separation of Powers Ideals in the States*, 52 Vand. L. Rev. 1167, 1172 (1999).

108 *Stofer v. Motor Vehicle Casualty Co.*, 369 N.E.2d 875, 879 (1977).

109 See Barry Friedman & Maria Ponomarenko, *Democratic Policing*, 90 N.Y.U. L. Rev. 1827, 1843 (2015) ("As compared with the regulation of almost any other aspect of society that fundamentally affects the rights and liberties of the people, rules adopted by democratic bodies to govern policing tend to be few and far between.").

110 John Hart Ely, *Democracy and Distrust: A Theory of Judicial Review* 181 (1980) (describing the "representation-reinforcing theory of judicial review" as "one that bounds judicial review under the Constitution's open-ended provisions by insisting that it can appropriately concern itself only with questions of participation, and not with the substantive merits of the political choice under attack").

111 I have expounded on Ely's theory as applied to programmatic surveillance and other suspicionless searches and seizures in Christopher Slobogin, *Government Dragnets*, 73 L. & Contemp. Probls. 107, 131–138 (2010); Slobogin, *Panvasive Surveillance*, supra note 54, at 1733–58.

8. Volunteer-Driven Virtual Searches

1 *Skinner v. Railway Labor Execs. Ass'n*, 489 U.S. 602, 614 (1989).

2 Id.

3 Id. at 615.

4 Id. at 615–616.

5 Paul Ohm, *The Fourth Amendment in a World Without Privacy*, 81 Miss. L.J. 1309, 1338 (2012) (describing the "coming world" in which "police outsource [almost all] surveillance to private third parties").

6 *Coolidge v. New Hampshire*, 403 U.S. 443, 488 (1971).

7 Barton Gellman, *U.S. Surveillance Architecture Includes Collection of Reveal Internet, Phone Metadata*, Wash. Post (June 15, 2013), at www.washingtonpost.com.

8 Julia Angwin et al., *NSA's Spying Relies on AT & T's "Extreme Willingness to Help*," ProPublica (Aug. 15, 2015), www.propublica.org.

9 See *ACLU v. Clapper*, 959 F.Supp.2d 724, 749–752 (2013) (relying on *Smith v. Maryland*).

10 Julia Angwin et al., *AT&T Helped U.S. Spy on Internet on a Vast Scale*, N.Y. Times, Aug. 16, 2015, at A1, at www.nytimes.com.

11 15 U.S.C. § 1841 et seq.

12 Id., § 1841(4)(A).

13 Id. § 1861.

14 Siobhan Gorman & Jennifer Valentino-DeVries, *New Details Show Broader NSA Surveillance Reach*, Wall. St. J (Aug. 20, 2013), at www.wsj.com.

15 James Bamford, *The Most Wanted Man in the World*, Wired (Aug. 22, 2014, www.wired.com (noting that the tipping point for Snowden was when Director of National Intelligence James Clapper told the Senate that the NSA did not "wittingly" collect data on millions of Americans, something that would have been known had it been approved by legislation).

16 See Yan Zhu, *Security Experts Call on Tech Companies to Defend Against Surveillance*, Electronic Frontier Foundation (Feb. 26, 2014), https://perma.cc/R6QL-C77J (noting that "trust in technology companies has been badly shaken" in the wake of the Snowden disclosures); see also Claire Cain Miller, *Revelations of N.S.A. Spying Cost U.S. Tech Companies*, N.Y. Times (Mar. 21, 2014), https://perma.cc/7MMV-K9PK.

17 Alan Z. Rozenshtein, *Surveillance Intermediaries*, 70 Stan. L. Rev. 99 (2018).

18 S. Rep. No. 94–755S. Rep. No. 94–755, bk. 3, at 765, 767–69, 771, 776 (1976).

19 Ali Winston, *Oakland Cops Quietly Acquired Social Media Surveillance Tool*, East Bay Express (Apr. 13, 2016), at https://eastbayexpress.com.

20 Matt Cagle, *Facebook, Instagram, and Twitter Provided Data Access for a Surveillance Product Marketed to Target Activists of Color*, ACLU N. Calif (Oct 11, 2016), at www.aclunc.org.

21 Sam Biddle, *Police Surveilled George Floyd Protest with Help From Twitter-Affiliated Startup Dataminr*, The Intercept (July 9, 2020), https://theintercept.com.

22 Alex Kozinski & Mihailis E. Diamantis, *An Eerie Feeling of Déjà vu: From Soviet Snitches to Angry Birds*, in *The Cambridge Book of Surveillance Law* 420, 423 (David Gray & Stephen Henderson, eds. 2017).

23 Id. at 424.

24 Chris Jay Hoofnagle, *Big Brother's Little Helpers: How ChoicePoint and Other Commercial Data Brokers Collect and Package Your Data for Law Enforcement*, 29 NC J Intl L & Comm Reg 595, 600 (2004).

25 See Andrew Ferguson, *Big Data Surveillance: The Convergence of Big Data and Law Enforcement*, in *The Cambridge Book of Surveillance Law* 171, 175–178 (David Gray & Stephen Henderson, eds. 2017).

26 Id. at 193.

27 Id. at 191.

28 Id. at 181.

29 Id. at 188.

30 Joshua L. Simmons, Note, *Buying You: The Government's Use of Fourth-Parties to Launder Data About "The People,"* 2009 Colum. Bus. L. Rev. 950, 976.

31 See Kiel Brennan-Marquez, *The Constitutional Limits of Private Surveillance*, 66 Kan. L. Rev. 584 (2018).

32 Elizabeth Joh & Thomas Joo, *The Harms of Police Surveillance Technology Monopolies*, Den. L. Rev. F. (2021), www.denverlawreview.org.

33 Id. at 2–3.

34 See John Herrman, *Who's Watching Your Porch?*, N.Y. Times (Jan. 19, 2020), at www.nytimes.com [https://perma.cc/A7B3-5RDP]; Kate Cox, *It's the User's Fault if a Ring Camera Violates Your Privacy, Amazon Says*, Ars Technica (Nov. 20, 2019), at https://arstechnica.com/tech-policy (noting Amazon has partnerships with over 600 police departments).

35 See *Ring Launches Request for Assistance App on the Neighbors App* (June 3, 2021), https://blog.ring.com.

36 See www.facebook.com/notes/city-of-rancho-palos-verdes-ca/ringcom-security-camera-products-city-incentive-program/1349042348506873 (indicating that the city of Rancho Palo Verdes allocated $100,000 for a limited number of $50 incentives to buy Ring).

37 *Hoffa v. United States*, 385 U.S. 293 (1966).

38 Id. at 302.

39 *Lopez v. United States*, 373 U.S. 427 (1963); *Lewis v. United States*, 385 U.S 206 (1966); *United States v. White*, 401 U.S. 745 (1971).

40 See chapter 2.

41 Hoffa, 385 U.S. at 302 (noting that federal agents asked Partin to keep them informed about any actions by Hoffa consistent with jury tampering, but also stating that Partin acted "voluntarily").

42 Mary Irene Coombs, *Shared Privacy and the Fourth Amendment, or the Rights of Relationships*, 75 Cal. L. Rev. 1593, 1643–44 (1987) ("To deny even the possibility of such a decision [to cooperate] is to turn a freely chosen relationship into a status, denying one person's full personhood to protect another's interests.").

43 *United States v. White*, 322 U.S. 694, 698 (1944) ("The constitutional privilege against self-incrimination is essentially a personal one, applying only to natural individuals."); *United States v. Morton Salt Co.*, 338 U.S. 632, 652 (1950) ("[C]orporations can claim no equality with individuals in the enjoyment of a right to privacy. They are endowed with public attributes. They have a collective impact upon society, from which they derive the privilege of acting as artificial entities.").

44 Hoofnagle, *Big Brother's Little Helpers*, supra note 24, at 617–18; Avidan Y. Cover, *Corporate Avatars and the Erosion of the Populist Fourth Amendment*, 100

Iowa L. Rev. 1441, 1445 (2015) (describing the economic and legal incentives that technology companies have to "cooperate" with the authorities).

45 Jack M. Balkin, *Information Fiduciaries and the First Amendment*, 49 U.C. Davis L. Rev. 1183 (2016) (discussing the concept of information fiduciaries).

46 18 U.S.C. § 2702(b)(7).

47 *Model Rules of Prof'l Conduct*, Rule 1.6(b)(1)(2) ("A lawyer may reveal information relating to the representation of a client to the extent the lawyer reasonably believes necessary . . . to prevent reasonably certain death or substantial bodily harm"); Fla Sta. Ann. § 394.4615(3) ("when a patient has declared an intent to harm other persons," the therapist may release "sufficient information to provide adequate warning to the person threatened.").

48 *Model Rules of Prof'l Conduct*, Rule 1.6(b)(3) ("A lawyer may reveal information relating to the representation of a client . . . to prevent, mitigate or rectify substantial injury to the financial interests or property of another that is reasonably certain to result or has resulted from the client's commission of a crime or fraud in furtherance of which the client has used the lawyer's services").

49 31 U.S.C. §5313(a).

50 Tamara Gane, *Should Police Turn to Crowdsourced Online Sleuthing?*, Ozy (Aug. 13, 2018), www.ozy.com [https://perma.cc/YVS7-GZKV].

51 Sara E. Wilson, *Cops Increasingly Use Social Media to Connect, Crowdsource*, Gov't Tech (May 5, 2015), www.govtech.com [https://perma.cc/2M67-RYQ3].

52 See www.equitynet.com/c/vizsafe-inc; Jon Glasco, *How Crowdsourcing and Incentives Improve Public Safety*, Bee Smart City (Mar. 10, 2019), https://hub.beesmart.city [https://perma.cc/2VX5-MPWS].

53 Wayne Logan, *Crowdsourcing Crime Control*, 99 Tex. L. Rev. 137, 163 (2020).

54 *United States v. D'Andrea*, 648 F.3d 1, 10 (1st Cir. 2011).

55 256 U.S. 465 (1921).

56 Id.

57 *Restatement (Second) of Torts*, § 652B (1977).

9. Making It All Happen

1 Matthew Claire & Amanda Woog, *Courts and the Abolition Movement*, 110 Calif. L. Rev. Part II (2022), at https://papers.ssrn.com (describing movement to abolish police and prisons and making the argument that "the courts must also be critiqued using an abolitionist framework, as the court system largely legitimizes and perpetuates the racialized violence and control of police and prisons widely criticized by abolitionists").

2 Jessica Reilly, Muyau Lao & Jessica Robertson, *China's Social Credit System: Speculation v. Reality*, The Diplomat (Mar. 30, 2021), at https://thediplomat.com.

3 Patrick Howard O'Neill, *Tor's Ex-Director: The Criminal Use of Tor Has Become Overwhelming*, Cyberscoop (May 23, 2017), at www.cyberscoop.com.

4 See Berkman Center for Internet and Society, *Don't Panic: Making Progress on the "Going Dark" Debate* 10 (Feb. 1, 2016) (noting that end-to-end encryption poses a serious impediment to law enforcement, but also stating that current company business models discourage implementation of end-to-end encryption and other technological impediments to company, and therefore government, access).

5 See Jane Bambauer & Tal Zarsky, *The Algorithm Game*, 94 Notre Dame L. Rev. 1, 33–43 (2018) (describing how privacy rights and a privacy-centric architecture "might enable gaming at a cost to accuracy or fairness").

6 Laura Bowen, *Bans on Facial Recognition Technology Spread Across U.S.*, The Crime Report (Sept. 17, 2020), at https://thecrimereport.org; Julie Carr Smith, *States Push Back against Use of Facial Recognition by Police*, PBS News (May 5, 2021), at www.pbs.org (noting 20 states are considering legal limitations on FRT).

7 Ali Winston, *Oakland City Council Rolls Back the Domain Awareness Center*, East Bay Express (Mar. 5, 2014), at https://eastbayexpress.com.

8 Nathan Sherard, *Officials in Baltimore and St. Louis Put the Brakes on Persistent Surveillance Systems Spy Planes*, Electronic Frontier Foundation (March 28, 2021), at www.eff.org; Associated Press, *Seattle Mayor Ends Police Drone Efforts* (Feb. 7, 2013), at www.usatoday.com/story/news/nation/2013/02/07/seattle-police-drone-efforts/190078.

9 See Andrea Cipriano, *Chicago's Red-Light Cameras Raise Cost of Driving in Black Communities*, https://thecrimereport.org (reporting that while Chicago has retained its red-light cameras, a number of jurisdictions have discontinued them largely because the financial harm to residents of low-income neighborhoods outweighed any safety benefits).

10 Perhaps also relevant is the belief that data accessed will be data de-identified. See Paul Ohm, *Broken Promises of Privacy: Responding to the Surprising Failure of Anonymization*, 57 UCLA L. Rev. 1701, 1706 (2010) (asserting that "advances in reidentification thwart the aims of nearly every privacy law and regulation").

11 See Rachel Levinson-Waldman, *NSA Surveillance in the War on Terror*, in *The Cambridge Handbook of Surveillance Law* 7, 41 (David Gray & Stephen E. Henderson, eds., 2017) (recounting the NSA's evasions and concluding "the intelligence communities agencies have repeatedly violated the promises they have made to the courts, to Congress, and implicitly to the American people, exceeding the lawful boundaries of their surveillance authorities and concealing that information from their overseers").

12 U.S. Senate Permanent Subcommittee on Investigations, *Federal Support for and Involvement in State and Local Fusion Centers* 1, 2 (Oct. 3, 2012), at www.hsgac.senate.gov (finding, inter alia, that the Department of Homeland Security "kept most of the troubling reports from being released outside of DHS, . . . slowed reporting down by months, and . . . continued to store troubling

intelligence reports from fusion centers on U.S. persons, possibly in violation of the Privacy Act.").

13 Jay Stanley, *Baltimore Aerial Surveillance Program Retained Data Despite 45-Day Privacy Policy Limit*, ACLU (Oct. 25, 2106, https://perma.cc/M8AK-AGNW.

14 Sarah Brayne, *Predict and Surveil: Data, Discretion and the Future of Policing* 130 (2021) ("Not one person I spoke with could identify a single instance in which a Palantir use audit had been conducted.").

15 Christopher Slobogin, *Why Liberals Should Chuck the Exclusionary Rule*, 1999 U. Ill. L. Rev. 363, 368–392.

16 Id.

17 *City of Los Angeles v. Lyons*, 461 U.S. 95 (1983).

18 Cf. *Screws v. United States*, 325 U.S. 91 (1945).

19 For some suggestions in this regard, see Slobogin, *Why Liberals Should Chuck the Exclusionary Rule*, supra note 15, at 405–406.

20 18 U.S.C. § 2518(10)(a) (exclusion); §§ 2511, 2520 (criminal and civil damages); § 2518(8).

21 18 U.S.C. § 2518(8)(d).

22 ALI, *Principles of the Law: Policing*, § 6.03(d)(1) ("individuals whose information is in a policing database . . . should be notified of that fact whenever the information is used as a basis for an adverse action against them involving a deprivation of liberty or property").

23 *Herring v. United States*, 555 U.S. 135, 146–147 (2009). See also Erin Murphy, *Databases, Doctrine and Constitutional Criminal Procedure*, 37 Fordham Urb. L.J. 803, 829 (2010).

24 18 § U.S.C. 2519(1).

25 Id. at (2)(b).

26 Accord, ALI, *Principles of the Law: Policing*, § 6.06(c).

27 Blurb for David Brin, *The Transparent Society: Will Technology Force Us to Choose Between Privacy and Freedom?* (1999).

28 Yihyun Jeong, *For Now, Nashville Shelves License Plate Readers*, The Tennessean 10A (Apr. 25, 2021),

29 See https://www.nashville.gov/sites/default/files/2021-08/Comparison-License-Plate-Reader-Policies-8-26-21.pdf.

30 Comparison-License-Plate-Reader-Policies-10-25-2021.pdf, www.nashville.gov/.

31 Cassandra Stephenson, License Plate Scan Plan Wins Approval, The Tennessean, Feb. 4, 2022.

Index

About the Author

CHRISTOPHER SLOBOGIN is Milton Underwood Professor of Law at Vanderbilt University. He has authored more than 200 works on topics relating to criminal law and procedure, mental health law, and evidence. He is one of the five most-cited criminal law and procedure law professors in the country and one of the sixty most-cited law professors overall, according to Hein Online.